CW00684659

TIGER, LION AND BLAKE
1942 – 1986

The Royal Navy's Last Cruisers

Neil McCart

FOREWORD BY
REAR-ADMIRAL M. L. STACEY CB

TIGER, LION AND BLAKE
1942 – 1986

The Royal Navy's Last Cruisers

Neil McCart

HMS *Blake* at sea following her conversion to a helicopter cruiser.

(Rear-Admiral D. M. Eckersley-Maslin)

To All Those Who Have Served In HM Ships
Tiger, Lion and *Blake* 1959-1979

Front Cover: A magnificent watercolour painting of HMS *Tiger* by artist Brian Conroy, Greatham, Hampshire.

Cover Design by Louise McCart
© Neil McCart/FAN PUBLICATIONS 1999
ISBN: 1 901225 03 8

Typesetting By: Highlight Type Bureau Ltd,
Clifton House, 2 Clifton Villas,
Bradford, West Yorkshire BD8 7BY

Printing By: The Amadeus Press Ltd,
517 Leeds Road,Huddersfield,
West Yorkshire HD2 1YJ

Published By FAN PUBLICATIONS
17 Wymans Lane, Cheltenham, GL51 9QA, England. Fax & Tel 01242 580290

Contents

Foreword
by Rear-Admiral M. L. Stacey CB

I enjoyed immensely the privilege of commanding HMS *Tiger* from 1973-1975 and thus was delighted to be invited to write the foreword to this story of the Royal Navy's last cruisers, HM Ships *Tiger, Lion* and *Blake.*

Lacking the majesty of the battleship or the glamour of the destroyer, cruisers have until recently traditionally provided the means whereby Britain's maritime influence has been deployed throughout the oceans of the world to maintain the naval presence required in support of our foreign policy, to protect our vital trade routes and to defend our essential interests in war. To meet these criteria the design requirement for these ships has generally produced a vessel of about eight to ten thousand tons with high speed and endurance and capable of operating worldwide. Surface and air defence gunnery was a prerequisite with an operations and communication capability able to command and control additional forces deployed in support. Overall there was a need for a large ship's company ensuring maximum self-support with minimum dependence on dockyard or external overseas support facilities.

The service of these ships spanned nearly four decades, from 1942 to 1980, which were particularly momentous years in the Navy's history, since it was during this period that the current strategic roles and structures of the Navy as we know them today were developed. These ships started their lives in the days when battleships still reigned supreme when they played their traditional role of providing a presence in distant waters. Thereafter in a changing Navy they became more integrated with the fleet providing seagoing flag officers with accommodation and command facilities, heavy surface and air defence gunfire support and in the case of *Tiger* and *Blake* the ability to deploy into deep water the increasingly potent Sea King anti-submarine helicopter. This extremely important capability went some way to filling the gap between the demise of the anti-submarine warfare capability of the large fleet aircraft carriers and their replacement by the smaller Invincible-class carriers of today.

This book tells the story of these three ships in an accurate and highly readable style, some of which now belongs to the Navy of yesterday, but much of which has continuing application and relevance to today. Ship's programmes have always been tight with exercises interwoven with foreign visits aimed at maintaining readiness for war within our international treaty commitments and sustaining our relationships with friendly and allied nations. And our sailors have always been busy, flexible and slightly stretched with the ability quickly to change from battle dress for action stations to pirate's rig for a children's party.

It also tells - with its many personal recollections - how much of the detail has changed over the years, but how the greatest single factor - the sailor - remains generally unchanged. He continues to stand as high as ever in terms of his professionalism in the art of maritime warfare as well as his ability to act overseas as a cheerful and diplomatic representative of our country. We owe to him a great deal as well as to his wife and his family - who are so frequently left for long periods on their own at home.

And finally, to any readers who served with me in *Tiger* I send my best wishes and join in happy memories of the old lady we loved - ugly though she undoubtedly may have been in her later years.

Michael L. Stacey
Rear-Admiral

A Confusing Start

The story of these three vessels, the Royal Navy's last big-gun warships, goes back to the spring of 1941 when the War Cabinet approved the construction of three 6-inch cruisers which were described as being of an 'improved Fiji class'. However, only two of the class were built, and these became the *Swiftsure* and *Minotaur*. Later that year, on 24 November 1941, approval was given for the construction of a further three such cruisers which were now described as 'modified Fiji-class' ships and they were to be named *Defence, Superb* and *Tiger*. Five months later, in April 1942, the Admiralty sought permission to build six more such cruisers, but only two of these were ordered, HMS *Blake* from the Govan shipyard of Fairfield & Co, and yard number 596 which was ordered from Alexander Stephen & Sons at Linthouse, but which was subsequently cancelled. However, with the outbreak of war in South-East Asia there was an urgent need for aircraft carriers and it was decided that the construction of nine light fleet carriers would take priority over the cruisers, although this led to some concern in the government and a committee was set up to investigate the possibility of building both the carriers and the cruisers. As a result of their deliberations it was decided to build three more light fleet carriers, and retain only one cruiser, which was the *Hawke,* the keel of which was laid at Portsmouth Dockyard in September 1943. At this stage the keels had been laid for four of the 1942 cruisers; the *Tiger* at John Brown's Clydeside shipyard on 1 October 1941; the *Superb* at Swan Hunter's Wallsend shipyard on 23 June 1942; the *Defence* at Scott's Greenock shipyard on 24 June 1942, and the *Blake*, whose keel had been laid at Fairfield's yard on 17 August 1942.

As the Second World War progressed consideration was given to various designs of cruiser, including a Neptune class which would have consisted of four new vessels, *Centurion, Edgar, Mars* and *Neptune,* together with a fifth ship, the cancelled *Bellerophon* from the 1942 building programme. The design of the new vessels, proposed in 1944, owed much to the US campaign in the Pacific, particularly around the Solomon Islands. The main 6-inch armament was to be very similar to the US Navy's cruisers

A rare view of the *Defence* laid up in Gareloch during September 1954. She had been launched ten years before this photograph was taken, in September 1944. *(Maritime Photo Library)*

of the Brooklyn class, but in the event they were all cancelled and replaced by six units of the Minotaur class which, in 1947, was also cancelled, but the newly designed armament for this class would eventually live on in the Tiger-class cruisers.

Work on the four hulls which had already been laid down went ahead, their design being based on that of the very successful Fiji-class cruisers which had all been completed in the early 1940s. The first of the four to be launched was the *Superb* which took to the waters of the River Tyne on Tuesday 31 August 1943. In the event she was the only one of the four cruisers which was completed to the original design with armament made up of nine 6-inch guns in three Mk 24 triple turrets, ten 4-inch guns in five Mk 19 twin mountings and quadruple power-worked 21-inch torpedo tubes. HMS *Superb* joined the fleet in December 1945, not in time to see any action, and in 1946 she was the flagship of the 2nd Cruiser Squadron.

Meanwhile work had been proceeding on the remaining three cruisers and the next to be launched, amid tight security, was the *Defence* from Scott's shipyard. She was christened on Saturday 2 September 1944 by Mrs J. Edelston, the wife of Rear-Admiral John Edelston (later Admiral Sir John Edelston), an Assistant Chief of Naval Staff with responsibility for U-boat warfare and trade. The third of the cruisers to take to the water was the *Tiger* and she was launched on Thursday 25 October 1945 from John Brown's Clydebank shipyard by Lady Stansgate, the wife of the Secretary of State for Air, Viscount Stansgate, and the mother of the Rt Hon Tony Benn MP. Viscount Stansgate had had a distinguished military career during the First World War, first in the Middlesex Yeomanry during the Gallipoli campaign and later as an observer with the Royal Naval Air Service in the Middle East. On the outbreak of the Second World War, at 52 years of age, he had enlisted as a pilot officer in the Royal Air Force and rose to the rank of air commodore, before being called to the House of Lords as the first Viscount Stansgate.

The last ship of the class to be launched was HMS *Blake* and she was sent down the slipway at Fairfield's Govan shipyard on Thursday 20 December 1945 by Lady Jean Blake, the wife of Vice-Admiral Sir Geoffrey Blake. Admiral Blake had joined the Navy in 1897 and he had served as the Gunnery Officer in the battleship HMS *Iron Duke* at Jutland. Between 1942 and the end of the Second World War he had served as a liaison officer to the US Navy in Europe, for which he had been awarded the Legion of Merit. At the luncheon which followed the *Blake's* launching ceremony came the first hints that the Tiger-class cruisers might not, after all, join the fleet in 1947 as had been originally planned, when the Controller of the Navy told his audience that new construction was to be very much reduced and there would be far fewer ships entering service. He went on to say that the 'atomic era'

would have far-reaching effects on naval construction and much energy would have to be devoted to research and development. Only seven months after the launch of the *Blake* the Controller's broad hints became a reality when it was announced that work on the *Tiger* and *Defence* would be suspended indefinitely, while the *Blake* would only be brought up to a similar stage of construction as her earlier sisters and then be laid up as well.

For seven years the three half-finished cruisers were laid up either on the Clyde or in Gareloch and as the years passed by it seemed less and less likely that they would ever be completed. However, in the meantime, in early 1951 the drawings for the three ships were resurrected by the Director of Naval Construction, and completely new designs were drawn up which were approved by the Admiralty Board on Thursday 14 October 1954, following which the decision was made to complete the three cruisers. Speaking at the annual dinner of the RNVR Club in London on the following day, the First Lord of the Admiralty, Mr J. P. L. Thomas, gave his audience an idea of the design changes which had been made to the cruisers, and in particular the new armament which was to consist of two twin 6-inch, Mk 26 turrets, which was a reduction from the original design of three triple 6-inch turrets. However, he went on to say, 'The greater improvement in this 6-inch gun armament lies in its increased rate of fire, which in these ships will deliver some five tons of shell on the target at a range of 13 miles every minute. The guns of these ships will be directed by the latest fire control equipment, which reaches out far beyond the range of the guns themselves and which will be equally effective under both visual and blind conditions. These ships will not only be very useful in the Cold War but their heavy guns will be of the greatest value for bombardment purposes should there be another outbreak of local war like Korea.' He then came to the most significant part of his speech, declaring to his audience something which most naval observers must have suspected in an age when guided missiles were rapidly being developed: 'Yet these ships may well be the last purely gunned cruisers which will be built for service in our Navy.'

The new cruisers would have an overall length of 555ft - 6in, a breadth of 64ft and a draught of 22ft - $2^{1}/_{2}$in. They would have a light displacement of 9,330 tons and a deep displacement of 11,900 tons. They were to be four-shaft ships, powered by the same number of single-reduction geared steam turbines which developed 80,000 SHP, allowing for a maximum speed of $30^{1}/_{2}$ knots, which was less than that of the Soviet Sverdlov-class cruisers. The steam for the main engines was provided by four Admiralty three-drum, oil-fired, superheat boilers, and a proposal to re-boiler the ships was turned down by the Admiralty Board. The modernization of the three cruisers was extensive, amounting almost to a complete redesign that involved stripping out the entire superstructure, the bridge,

This view of the cruiser HMS *Superb* gives some idea of how the *Tiger, Lion* and *Blake* would have looked had they been built to their original design. *(Maritime Photo Library)*

the gun supports, some minor bulkheads in the hull, and most of the services, which had already been installed. In addition to this a great deal of the auxiliary machinery and equipment was either replaced or modified to suit an entirely AC electrical power system. As well as the modification of the main armament, which reduced the original three 6-inch triple turrets to two 6-inch twin turrets, the five 4-inch twin mountings were changed to three 3-inch twin mountings. It had originally been intended to fit the three cruisers with quadruple power-worked torpedo tubes, and in the redesign it was decided that if weight margins allowed they could be fitted at the after end of the quarterdeck which, in the event, was not feasible, not only because of the weight, but also the fact that there was no space for torpedo spares and maintenance, and so they were left out.

As regards ammunition, a full outfit of 800 rounds of 6-inch ammunition was catered for in the magazines and shell rooms, with the cordite being stowed in cartridges on open racks so that the required rate of supply to the guns could be maintained. The main armament was impressive, with each water-cooled six-inch barrel capable of delivering 20 rounds per minute, while each 3-inch barrel could, in theory, deliver up to 120 rounds per minute, although in practice 90 rounds per minute was the best they achieved.

As to fire control systems, each of the main 6-inch and 3-inch mountings was fitted with MRS3 Mk 1 fire control sets, which were similar to the US Navy's Mk 56 with a Type 903-dish radar scanner. Two of these were fitted above the bridge superstructure, two amidships on either side of the after funnel and one aft. The radar scanners included a Type 960 for air warning, with a range of 170 miles, and a Type 992 for surface searching, with a range of 30 miles, both at the masthead.

Accommodation was provided for a full war complement of 73 officers, 215 senior rates and 593 junior rates, but the heavy demands on space for gun control equipment and auxiliary machinery, which included air-conditioning equipment, together with workshops and maintenance spaces, reduced the available area to approximately 16 square feet per junior rating and 18 square feet per senior rating, which meant that the three vessels would never be described by their ships' companies as 'comfortable'. Apart from a cinema there was no other recreational area for ratings outside their messdecks and inevitably they will be largely remembered as congested ships. Indeed, the author's memories of the very short time he spent in HMS *Lion* on the Far East Station are of the overcrowding and the fact that literally every nook and cranny seemed to be packed with machinery. A

HMS *Tiger* laid up in Dalmuir Basin on the Clyde in August 1947. She is alongside, and dwarfed by, the troopship *Empire Fowey*, which was formerly the German passenger liner *Potsdam*. *(Glasgow University)*

contemporary, tongue-in-cheek, article about the *Tiger* in the magazine *Punch* seemed to sum up this sense of overcrowding: 'There is no need to be ashamed of a momentary loss of one's sense of direction in this ship. Her hull was laid down at the end of the last war, and for over 13 years experts of one kind or another (gunnery, radar, electrical, radio, engineering, anti-atomic, cooking, laundering, sixpence-in-the-slot and just plain designers of lumps of metal) have been thinking up things to put in her. The result is she is now full. When they had filled her up to main-deck level there was still such a pile of stuff to be got in that Messrs John Brown had to build on a whole series of extra decks, towers, blockhouses, outhouses and other obstructions, with the result that there is no place on board where one can stand off and see the ship as a whole. It is useless to pop out into the open air with the idea of getting port and starboard sorted out, as one can do on an aircraft carrier for instance, because as likely as not you will find yourself in a kind of metal cul-de-sac and nowhere to go but up a ladder leading to a small decklet from which the only exit is a narrow doorway - and there you are inside again, with 350 electric cables swarming along just overhead.'

There were other limitations of which the Admiralty Board were well aware, one of the most significant points being the pre-war hull design which meant that full Atomic, Biological and Chemical Damage Control (ABCD) measures could not be implemented without re-boiling the ships, which in turn would mean the speed and endurance being affected by the increased auxiliary machinery load on the boilers and, as the hulls would have been in the water for at least 14 years by the time they were completed, there would be some reduction in the expectation of life for the cruisers. The function of the three ships was to provide close-range cover and anti-aircraft support to convoys and to aircraft carrier task groups, but there were many who opposed the spending of such large amounts of money on ships, which, it was argued, were already obsolete.

Within days of the announcement that the three cruisers were to be finished, there came a further statement that although the *Tiger* and *Blake* were to be completed by the original builders, HMS *Defence* had been put into the hands of Swan Hunter & Wigham Richardson Ltd at Wallsend on Tyne, although it was to be another nine months before

A crowded and busy flight deck on board HMS *Tiger,* and...

...A very smart flight deck for Procedure 'Alpha'. *(Rear-Admiral M. L. Stacey)*

work on her recommenced. It was in July 1955 that tugs took the *Defence* in tow for her first sea passage from the Clyde to the River Tyne, by way of the Pentland Firth. Her arrival alongside the fitting-out berth at Wallsend on Thursday 7 July 1955 signalled a boost to the river's shipbuilding industry where it was thought that she would provide two years' work for several hundred Tyneside shipyard workers. In the event it was to be over five years before she was commissioned into the Royal Navy.

Meanwhile, just eight days after *Defence's* arrival in the River Tyne, back on the Clyde fire broke out in the *Blake* as she lay in the fitting-out basin at Fairfield's shipyard and although the Glasgow City Fire Brigade and river fire floats were soon on the scene, they were not in fact required as the blaze was soon extinguished. Two years later, in October 1957, to keep alive the famous four-century old ship name *Lion* in the Royal Navy, the Admiralty, with the Queen's approval, changed the name of the *Defence*. However, seven months later on Thursday 22 May 1958, fire broke out on board the *Lion* as she lay alongside her Tyneside fitting-out basin. Firemen were soon on the scene, and wearing breathing apparatus they made their way down three deck levels to rescue a workman who was trapped in a compartment by dense smoke. The fire had started when sparks from a welding torch ignited a pile of tarpaulins, but fortunately the man was led to safety and damage to the cruiser was not serious.

Despite the constant assurances from the government that work was proceeding to schedule, it was 15 years from the initial launching in 1944 before the first of the three cruisers was ready to commission and to take her place in the fleet.

The *Defence* alongside a fitting-out berth at Wallsend on Tyne. Her superstructure has been entirely stripped away and it was rebuilt to a completely different design. *(Glasgow University)*

HMS *Tiger* at sea on her Contractor's Trials in February 1959.

(Imperial War Museum A34144)

HMS *Tiger* leaving Cape Town on Monday 9 July 1973. *(D. Smith)*

With not much room to spare a Sea King lands on the *Tiger's* flight deck.

(Rear-Admiral M. L. Stacey)

Part One

HMS *Tiger* 1959-1978

Chapter One

HMS *Tiger* – First Commission 1959-1960

The first of the Tiger-class cruisers to be commissioned was HMS *Tiger* herself, with the advance party having joined the ship in late 1958 and in January 1959. One of those key ratings was Derek Brook who, as an ERA, remembers the early days: 'I was one of a group of about a dozen senior engine room ratings who joined the *Tiger* at John Brown's Clydebank shipyard on Friday 23 January 1959. We had all travelled by rail from our various depots, which in my case was Chatham. We were immediately given an address to go to and I was lucky to get a very nice place with a family who lived close to Hampden Park football ground. It was to be my lodgings until shortly before the ship commissioned when we all moved on board. Although I had a long journey into the yard each day, it was made easier by the fact that I was staying at the home of one of the yard's overseers and he used to give me a lift to work each morning. The *Tiger*

herself had just returned to John Brown's from her initial builder's sea trials during which it had been discovered that, amongst other defects, the captain could not see the after end of the ship from the navigation bridge. One of the first tasks for the builders was to construct a "flying bridge" on either side of the main bridge position. Our office accommodation at the shipyard was very makeshift, and I doubt that it would be considered acceptable these days. The Engineers' Office was in a cabin mock-up area for a large oil tanker which was also under construction and the Senior Engine Room Ratings' restroom consisted of a large square of wooden boxes containing gear wheels, surrounded by and roofed over with a large sheet of tarpaulin. Inside we had a very basic wash basin and a hot water heater. Each day we ate our lunch in the Works' Canteen, which cost us one shilling and sixpence ($7\frac{1}{2}$p), and to ensure that we had sufficient funds for this we were

The *Tiger's* Commissioning Ceremony took place on the morning of Wednesday 18 March 1959 on the jetty alongside the ship. This view shows the ship's company marching off at the conclusion of the ceremony. *(D. Brook)*

paid the princely sum of seven shillings and sixpence (37¹/₂p) every Monday morning.'

The great majority of the ship's company joined the *Tiger* on Tuesday 17 March and after marking their kitbags and baggage with coloured ribbons, and the number of their mess, they were shown to their new homes by members of the advance party. The Commissioning Ceremony took place on the jetty alongside the *Tiger* at 11am on Wednesday 18 March 1959, in the presence of the Flag Officer Scotland, Vice-Admiral J. D. Luce CB. The ceremony, which started with a short address and the reading of the Commissioning Warrant by Captain Washbourn DSO OBE RN, the cruiser's first commanding officer, was followed by a religious service conducted by The Reverend R. W. Pope RN, the ship's chaplain. Captain Washbourn, who had been appointed to his command from the Directorate of Naval Ordnance in the Admiralty, told his ship's company, 'There is no doubt that the Admiralty made the right decision in going ahead with these ships. Guided missiles at this stage have their disadvantages. The fully automatic guns combine the best of both worlds. Press-button warfare is here.' Following this there was a march past before the ship was opened to the ship's company's families and guests.

Captain Washbourn was born in Auckland, New Zealand, and he had joined the Royal Navy in 1927. In the pre-war years he had served in the elderly monitor HMS *Erebus,* the battleship *Warspite* and the cruisers *Diomede* and *London.* In 1939 he was appointed to the cruiser *Achilles* as the gunnery officer and he was aboard her during the Battle of the River Plate, subsequently being awarded the DSO for his part in the action. He was still serving in the *Achilles* when, in October 1941, she was lent to the newly formed New Zealand Navy. Later in the war he served in the battleship *Anson* and the cruiser *Bellona,* and in 1953 he commanded the fast minelayer *Manxman* before being appointed as the Chief Staff Officer to the Flag Officer (Flotillas) Mediterranean.

Just five days before the Commissioning Ceremony the *Tiger's* Royal Marines Detachment held its passing-out parade at the RM Barracks, Eastney, before travelling to Scotland to join the ship. The cruiser was unique in that it was the first ship, other than a flagship, to have its own Royal Marines Band, and during the parade at Eastney with the Detachment the drum major of the band was presented with a highly appropriate tiger skin to wear in place of the traditional leopard skin. Some idea of the conditions on board the *Tiger,* and the effort required to make the vessel shipshape, is given by one of the cruiser's Marines who recalls, 'Some revolutionary ideas were tried at first, such as "cleaning stations" from 7.30am to 9.30am, in which the whole ship's company pitched in and cleaned the ship, after which everyone was engaged on maintenance work; but this soon fell by the wayside, and we went back to the old routine of "flat sweepers". However, one-third of the Detachment were still employed on maintenance as Y turret ordnance party, the only armament we manned. Our other duties were as boats' crews and watchkeepers.' The living conditions on board definitely met with approval, as the Marine remembers: 'Some of the new features of this ship which made life more bearable were bunks and bedlights, large kit lockers, in which we could stow our suits, and cafeteria messing. But some of the older members maintained that their previous ships were better.'

Three days after the Commissioning Ceremony, at 8.16am on Saturday 21 March, with the tug *Flying Duck* forward, and the *Flying Dipper* and *Flying Drake* aft, the *Tiger* slipped her moorings and six minutes later, after clearing the basin, she set course downriver for Greenock. By 8.50am she was abeam of the Erskine Ferry and at 10.10am she passed Greenock's Princes Pier before anchoring just over 20 minutes later in the Firth of Clyde. After carrying out compass adjustments, she weighed anchor at 11.30am to carry out six hours of full-power trials off the Arran measured mile. That afternoon, at 4.30pm, she anchored off Greenock once again and there she remained for three days whilst the workers from John Brown & Co put the finishing touches to the cleaning up process. One of the main problems from the engineers' point of view is recalled by Derek Brook: 'On leaving John Brown's yard the main problem for us all in the engine room department was continual thick black smoke belching from the funnels for which, try as we might, we could not find a cause. Needless to say we were not popular with the seamen. On the first night out at sea we gave the boilers a "water-wash" in order to try to eliminate the sooty deposits which were gathering on the beautiful new paintwork. Unfortunately, this was no good at all and the black smoke just kept belching out. It actually took weeks of hard work by all the ship's engineering department, and staff from the Admiralty who were boiler specialists, to discover that the cause was actually drilling "rags" which had been left in the oil return column, thereby preventing excess fuel from draining away quickly. Once they were removed we had no more black smoke and our popularity with the seamen was restored.' During the afternoon of Sunday 22 March most of the Clydeside workers were disembarked and at 4.30am on Tuesday 24 March the *Tiger* weighed anchor once again and steamed south. Seven hours later, at 11.36am, she stopped in Liverpool Bay in a position Lat 53° - 39.5'N/Long 03° - 46.7'W, and she was officially accepted into naval service, whereupon the White Ensign was hoisted at the masthead for the first time. That same afternoon, as she steamed south again, gun functioning trials were carried out, and at 9.35am on Wednesday 25 March the cruiser stopped in Sandown Roads where side parties spruced up the hull in preparation for her first ceremonial entry into Portsmouth Harbour. By

A brand new *Tiger* on Commissioning Day, still firmly alongside John Brown's fitting-out wharf on the River Clyde.

(D. Brook)

11.41am the ship's company had manned ship and 20 minutes later the pilot was embarked as she steamed through Spithead and past Southsea seafront where she fired gun salutes to the C-in-C Home Fleet and the C-in-C Portsmouth. Finally, at 12.34pm, she secured alongside North Corner Jetty in Portsmouth Dockyard and the main leave parties left the ship for their seasonal leave. Three days later, during the Easter weekend holiday, the gangways were thrown open to Navy Days visitors and over 12,000 people took the opportunity to visit the first new cruiser to be commissioned into the Royal Navy for 15 years. Among the visitors that weekend was the Russian Naval Attaché, who could not fail to be impressed by the new ship.

After 19 days alongside in Portsmouth it was time for work to begin in earnest and on the morning of Monday 13 April the *Tiger* left North Corner Jetty to begin an arduous period of trials and working up which began in the Channel with the ship anchoring at Spithead on most evenings. During the exercises and manoeuvres long sessions were spent off Portland and Weymouth, with the occasional weekend alongside in Portsmouth, and for many members of the ship's company it seemed as though the

exercises would never end. The only real break was a 59-hour Whitsun weekend visit to St Peter Port, Guernsey, from the morning of Saturday 16 May to the evening of Monday 18 May. The middle of June saw the *Tiger* at sea off the south of Ireland and after three days of gunnery exercises in the area, during the afternoon of a sweltering Friday 19 June she set course for Avonmouth where she secured alongside P berth in the port's Royal Edward Dock during the evening. In those days, before the building of the Portway Road between Bristol and Avonmouth, the journey into the city was slow, but nevertheless the ship's company made the most of their weekend break. Amongst the guests invited to tour the ship was a group from the Admiralty offices in nearby Bath, many of whom had been responsible for designing the cruiser, and at last they were seeing for the first time the results of their work. However, according to one engineer officer not all of them recognized the areas they had designed: ' "Excuse me, is this the Engineer's Office?" asked a dapper man, peering in from 3M flat. I thought this a strange question to ask someone in overalls, sitting in a compartment with its traffolite nameplate on the door. My assurance that it was, brought no relief to the puzzled look on the man's face: he merely commented, "Strange, I didn't think it looked anything like this."' After leaving Avonmouth on the morning of Monday 22 June the *Tiger* steamed round to Portsmouth to secure alongside North Corner Jetty the following morning.

The next phase of the work-up took place during the middle two weeks of July 1959, with weekends alongside in Portsmouth Harbour. Once again the schedule was arduous with long hours worked by the ship's company. Fortunately, however, the waters of Spithead were warm enough for Captain Washbourn to pipe 'Hands to Bathe' on most afternoons. During her weekends alongside North Corner Jetty a stream of VIPs visited the ship, including the Minister of Defence, The First Lord of the Admiralty and the C-in-C Home Fleet. On Monday 20 July the *Tiger* went into D lock dry dock at Portsmouth for hull maintenance and the ship's company were able to take some leave. At this stage the first change of command took place when, on Tuesday 21 July 1959, Captain Washbourn left the ship on promotion to Commodore and his place was taken by Captain R. E. Hutchins DSC RN, who had first gone to sea in the Merchant Navy at 11 years of age. In 1928, then aged 17 years, he had joined the Royal Navy as a Boy Seaman at HMS *St Vincent* in Gosport. Five years later, having passed the necessary examinations, he was awarded a commission and two years later, as a Sub Lieutenant, he joined the submarine *L27* which patrolled the Red Sea during the Abyssinian crisis. In 1938 he qualified as a gunnery officer and served in the cruisers *Hawkins* and *Glasgow,* seeing action on board the latter against German destroyers in the Atlantic on 28 December 1943 for which he was subsequently awarded the DSC. Promoted to Captain in 1951 he served in the Admiralty, and in 1952 took up his first command as Captain, Minesweepers, Mediterranean. The *Tiger* was to be his final appointment.

The work-up continued throughout August and September with the ship spending more long periods at sea off Portland and Weymouth under the aegis of Flag Officer Sea Training, although during the weekend of 5/6 September she anchored off Milford Haven. To everyone's great relief, on the morning of Friday 25 September 1959, when the *Tiger* was moored in Portland Harbour, the Flag Officer Sea Training was embarked and the ship left harbour to undergo her Operational Readiness Inspection, which was successfully completed by 5.15pm that day and after disembarking FOST and his staff at Portland, the *Tiger* left for Portsmouth where she spent the night anchored at Spithead. Next morning she steamed up harbour to secure alongside South Railway Jetty, the work-up finally over.

Following this hectic initial start to her career it was time for some relaxation, and this came in the form of a 'Showing the Flag' cruise to the Baltic which proved a welcome diversion for the ship's company after so much time around Weymouth and Portland. At 7.30am on Tuesday 6 October 1959 the *Tiger* slipped her berth at South Railway Jetty, and after steaming into the Channel she set course for the German port of Brunsbüttel at the mouth of the Kiel Canal. Next morning, at 6.30am, she embarked the canal pilot and throughout the day she steamed past the countryside of Schleswig Holstein, before leaving the canal that evening and setting course for Gdansk in Poland. The *Tiger* was the first British warship to visit the port for many years and she secured alongside French Quay in the port at 11am on Friday 9 October. Needless to say the new cruiser was an unusual sight in the Polish port and she was a great attraction for the local people, with the jetty sentry especially attracting crowds of fascinated sightseers. During the visit the Royal Marines Detachment took part in many ceremonial occasions, including a Guard of Honour at a Polish war cemetery outside Gdansk where Captain Hutchins laid a wreath, and another at a British war memorial at Malbork. During the weekend of 11/12 October the ship was opened to visitors, and a children's party for 200 young orphans was held on board. Finally, at 10am on Tuesday 13 October, the *Tiger* left Gdansk and set course north through the Baltic Sea to Stockholm where she arrived at 11am the next day. Once again there was a busy round of official and social events, and almost 4,000 people went on board to view the ship. After six days in the Swedish capital the *Tiger* set course for Kiel again and at 9.15am on Thursday 22 October she secured alongside the Tirpitz Mole of the German naval base where she proved to be a major attraction. After leaving the naval base she made her southbound transit of the Kiel Canal and two days later, at 6.07am on Thursday 29 October, she anchored off the Ostend Lightship before making a passage up the Westerschelde to secure alongside 21 Berth in Antwerp City Docks at 5.15pm that afternoon. Although the visit was marred somewhat by foul weather, once again the *Tiger* proved to be the main attraction in the port and on Sunday 1 November, when she was opened to visitors for just three hours, almost 2,700 people looked round the ship. After leaving Antwerp at 12.45pm on Tuesday 3 November she steamed straight back to Portsmouth and after a full ceremonial entry into harbour she secured alongside North Corner Jetty at 8am on Wednesday 4 November. No sooner had she tied up alongside than the first main leave parties left the ship to take some General Service Leave before the next deployment, to the Mediterranean.

During her time alongside the Chaplain of the Fleet dedicated the ship's chapel, and after many tearful partings the cruiser left Portsmouth at just after 9am on the morning of Friday 27 November 1959 and set course for Gibraltar, where she arrived on Monday 30 November, securing alongside the sheerlegs berth at 3.15pm. Here

At about midday on Wednesday 25 March 1959 the *Tiger* made her first ceremonial entry into Portsmouth Harbour. She had been accepted into service from the builders the day before these photographs were taken.
(Maritime Photo Library)

Rear-Admiral R. A. Ewing DSC CB, Flag Officer Flotillas (Mediterranean), hoisted his flag in the cruiser. For many members of the ship's company this stop at Gibraltar would have been the first foreign visit of their service, and no doubt memories still abound of the 'social' that was arranged with members of the *Hermes'* ship's company in the colony's Café Universal. After leaving Gibraltar at 11am on Wednesday 2 December the *Tiger* made good time to Malta, arriving on the morning of Saturday 5 December for a ceremonial entry into Grand Harbour before securing at No 8 buoy.

During the period before Christmas the *Tiger* carried out a number of exercises at sea with the 2nd Destroyer Squadron and the 4th Frigate Squadron, which included the destroyers *Daring, Defender, Delight* and *Battleaxe,* and the frigate *Eastbourne.* During a night encounter exercise on Wednesday 9 December the *Delight* exploded a shell just 20 yards off the *Tiger's* port bow and shrapnel from the shell flew on board the cruiser, narrowly missing an able seaman. On Wednesday 16 December she flew the flag of the C-in-C Mediterranean Fleet, Admiral Sir A. N. C. Bingley, for the day while she carried out gunnery exercises in the areas off Malta, but on the following day she finally returned to Grand Harbour for the Christmas period. For 12 days a very good time was had by all, mainly on Strait Street. A 'top secret operation' was also mounted to return the compliment of the *Delight's* stray shell when the *Tiger's* pinnace carried out a surface attack on the destroyer which was moored in Sliema Creek. The action took place at midnight with thunderflashes and bags of white flour for ammunition, while the destroyer's complement were

suitably serenaded with bugles and cymbals; some counter-fire ensued, however, when a number of large, well-aimed 'spuds' hit the pinnace. At the conclusion of the 'battle' the able seaman who was almost hit by the shrapnel was presented with the base of the 4.5-inch cartridge of the offending shell, which had been converted into an ash tray, by the *Delight's* ship's company. By the morning of 29 December, when the *Tiger* put to sea for more exercises, most of the ship's company were woefully counting their coppers and eagerly awaiting the next pay day. After 24 hours at sea in company with the *Daring* and *Defender,* during which the former made a torpedo attack on the cruiser, which she skilfully avoided, the *Tiger* returned to Grand Harbour for the New Year celebrations before shifting to Parlatorio Wharf for maintenance. On Monday 25 January 1960 Rear-Admiral Ewing struck his flag and left the ship to take up an appointment in the Admiralty, and Rear-Admiral D. P. Dreyer DSC CB hoisted his flag in the cruiser on his appointment as Flag Officer (Flotillas) Mediterranean. It was Tuesday 2 February before the *Tiger* completed her maintenance period and left Malta for more gunnery exercises, for it had become clear that the high rates of fire which had been expected from the main armament were not being achieved and there had been a lot of mechanical problems to be rectified. Next on the agenda were visits to La Spezia in Italy and to Menton in the south of France, not far from Monte Carlo. In the former port the *Tiger* was able to berth stern to on Bauchina Pier and as the accent was on relaxation there was little ceremonial which gave many of the ship's company the opportunity to undertake trips to such romantic places as Pisa, Florence and Genoa, whilst another more actively inclined group spent an exhausting day climbing in the mountains just outside La Spezia. After a very pleasant long weekend in the city and yet more exercises, the *Tiger* anchored off Menton, just a few miles into France from the Italian border, on the morning of Wednesday 17 February. This was the more popular of the two ports, mainly because of the close proximity of Monte Carlo and Nice, which were easily accessible by bus. A large number of the ship's company made an immediate beeline for the Casino at Monte Carlo, where most quickly lost their money at the gaming tables. Others went to Nice where they could join in the annual Flower Carnival which was in full swing at the time. On the ceremonial side the Royal Marines Detachment provided a Guard of Honour for the visit of Vice-Admiral Anderson, the commander of the US Navy's 6th Fleet, when he visited the ship, and ashore a Guard and Band paraded for the unveiling of a monument to Queen Victoria, which replaced an original that had been destroyed during the Second World War. After leaving Menton on Monday 22 February there were three more days of exercises before the *Tiger* returned to Grand Harbour on 25 February, for a ten-day maintenance period.

It was on Wednesday 9 March that the *Tiger* sailed from Grand Harbour, flying the flag of Admiral Dreyer, to take part in the fleet exercise 'Marjex', which also involved the carriers *Ark Royal* and *Albion,* with the *Ark* carrying out the first phase of her work-up. Also taking part were the destroyers *Daring* and *Dainty* and on the second day Admiral Bingley hoisted his flag in the *Tiger.* The manoeuvres ended on 17 March when she detached from the fleet to visit Valencia in Spain where she berthed alongside the Muelle de Pontiente at 9.20am that morning. The weather was excellent and the visit coincided with the local grand fiesta celebrations, during which there was dancing in the streets with lavish firework displays, accompanied by the consumption of copious amounts of wine. In return the *Tiger* herself proved to be a popular attraction for the local residents and over the weekend of 19/20 March over 3,000 visitors toured the ship. *Tiger* left the port on the morning of Monday 21 March and after rendezvousing with the cruiser *Bermuda* and the destroyers *Daring, Delight* and *Dunkirk,* course was set for Gibraltar where they arrived the following day to find 20 naval ships already in port preparing for the NATO exercise 'Dawn Breeze V'. No doubt the scene was reminiscent for the locals of those far-off pre-war days when the harbour was always full of naval ships. During the visit the Royal Marines Detachment combined with that from the *Bermuda* for the Ceremony of the Keys, with the band being provided by HMS *Tyne* from the Home Fleet. There was more ceremonial on 23 March when the First Lord of the Admiralty, Lord Carrington, paid a visit to the cruiser, and he was followed on the next day by the C-in-C Home Fleet. After leaving Gibraltar on 28 March some exercises were held before course was set for Palma, Majorca, which, in those days, had a reputation as being the 'poor man's Monte Carlo'. Here the ship's Royal Marines Band combined with a band which was being carried in the destroyer *Trafalgar* and together they laid on a magnificent performance of Beating Retreat. After leaving Palma on Monday 4 April the *Tiger* arrived back in Maltese waters two days later and after disembarking Admiral Dreyer and his staff in St Paul's Bay, she entered Grand Harbour on 7 April to begin a seven-week maintenance period. During the refit the *Tiger* was docked down in Malta Dockyard's No 9 dry dock for a routine scraping and painting, then on Monday 16 May the cruiser returned to No 8 buoy in the harbour and preparations went ahead to get her ready for sea.

Finally, at 8.30am on Tuesday 24 May the *Tiger* slipped her moorings and left Grand Harbour to rendezvous with the aircraft carrier *Ark Royal* which had steamed east from Gibraltar to carry out a 'Shop Window' display for a number of senior British Government and military personnel, including the First Lord of the Admiralty, the Chief of the NATO Staff and the GOC Malta. The *Tiger* was also carrying a contingent of important passengers, namely relatives and friends of the ship's company who were embarked for a day at sea. During the manoeuvres they were able to watch the normal functions of a peacetime ship on exercises, such as jackstay transfers, A and Y turrets firing bombardment salvoes and the *Ark Royal's* aircraft firing at a splash target towed astern of the cruiser. The Royal Marines Detachment gave a display of their various weapons and invited members of the audience to fire a Bren gun. That afternoon, at 4pm, the cruiser stopped off Grand Harbour where the families were disembarked before she got under way again to carry out exercises for the benefit of Air Vice Marshal Sir Walter Cheshire, the AOC Malta.

On Friday 27 May the *Tiger* steamed into Grand Harbour to embark stores, before leaving three days later to rendezvous with the *Ark Royal,* the destroyer *Scorpion,* the experimental guided missile ship *Girdle Ness,* the heavy repair ship *Ausonia* and three RFAs, for three strenuous days of fuelling at sea, embarking ammunition and fleet manoeuvres, before setting course for a much-publicized visit to Barcelona. It was the most powerful force to have visited the Spanish port for many years and it had been arranged to coincide with the annual Barcelona Trade Fair and particularly with British Day. The fleet of ships arrived off Barcelona on the morning of Friday 3 June, and after embarking 150 guests outside the port, the *Tiger* and *Ark Royal* put to sea where they staged a spectacular gunnery and flying display about 20 miles offshore. Following the display the *Tiger* entered the port while the *Ark Royal* anchored just outside the harbour's main mole. For the ship's company there was a mix of ceremonial and relaxation with guards of honour and an enjoyable daily routine which became known as 'Spanish Routine', with reveille at 7.15am and a make and mend each afternoon. On British Day the Royal Marines Band combined with their counterparts from the *Ark Royal* and played at the hoisting of the Union Flag, then the Detachment gave an exhibition of marching and countermarching before a very enthusiastic holiday crowd. On Whit Monday, 6 June, the combined band put on a magnificent evening performance of Beating Retreat in the city's vast central square, the Plaza Cataluna. The ceremony was conducted by Commissioned Bandmaster Sumner and it was here that members of the Detachment who had gathered to watch the ceremony had to pitch in, in the absence of sufficient local police, and control the large crowds. For many members of the ship's company the highlight of the visit was the night life, with many bars remaining open until 4.30 each morning, and despite the fact that the US Navy's 6th Fleet commuted between the port and Naples, prices were cheap. The Barcelona Trade Fair was a major event in Europe, occupying 65 acres, with 10,200 exhibitors and providing a major exporting opportunity for Britain at which the ships' companies of the *Tiger* and the other vessels conducted themselves as excellent ambassadors for their country.

It was with some regrets amongst the ship's company that the *Tiger* left Barcelona at 10am on Wednesday 8 June to rendezvous with the *Ark Royal* for exercises with the French Navy and the USS *Forrestal* before the two British ships went their separate ways, with the *Ark Royal* setting course for Gibraltar and the *Tiger* heading for Villefranche on the French Riviera. It was at 8am on Friday 10 June that the *Tiger* slid into the anchorage past Cap Ferrat and anchored near the cruiser, FS *Colbert,* in Villefranche Bay, which was over a mile offshore. However, after the flag deck reported 'bikinis galore' on the beaches most of the ship's company wanted to make the trip. After official visits to the ship by the Mayors of Villefranche and Nice the gangway was opened to liberty men and although, viewed from the ship, there didn't appear to be much there, the town of Villefranche turned out to be well stocked with pavement bars and cafés. For most the main attraction was Nice, which was about four miles away and as always the Royal Marines Band Beat Retreat, this time on the city's Promenade de Anglaise. Back on board, the ship was opened to visitors during the afternoon of Saturday 11 June, and despite the fact that she was anchored well offshore over 500 people visited the cruiser. Two days later there was a very successful party for 200 local children, and on the following day, Tuesday 14 June, the *Tiger* slipped her moorings at 6pm and put to sea where she rendezvoused with the frigates *Eastbourne, Chichester* and *Zest* to carry out gunnery exercises en route to Palmas Bay, Sardinia. It was at 6am on the morning of Saturday 18

June that she arrived off this final port of call and anchored in Palmas Bay. This was purely a recreational visit with banyan leave expiring at 8pm each evening, and with the emphasis on swimming and beachcombing. Fortunately the weather was obliging with wonderful blue skies and even bluer seas, but as it was only a weekend break it was back to sea on Monday 20 June with course set for Malta where she arrived the following morning.

After only ten days in Malta the *Tiger* left on Friday 1 July for another flag showing cruise to Mediterranean ports, the first of which was Venice where she arrived alongside at 9am on Monday 4 July for a four-day visit which was every bit as romantic as the travel brochures suggest, but extremely hard on the wallets. After leaving the city at 9am on Friday 8 July the *Tiger* steamed south through the Adriatic to the Italian naval base of Ancona where, despite local strikes, most members of the ship's company enjoyed themselves at the annual festival. After three days alongside the next stop was Lemnos Bay on the island of Mudros (Maudhros), where the cruiser anchored on the morning of Thursday 14 July. It was during the banyan leave which was organized here that many members of the ship's company found they had lain in the sun for too long and as a result were afflicted by very red and sore torsos for the next stop, Salonika (Thessalonika) on the Greek mainland where the ship anchored in Ormos Bay on the morning of Tuesday 19 July. During the four-day visit the ship's band and a guard of honour took part in a remembrance ceremony in a large British war cemetery just outside the town. The next, and final, visit on the cruise was to a rather bleak and desolate anchorage off Navarino, where there was recreational leave only. After three days in Navarino Bay the *Tiger* weighed anchor at just before 2pm on Wednesday 27 July, and a few hours later, at just before 6pm, she rendezvoused with the *Ark Royal,* which had visited Piraeus, for two days of exercises before the *Tiger* returned to Grand Harbour during the afternoon of Friday 29 July.

Once again the cruiser's stay in Malta was limited to ten days and then at 9am on Monday 8 August she left harbour for another cruise to more Mediterranean ports. This time the first port of call was Cannes on the French Riviera, a visit which had been eagerly anticipated by the ship's company, and the *Tiger* arrived just 48 hours after leaving Malta. As there was no film festival on at the time there were no film stars sunning themselves on the beaches, but nevertheless everyone enjoyed the run ashore despite the very high prices. On the ceremonial side the band Beat Retreat in the city square and a contingent of seamen and the Royal Marines Detachment provided a Guard for an international naval parade. After five very expensive days in Cannes the *Tiger* weighed anchor at 8.20am on Monday 15 August to steam south-west just seven miles down the coast to the town of Theoule where she anchored 40 minutes later. The object of this visit was to provide British

The *Tiger* makes her first ceremonial entry into Malta's Grand Harbour during the morning of Saturday 5 December 1959. A Daring-class destroyer is moored in the background.

(M. Cassar)

representation at a ceremony to celebrate the anniversary of the first Allied landings in the south of France on 15 August 1944, when US and Free French forces, commanded by Lt General A. M. Patch, landed in the Cannes-Toulon area prior to advancing north in an operation designed to extend the German Army further, when they were already trying to cope with the Allied forces in northern France. Unfortunately the ceremony itself was marred by heavy rain, but members of the Guard and Band who attended from the *Tiger* did get a close-up view of the actor Douglas Fairbanks who had commanded a US Navy warship during the landings. At sea a wreath-laying ceremony was held on the quarterdeck of the French cruiser *Colbert*. Leaving Theoule at midday on Tuesday 16 August the *Tiger* steamed south-east to Ajaccio in Corsica and from there she set course for Aranchi Bay for recreational leave and to spruce up the ship's paintwork for the next port of call, Naples. After an overnight passage the

Tiger secured stern to, at the end of 71 Quay on the Molo Angiono, very close to the Greek royal yacht, *Polemistis,* at 9.30am on Tuesday 30 August for a visit that was to last for six days. This visit coincided with the Rome Olympic Games and the Olympic Sailing Regatta which was being held at Naples, and it was these events which had brought the Greek royal family and many other VIPs, including Prince Rainier and Princess Grace of Monaco, the Dutch royal family and the millionaire, Aristotle Onassis, to the city. The games were held at the height of a scorching Mediterranean summer, to the detriment of many performances, but nevertheless they were a spectacular success and were in fact the first to have saturation television coverage which was broadcast worldwide. British gold medallists at the games were the swimmer Anita Lonsborough and the marathon walker Don Thompson, while a young light-heavyweight boxer, Cassius Clay, showed an unusual fleet-footed style on his way to a gold medal for the USA. Some people predicted that one day he might even be a world champion. For the *Tiger's* ship's company the visit to Naples offered a unique opportunity to attend the Olympic Games, and many took advantage of it. Parties also went over to Capri, up to Rome, and to Sorrento, Pompeii and Vesuvius.

After leaving Naples on the morning of Monday 5 August, the *Tiger* arrived back in Grand Harbour the following morning to prepare for her Sea Inspection by Admiral Dreyer. The inspection itself took place on Thursday 15 September with a full day at sea, and for the next three weeks the *Tiger* was in and out of Malta continuously carrying out gunnery exercises. Although the Admiralty was keeping very quiet about the subject, neither the 6-inch guns of the *Tiger's* main armament nor the secondary 3-inch armament had proved to be fully satisfactory and it was clear that with the end of the commission in sight and a long refit scheduled, modifications would have to be made to the control machinery. The cruiser left Grand Harbour for the last time in the commission during the morning of Tuesday 11 October, and set course for Cartagena in Spain and Palma, Majorca, which were the last 'foreign' visits. After leaving Gibraltar on Thursday 27 October she set course into the Atlantic and headed for Devonport, where she anchored in

Plymouth Sound at 7pm on Sunday 30 October to embark Customs officials. Next day, at 2pm, she weighed anchor and with the ship's company manning the decks she steamed up harbour to secure alongside No 5 wharf at 2.45pm. Since Captain Hutchins had taken command during the *Tiger's* trials the ship had steamed 28,000 miles, and had visited 25 seaports. Captain Hutchins summed up the commission thus: 'I believe that the first commission of the twelfth *Tiger* has been particularly successful on two counts. First, for the commendable way in which the technical problems, which are inevitable in the first of a new class of warship with so much new and complex equipment, have been mastered by her ship's company. Second, that despite these technical problems the ship has been able to visit so many foreign ports with such outstanding success. The ship's company can therefore take justifiable and lasting pride in the achievements of this ship in the material field and in the highly successful contribution they have made in *Tiger* to the principal peacetime task of the Royal Navy - namely, that of showing the flag.'

Although it was the end of a successful first commission it was marred by controversy as the press had learned of the problems with the armament and the Admiralty was desperately staving off rumours that the *Tiger* and her newly commissioned sister ship, *Lion,* were to be paid off.

This unusual shot is a sign of things to come. The photograph was taken during the early afternoon of Tuesday 29 December 1959, shortly after Rear-Admiral Ewing, the FOF (Med), embarked by Whirlwind helicopter, which sits snugly on the *Tiger's* quarterdeck.   (M. Cassar)

Chapter Two

HMS *Tiger* – Second Commission 1961-1963

Following her return to Devonport in October 1960, the *Tiger* remained in dockyard hands for seven months whilst essential maintenance and repair work was carried out. On Saturday 22 April 1961, at 10.35am, Captain P. W. W. Graham DSC RN assumed command and just over an hour later Captain Hutchins left the ship. Before the Second World War the commissioning of a capital ship, including the changeover of a ship's company, took place on one day and in order to achieve this a full complement for a battleship was held permanently in reserve in each of the three barracks, Portsmouth, Devonport and Chatham. However, this was not possible with the shortages of manpower in the 1960s and the *Tiger's* new ship's company had been steadily trickling on board since the start of the refit. There is always a feeling of apprehension on joining a new ship, but on this occasion

the feeling was stronger because of the continuing controversy surrounding the Tiger-class cruisers and their armament which had been widely reported in the press during the first commission. Comments had ranged from, 'The Gunnery Systems of *Tiger* Have Developed Defects', to 'Wonder Ships Are Faulty' and 'Toothless *Tiger*'. Those who joined the ship at Devonport were greeted by the sight of a spare gun turret and a spare propeller lying on the jetty alongside the ship, but fortunately they were not destined for the *Tiger* and her refit was progressing to schedule. However, with the ship in dockyard hands life on board was barely tolerable, with nowhere to eat, nowhere to wash and with no heating or ventilation. Conditions became so bad that the ship's company moved into accommodation in the nearby barracks, where the population was increased by 600 in one day, but even so life was far more

HMS *Tiger* recommissions at Devonport on 2 May 1961.   *(Author's collection)*

comfortable. On Monday 17 April 1961 the ship was shifted out of No 5 basin and tied up alongside No 5 sea wall wharf, and next day the ship's company moved back on board.

The *Tiger* was commissioned at Devonport on Tuesday 2 May 1961, which turned out to be a very wet and blustery day so a 'drill-shed', as opposed to a 'jetty', ceremony was ordered at short notice. At 9.40am the ship's company marched up to the barracks by Divisions, and their families and other spectators were diverted there from the main gate. Soon after this the parade formed up and the VIPs, including the C-in-C Plymouth, Vice-Admiral Sir Charles Madden, and Major-General Cartwright-Taylor, Commanding Officer of the Royal Marines Plymouth arrived. Captain Graham read the Commissioning Warrant and this was followed by a short religious service conducted by the ship's Chaplain, with the music being provided by the Royal Marines Band. Vice-Admiral Madden then gave a short address to wish the ship's company well and once the parade had been dismissed, officers and men were free to entertain their guests on board or, following the cancellation of a sports event which had been arranged, to go ashore. One event which the weather could not spoil, was the Ship's Company Dance that was held in the Plymouth Guildhall and which was acknowledged by everyone to have been a great success.

It was almost four weeks after recommissioning, at 11.45am on Monday 29 May, that the *Tiger* finally slipped her moorings and steamed to C buoy in Plymouth Sound to carry out compass adjustments, then in the days that followed the ship's company found their sea legs as the cruiser carried out her sea trials in the Channel. On Monday 5 June a Families Day was held on board, and at 9am the relatives came out by Admiralty tugs to the ship which was moored in the Sound. Once on board it was not long before mums, dads, wives, children and sweethearts were dispersed around the ship and drinking the first of many cups of tea. Whilst the ship was made ready for sea the Royal Marines Band played on the quarterdeck and as the weather was fine there was also a small arms and diving equipment exhibition. At sea came a gunnery display and after lunch many chose to sit quietly on the quarterdeck listening to more music. Finally, at 4.15pm, after tea and a draw for the raffle, the *Tiger* passed Plymouth breakwater where the visitors were able to watch the ship's company man the decks as the cruiser steamed up harbour to secure alongside No 5 wharf at precisely 5pm, where a lot of tired, but happy, families left the ship. The sea trials continued into July with visits to Portland and Portsmouth and in the middle of the month Captain Graham announced to the ship's company that the *Tiger* had been chosen to act as Guard Ship in the Solent for Cowes Week, which would be the cruiser's first assignment of the commission. First, however, came a visit by the C-in-C Plymouth, who

hoisted his flag in the *Tiger* at 10am on Monday 17 July for a day at sea where the guns' crews were put through their paces in the exercise areas off the coast of Cornwall. Four days later the *Tiger* berthed alongside at Devonport for a seven-day break during which the ship was painted and additional floodlighting gear was embarked. Finally, looking very smart, the *Tiger* left Devonport on the evening of Friday 28 July to make an overnight passage to the Solent, where she anchored in Cowes Roads at 5.30am the following morning. The five days spent at anchor off what is usually a sleepy little town were extremely busy as Cowes was transformed into the 'Mecca' for the world's yachtsmen. The *Tiger* wore the flag of Admiral Sir Manley Power, the C-in-C Portsmouth, and the Royal Marines, both Detachment and Band, the quarterdeck staff and the boats' crews had their first experience of the ceremonial duties of a flagship. Each day the cruiser was surrounded by what appeared to be a hopeless jumble of yachts, but by the end of the visit most of the ship's company could identify the various classes. During the evening of Monday 31 July, the Duke of Edinburgh, Princess Marina and Princess Alexandra paid a forty-five minute visit to the cruiser when they attended a reception given by the C-in-C. Next day the ship was opened to visitors, where one of the most popular guests was the Regatta Beauty Queen. A festive and international atmosphere ashore was generated by liberal licensing laws, the presence of a number of foreign warships and several thousand holidaymakers, with the result that Cowes was voted a good run ashore. The cruiser's duties ended on the evening of Wednesday 2 August, when Admiral Power struck his flag and next morning, at 10am, the *Tiger* weighed anchor to make a fast, uneventful, seven-hour passage from the Needles to Devonport.

Two days after arriving alongside No 5 wharf in Devonport Dockyard the *Tiger* was once again opened to visitors for the summer Navy Days, during which nearly 13,000 people went on board the cruiser. With the excitement of Navy Days over there were just seven days to prepare the ship for the overseas leg of the commission, a four-month Mediterranean deployment which unfortunately did not get off to a good start. It was at 4.30pm on Monday 14 August that the *Tiger* slipped her moorings, but in the process the port anchor came loose and struck the ship's side, causing a one-foot square hole and split just forward of No 6 bulkhead. As a result the *Tiger* had to anchor for three hours in Cawsand Bay so the shipwrights could make temporary repairs by welding a three-foot square steel plate over the hole. Finally at 6.45pm that evening the *Tiger* was able to weigh anchor and set course for the Mediterranean. Heading south from Plymouth the sea became steadily bluer, the night sky clearer and the ship's company gradually more sun-tanned. By the time the cruiser entered the Strait of Gibraltar they had changed into whites and upper deck games were in full swing.

Whenever possible during the dog watches the ship would stop for 'Hands to Bathe' to be piped and the quarterdeck was converted to a hockey pitch. After six days at sea the first sight of Malta was glimpsed with their arrival at the Marsaxlokk anchorage during the afternoon of Sunday 20 August where, after anchoring, recreational leave was granted. Next day, however, came the serious business of the work-up, which started with naval gunfire support exercises over four days before the *Tiger* made a ceremonial entry into Grand Harbour where she secured to No 7 buoy, aft of the *Lion* which was at No 8 and flying the flag of the C-in-C Mediterranean. The *Tiger* enjoyed a long weekend break before putting to sea again to continue her work-up exercises, during which each department received the polishing necessary for the Sea Inspection of the Flag Officer Flotillas (Mediterranean). At sea under way replenishment teams were kept busy with fuel, ammunition and stores transfers, the guns' crews were exercised under battle practice conditions, the ship's divers carried out what seemed to be endless 'Awkward' exercises, searching the cruiser's underwater hull, and the Royal Marines Detachment successfully 'captured' Marsaxlokk, on a particularly foul day when Malta's six-month-long drought finally broke. To everyone's relief the Sea Inspection went off without a hitch and on the afternoon of Friday 15 September the *Tiger* secured alongside Malta's Parlatorio Wharf for a 13-day maintenance period, before the first 'foreign' visit of the commission.

On the morning of Thursday 28 September the *Tiger* left Grand Harbour and set course for the Greek island of Leros and its picturesque and secluded anchorage of Port Laki, where the cruiser had an appointment to meet her sister 'cat', *Lion,* for an old-style fleet regatta. During the early morning of 30 September the two cruisers rendezvoused off Leros, the *Lion* having left Rhodes the previous day, and just as soon as they were firmly anchored the forenoon was spent rigging the necessary equipment for the aquatic sports and laying the dan buoys for the sailing races. A swimming enclosure was created, with diving boards and waterborne cycles, which the Ordnance Artificers had converted from pusser's 'iron horse' bicycles for the obstacle races. During the afternoon all the contestants took to the water and the tranquillity of Port Laki was shattered by sailing and swimming races, although the lack of wind hindered the former somewhat. In the event the *Tiger's* sailing club beat their counterparts in the *Lion* after the complete absence of even the slightest breeze meant the last race had to be abandoned. Regardless of the fact that there were few bright lights on the remote Greek island, a few liberty men hired motor scooters and explored the highways and byways and on Sunday evening there was a mass migration from both ships as inter-ship visiting took place and uckers, darts and deck hockey tournaments flourished, which provided a suitable conclusion to an energetic, but enjoyable weekend. The next stop on the agenda was Salonica, and after an overnight passage the two cruisers anchored offshore from Greece's second largest city. For most the local bars and the 'deadly' ouzo were sufficient to keep them occupied, but a few hardy souls insisted on climbing Mount Olympus and making camping expeditions into Macedonia. The Royal Marines Band, under Bandmaster Ray Banning, entertained the local population in the city's main square, but official entertainment was limited because of impending Greek elections. After leaving Salonica both cruisers carried out 'Exercise Aegis', during which the Flag Officer Flotillas (Med), Rear-Admiral Bush, transferred by jackstay from the *Lion* to the *Tiger* and hoisted his flag in the latter.

Following a two-day break in Grand Harbour the *Tiger,* now wearing the flag of FOF (Med), sailed on the morning of Thursday 12 October for Palermo, the largest town in Sicily, where she secured alongside the next morning. During the three-day visit there was a coach tour to the catacombs, the Greek temple and the Roman amphitheatre at Segasta. After leaving Palermo on Monday 16 October the *Tiger* carried out air defence exercises, before returning to Grand Harbour four days later where she remained until the end of the month carrying out maintenance. The first few days of November were spent at sea with the destroyer *Duchess,* but on Monday 6 November she left Malta for a 22-hour passage to the Italian naval base of Taranto. The base consists of two harbours, the Mar Grande and the Mar Piccolo, and they are joined by a narrow canal across which is a large swing bridge, with 'traffic lights' to control the ships entering and leaving the little sea. The *Tiger* was greeted by the Italian cruiser *Guiseppe Garibaldi,* after which she entered the canal to secure alongside No 25 berth in the Mar Piccolo. It was here that the ship hosted its first children's party, for 80 orphans, who thoroughly enjoyed the entertainment and games, not to mention the splendid tea, which was provided by the catering department. Everyone enjoyed the visit to Italy's premier naval base, but it was considered discreet to leave the port on the morning of Friday 10 November, the eve of Taranto Day, in readiness for more exercises off Malta, this time with the aircraft carrier *Centaur* which was en route to the Far East Station, and the destroyer *Diamond.*

The *Tiger's* homeward run from the Mediterranean began on Monday 27 November, but with a passage in the wrong direction. The Royal Marines of 40 Commando had embarked in Malta in order to hitch a lift to Tobruk in Libya. In all some additional 350 officers and men were embarked and they were soon absorbed into the ship's routine, despite the overcrowding. To alleviate any possible boredom the guests were kept fully entertained by record programmes on the ship's tannoy, tours of the ship, quizzes and, as it must have seemed to the chefs, a non-stop serving of meals. There was some relief, however, when the

The *Tiger* leaving Portsmouth for trials early in her second commission.

(*Maritime Photo Library*)

passengers were delivered to Tobruk Harbour after an uneventful voyage in bright sunny weather and calm seas. After leaving Tobruk at midday on Tuesday 28 November the *Tiger* set course for Naples and on the morning of Friday 1 December she rendezvoused with the aircraft carrier *Ark Royal* to make a ceremonial entry into the port where she berthed stern to at the port's new passenger terminal. The *Ark* was not so fortunate and she had to anchor in the Naples Roads, for what were to be four very full days. On the first evening the Royal Marines Band Beat Retreat on the jetty, under the sterns of a destroyer flotilla. This setting, together with the very effective lighting arrangements, made for a very impressive show which drew much favourable comment from the many NATO officials and guests who attended. With Christmas fast approaching the many large stores in the city did a roaring trade in toys of all descriptions. Despite the December drizzle many visited the seaside towns of Amalfi and Sorrento, the preserved Roman town of Pompeii and even the cause of its demise, Mount Vesuvius.

After leaving Naples the *Tiger* returned to Malta for a brief three-hour stay in Grand Harbour in order to refuel and to land FOF (Med) and his staff, before leaving at midday on Wednesday 6 December for a long weekend visit to Palma, Majorca. The passage west was made through severe gales and, off the coast of Sardinia, it became necessary to reduce speed to four knots owing to the short steep seas. The inclement weather meant a late arrival in Palma, but by that time the sun was shining and the winds had subsided, making it difficult to believe that Christmas was only 17 days away. The final call of the deployment was Gibraltar where, during a 28-hour stopover, there was time for some last-minute shopping. Finally, at 3.45pm on Thursday 14 December, the *Tiger* left Gibraltar and set course for Devonport where, at just after 10pm on Sunday 17 December, she anchored in Plymouth Sound. During the evening a carol service had been held in the Junior Rates' Dining Hall when the whole ship echoed to the strains of 'Ding Dong Merrily on High'. Next day at 2pm, after Customs clearance, the *Tiger* secured alongside No 5 wharf of Devonport Dockyard, where there were many happy reunions with wives and sweethearts. *Tiger* was home for Christmas.

The second, much shorter leg, of the *Tiger's* commission was to be spent with the Home Fleet and it got under way on Monday 22 January 1962 when, at 12.30pm, she left Devonport. The first duty was a sad one as it entailed holding the funeral ceremony for the late RO2 William Swann who had died unexpectedly in hospital at Devonport three days before Christmas. The *Tiger* came to a stop at 1.45pm and the ashes of RO2 Swann were scattered at sea off Eddystone, following which the cruiser returned to the Sound for the night. Next morning, upon her departure at 9am, the *Tiger* set course for Portland

where she was to spend ten days exercising, at one stage with the cruiser *Bermuda*. When this initial phase was completed on Friday 2 February, the *Tiger* secured alongside Portsmouth's South Railway Jetty for a weekend break. This was followed by the highlight of the home leg, a visit to Bremen, where she docked alongside the Europa Hafen at 3pm on Wednesday 7 February to be greeted by a large crowd of well-wishers. Some of the most popular spots turned out to be the city's beer gardens while the cruiser herself was popular with the locals, over 4,000 of whom visited the ship during the two afternoons that she was opened to the public. After sailing on the morning of Monday 12 February and steaming down the River Weser the *Tiger* was met by severe storms, with winds of up to Force 10 and mountainous seas, which made many on board wish that they had kept away from the beer gardens the previous evening. Later that afternoon, in the German Bight, the *Tiger* was called upon to stand by a badly listing coaster, and although she was unable to follow the small vessel because she was blown out of the swept channel into what had been a Second World War minefield, she was able to direct the lifeboat by searchlight. Fortunately the weather moderated soon afterwards and the cruiser was able to make up for lost time as she set course for Liverpool. Happily, all on board the coaster were rescued and the master of the vessel sent a signal to Captain Graham thanking the *Tiger* for her assistance. The passage to Liverpool was made by way of the Channel and the visit started at 11am on Thursday 15 February when the cruiser tied up alongside No 2 berth in the Canada Dock, just off the city's Regent Road. This visit was the last during the Home Fleet deployment and here too the *Tiger* proved to be very popular with the Scousers as hundreds of people had to be turned away when closing time arrived and long queues were still patiently waiting to look round the cruiser. After leaving Liverpool on the morning of Monday 19 February she steamed south and arrived alongside at Devonport at noon the next day, to prepare for service on the Far East Station.

The final, and longest, deployment of the *Tiger's* second commission started at 1pm on Friday 23 March 1962, when the cruiser slipped her berth at No 5 wharf and steamed down the Hamoaze, where several groups of well-wishers had gathered to wave her off, into the Sound and out into the Channel where she set course for Gibraltar. The crossing of the Bay of Biscay was quiet and after a weekend at sea she arrived in Gibraltar where, with dry weather, the paint-ship programme which had been started at Devonport was completed. On the third day of the stopover, the newest of the Tiger-class cruisers, HMS *Blake*, wearing the flag of FOF (Med), arrived in harbour, but it was to be a very brief meeting for next morning, at 7.30am, the *Tiger* left for Suez and Aden. During the afternoon of Thursday 5 April the cruiser embarked the Suez Canal pilot off Port Said and an hour later she secured to buoys off the Suez Canal Authority Building in the port to await a southbound convoy. Seven hours later, at 10.20pm, she slipped her moorings and began her transit of the canal. The first leg, as far as the Great Bitter Lake, was completed during the night and at 5am the next morning she anchored for seven hours. The second leg of the transit took just three hours and at 3.20pm on Friday 6 April she passed through Port Suez and set course for Aden. Between Suez and Singapore a series of deck games tournaments were organized for the long sea passage east, and each afternoon the upper decks were a hive of activity with hockey and volleyball matches and tug-of-war competitions. On Tuesday 10 April there was a 24-hour call at Aden which had little to commend it apart from the duty-free shopping, and on sailing the next day there were many new cameras in evidence.

At 8am on Saturday 21 April, ten days after leaving Aden, the *Tiger* arrived in the Johore Strait and once off Changi Pier the lower deck was cleared before the cruiser steamed ahead in style to secure alongside No 7 berth of the Stores Basin in Singapore Naval Base at 9am precisely. The change to tropical routine, with its early start and finish to the day was welcomed by everyone on board, especially the sunbathing and swimming addicts who had all the facilities of the pool at HMS *Terror* at their disposal.

After a two-week maintenance period in the naval base, the *Tiger* left harbour to steam north into the South China Sea to the exercise areas off the island of Pulau Tioman, situated about 30 miles off the northern coast of Johore. During the manoeuvres the main and secondary armament were fired on bombardment exercises and the first weekend of May was spent off Tioman and given over to banyans, sunbathing and swimming from the beaches of this idyllic tropical island. On Monday 7 May it was time to start work once again, and after rendezvousing with the frigates *Eastbourne* and *Plymouth* in the China Sea, all three ships threaded their way through the islands of the Pearl Delta to make their way to berths in Hong Kong's new naval dockyard at HMS *Tamar*. The base was officially opened on the day of the cruiser's arrival and having thrown its doors open to visitors, the *Tiger* opened her gangway to the sightseers as well. The crowds queued twenty deep to walk round the cruiser and, incredibly, almost 20,000 visited the ship in just over eight hours – which must be a record. Just a few hundred yards from the dockyard was the famous China Fleet Club which, with its well-stocked bar, bowling alley and cinema, was where most sailors started the run ashore. Just a little further up the road was the suburb of Wanchai with its bars, music and Chinese girls in cheongsams serving ice-cold San Miguel beer. The *Tiger's* next port of call was to be Inchon in Korea, and originally it had been intended that the C-in-C Far East Station would be on board for the trip. Unfortunately, the troubles

in what had once been French Indo-China were never far from the surface in the early 1960s, and on 6 May that year Communist guerrillas of the Pathet Lao had captured the government stronghold of Nam Tha in the north of Laos, near to the Thai border. At the time the United States was committed to preventing a communist takeover in South-East Asia and it was considered vital that a line was held in Thailand, South Vietnam and, if necessary, Cambodia. In response to the Pathet Lao victory in Laos the USA sent a force of 5,000 marines from its 7th Fleet to Thailand, and as a result of the military and diplomatic activity the C-in-C cancelled his visit, so the *Tiger* sailed from Hong Kong without him. It was on the morning of Tuesday 22 May that the cruiser anchored off Inchon, which is the port for the South Korean capital city of Seoul. Although it had been nine years since the end of the Korean War, during which Inchon had been razed to the ground by the Allied forces, the city was still virtually a collection of hovels, despite US efforts to redevelop it. However, thanks to the generosity of the US service personnel the *Tiger's* visit was a success, and many of the ship's company took away vivid memories of 'boneshaking' bus rides and a wide variety of entertainment, including a visit to the ship by a local singing and dancing troupe consisting of 144 children and 70 adults, which left little room on the quarterdeck for spectators.

After leaving Inchon on the morning of Saturday 26 May the *Tiger* set course for Japan and a cruise which all on board had been looking forward to. After steaming down the Yellow Sea, across the Korea Strait and into the Pacific Ocean, the cruiser entered Japan's Inland Sea by the Shimonoseki Strait to steam north towards Hiroshima Bay and the island of Eta Jima, the home of Japan's naval college, the equivalent to Dartmouth. Here the *Tiger* anchored for the day on Monday 28 May to allow visits by Japanese naval officers and, more popularly, girls in traditional costume. At 4pm that afternoon the cruiser weighed anchor and steamed through the Inland Sea once again, this time bound for Tokyo. As she sailed through Tokyo Bay and into the Sumida River, the *Tiger* was met by fire floats which, with hoses playing, escorted her to a berth at Mamuri at the end of one of the city's main shopping streets. A Japanese naval band welcomed the cruiser as she drew alongside, and very soon the Royal Navy's white uniforms were to be seen all round the city. In the bars the ship's company soon learned that the pretty, kimono-clad girls who served the saki were also adept at fleecing the unwary of their money, whilst in the city's main park the Royal Marines Band was kept busy playing to the local crowds. Other activities on offer were coach trips to Kamakura to see the Great Buddha, and to Enoshima, a nearby seaside resort.

After leaving Tokyo at 9am on Tuesday 5 June the *Tiger* made a 24-hour passage down the coast to Nagoya, a large industrial city, where she tied up alongside the Central Pier which was some way from the city centre. At first glance the port seemed to have little to commend it, but with cheap beer and friendly locals it was voted by some as the best run ashore in Japan. A reception held in the wardroom turned out to be rather unconventional when guests arrived with supplies of visiting cards which they distributed generously and then, with the awkward lack of conversation owing to language problems, mostly left an hour before the end of the party. After a five-day stop at Nagoya the *Tiger* left for a two-day passage to Sasebo on the island of Kyushu where, with the frigate *Plymouth,* she arrived at just after 10am on Wednesday 13 June and secured alongside No 6 berth of India Basin. Once again, thanks to the hospitality of the US naval base in the city, the ship's company were superbly entertained and also able to travel to the city of Nagasaki. The *Tiger's* sailing club enjoyed three splendid days racing against local and US Navy crews, during which they made many new friends. At 8.30am on Monday 18 June, escorted by the *Plymouth,* she left the picturesque natural harbour and rendezvoused with the frigates *Chichester, Rhyl* and HMAS *Yarra,* as well as US Navy units, including the aircraft carriers *Providence* and *Hancock* and the destroyer *Towers,* for exercises off the island of Okinawa, after which the British squadron set course for Singapore where they arrived on the morning of 29 June.

The *Tiger* was to spend the next seven weeks at Singapore or in the South China Sea off the east coast of Malaya, but for the first ten days she was alongside the dockyard carrying out maintenance with the ship working a tropical routine and many men spending their afternoons at the nearby swimming pools. This all came to an end on the morning of Thursday 12 July when, at 7.30am, the cruiser sailed for the Flag Officer's Tactical Exercises, 'Exercise Fotex 62', and at 6pm the next day she anchored off the island of Tioman. Soon afterwards the submarines *Ambush* and *Andrew* joined her and secured alongside where their companies were able to share the facilities on board their makeshift depot ship. Although some recreational leave was granted during the weekend, everyone was kept occupied with drills and exercises, and the following week was filled with fleet manoeuvres, gunnery exercises and anti-submarine measures. There was no respite during the hours of darkness either, with night encounter exercises dominating the night watches. To everyone's relief the fleet, including the two submarines, the aircraft carriers *Bulwark* and *Ark Royal,* the destroyers *Caprice, Carysfort* and *Cassandra,* and the frigates *Eastbourne* and HMAS *Yarra,* returned to Pulau Tioman during the early evening of Friday 20 July. This time, however, it was a much more relaxed weekend with two days of swimming, fishing, or just relaxing on the island, but on the morning of 23 July the holiday atmosphere came to an abrupt end when, wearing the flag of the Chief

of Staff Far East Station, Rear-Admiral B. C. Durant, the *Tiger* sailed with the rest of the fleet to take part in 'Exercise Hopalong', the purpose of which was to embark a battalion of the Royal Green Jackets, transport them up the east coast of Malaya to Kuala Trengganu, disembark them there and then assume the role of a military force command ship. The *Tiger* steamed south to the Johore Strait where at first light on Tuesday 24 July the troops were embarked, and by 8am she was heading north once again. Having carried out a similar exercise in the Mediterranean the whole operation went very smoothly, and at 6am on Wednesday 25 July the cruiser anchored off the town of Kuala Trengganu where LCAs from the *Bulwark* collected the troops and took them ashore into the Malayan rainforests where they were to spend the following 24 hours. All that day and well into the night the usually quiet waters off the isolated town reverberated to the clatter of helicopters and the roar of the *Ark Royal's* jets as they carried out strafing runs. Next morning the Green Jackets were brought back out to the *Tiger* and at noon the cruiser weighed anchor and set course for Singapore Naval Base, where she arrived eight hours later.

During the *Tiger's* three weeks at the base, seven days were spent in the massive King George VI dry dock, where a cracked port outer propeller was changed. To alleviate the unpleasant living conditions on board whilst the cruiser was under refit, arrangements were made for at least half of the ship's company to move into shore accommodation at HMS *Terror* at weekends and, with no reveille and use of the swimming pool, these breaks proved very popular. On Thursday 16 August the Flag Officer Second in Command Far East Station (FO2 FES), Vice-Admiral J. B. Frewen, hoisted his flag in the *Tiger* and two days later she sailed for Bangkok, with a small intrepid band going on ahead and making the 1,600 mile journey overland in the cruiser's Land Rover. The *Tiger* herself arrived at the mouth of the Chao Phraya River early on Tuesday 21 August, and began her run upriver on what was a fine, clear morning with the brightly painted houses and gilded temples contrasting starkly with the lush green river banks and the muddy waters of the river itself. Finally, at 11am she secured alongside Customs Quay in Bangkok's New Harbour. Most members of the ship's company took the opportunity to visit at least one of the city's impressive Buddhist temples and some went to pay their respects at the immaculately kept War Graves Cemeteries at Kanchanaburi and Chungkai, which were the last resting places of their compatriots who had died during the Second World War while working on the infamous Burma Railway. The city's nightlife proved a magnet to some and there were more than a few empty wallets when, at 1pm on Saturday 25 August, the *Tiger* left Bangkok to make a 48-hour passage to Singapore where she remained for less than 24 hours before sailing for Australia in company with the destroyers

Caprice and *Cassandra* and the frigate *Loch Killisport.* In the early hours of the next morning, at 3.20am, the *Tiger* crossed the equator in a position Long 106° - 59'E in the Karimata Strait between the town of Pontianak in Borneo and the Sumatran island of Kepulauan Lingga. Just over six hours later King Neptune's Court assembled on the quarterdeck and the 'victims' received their usual duckings as part of the Crossing the Line ceremony.

For ten days before her first Australian port of call the *Tiger* took part in the combined British and Australian fleet exercise code-named 'Tucker Box', which also included the aircraft carrier HMAS *Melbourne.* Finally, during the morning of Monday 17 September, the combined fleets arrived off Sydney Heads for what should have been an impressive entrance to the harbour in line astern, but strong winds and heavy rain squalls spoilt the occasion. However, at 2.30pm the cruiser tied up alongside the Oil Wharf at Garden Island, with a magnificent view of the harbour and the famous bridge. As always the people of Sydney were wonderful hosts and soon the slang 'Aussie' terms of 'cobber', 'dinkum' and 'pommie' became second nature to those on board. The first ship's company dance since leaving Devonport in March was held in Sydney's Victoria Army Barracks with the music being provided by the Royal Marines Band, augmented by the ship's instrumental group, the Federals, and the Moonrakers, who provided the vocals. There was also a beauty competition to find a 'Miss Tigress', which was won by Maureen Jones from the suburb of Canterbury. At the end of the *Tiger's* 11-day visit everyone was very sorry to be leaving the Commonwealth's second largest city when the cruiser slipped her moorings at 1pm on Friday 28 September and set course for the passage of the Tasman Sea and the city of Auckland.

It was early on the morning of Wednesday 3 October that the *Tiger* arrived off the beautiful Hauraki Gulf and the approaches to Auckland, and at 9am she berthed alongside Calliope Wharf at Devonport on the north side of the harbour which meant a ferry ride across to the city's main streets. The early pub closing hours - 6pm - were difficult for the ship's company to get used to, but the hospitality of the local people more than made up for this 'hardship'. The coach tours to Rotorua were very popular, as were trips to Mount Eden overlooking the harbour, and two dances were held for the ship's company. After leaving Auckland at 9am on Monday 8 October, the *Tiger* set course for Wellington and made the short passage in just 48 hours, securing alongside Clyde Pier, close to the town centre, opposite the frigate *Loch Killisport.* During open days the cruiser drew large crowds, and with no restrictions on entry to her pier almost 10,000 people visited her over two afternoons. Wellington was a 'quieter' run ashore than Auckland, but nevertheless everyone enjoyed their time there before sailing at 3pm on Monday 15 October for Lyttelton. If Wellington was a 'quiet' run then Lyttelton,

the port for Christchurch, was even more so, and the very English atmosphere of the place made it difficult to believe that one was on the opposite side of the world. After a stay of just three days the *Tiger* left for Dunedin, where the approach to the town along a very narrow and tricky channel under grey skies and steady drizzle conjured up the impression of arriving in Scotland. However, in spite of the inclement weather a small group of schoolchildren, enthusiastically waving their Union Flags, greeted the cruiser as she berthed alongside Victoria Wharf close to the town centre. Four days later, on 23 October, as the *Tiger* reluctantly left harbour and headed down the estuary, she was greeted by newly found friends and more schoolchildren waving, while car drivers sounded their horns to wish her Godspeed. At 8pm that evening the cruiser dropped anchor for a while before getting under way again just after midnight and setting course for the one-mile-wide and one-mile-high Milford Sound. During the morning, as the *Tiger* steamed in the magnificent fjord, Admiral Frewen re-embarked before the cruiser set course into the Tasman Sea and Australian waters.

After a choppy and uncomfortable four-day passage across the Tasman Sea the *Tiger* arrived at Hobart, and on a fine, clear morning she passed the Iron Port Lighthouse and steamed up the Derwent Estuary to berth alongside Princess Wharf. The cruiser's arrival coincided with the last day of the Hobart Show at the town's racecourse, and it proved to be a popular attraction for the ship's company. The Royal Marines Band made a major contribution to the show, and in the evening a ship's dance was held at the Town Hall. On the afternoon of Wednesday 31 October, after embarking fuel oil, the *Tiger* left Hobart to make a two-day passage to Melbourne and after passing Port Phillip Heads in the early morning of Friday 2 November, she drew alongside the outer berth of Station Pier at 9am. Tuesday 6 November was Melbourne Cup Day, and a public holiday, so taking advantage of a Sunday routine on board many of the ship's company joined the thousands of racegoers at Flemington Racecourse. The visit ended the next day and after an uneventful forty-eight hours at sea the cruiser secured alongside No 2 berth at Port Adelaide. The passage upriver, through a heavily industrialized area, was a complete contrast and a following wind whipped up clouds of dust from the surrounding sandy wastelands. The port is about ten miles from Adelaide, but the long, straight road which connects the two became very familiar to liberty men as they made their way to the city, where, as a reminder that Christmas was approaching, an enormous pageant was staged, with a two-mile-long procession of brightly coloured floats. The *Tiger* left Port Adelaide at 10am on Friday 9 November and steamed into the Great Australian Bight for fleet exercises during which the area lived up to its reputation for bad weather. During the following eight days the cruiser carried out exercises with

A magnificent study of the *Tiger* at sea in the Channel.

(FotoFlite)

the *Cavalier, Blackpool, Tapir, Anchorite, Quickmatch, Taranaki, Anzac* and the RFAs *Fort Charlotte* and *Wave Sovereign,* relieved only by short periods at anchor in King George V Sound and Geographe Bay on Australia's west coast. Finally, at just after 9am on Wednesday 21 November the *Tiger* and the other units arrived at Fremantle where the cruiser berthed alongside the North Wharf, opposite the port's new passenger terminal and astern of three large passenger liners which were providing additional accommodation for visitors to the Commonwealth Games, which the City of Perth was hosting. Altogether there were ten naval warships in harbour including the Australian units and the New Zealand frigate *Taranaki* which was secured alongside the *Tiger*. The day of the squadron's arrival saw the opening of the Games at the Perry Lake Stadium, and whilst they were in progress the *Tiger's* sports teams took part in the Naval Commonwealth Games at HMAS *Leuwin* in Fremantle. On Thursday 29 November HRH Prince Philip, who had opened the Commonwealth Games, was welcomed on board the *Tiger* by Admiral Frewen, and during his two-hour visit he also met the commanding officers of the other warships and the RFAs. At 1pm on Sunday 2 December the *Tiger,* accompanied by the other ships of the Far East Fleet, left for Singapore at the end of their detachment.

The passage back to the naval base at Singapore was spent in exercising and preparing for the Admiral's departmental inspections. In his farewell speech to the ship's company Admiral Frewen emphasized the importance of the flag-showing deployment to Australian and New Zealand ports, but political events in South-East Asia were soon to dominate the final months of the *Tiger's* service on the Far East Station.

In the early hours of Saturday 8 December 1962 a quasi-political organization with strong links to Indonesia's President Sukarno, called the North Kalimantan National Army, led by a politician, A. M. Azahari, seized the Seria Oilfield and a small coastal strip between Miri and Brunei town in the oil-rich British dependency of Brunei. This small sultanate was one of three British dependencies bordering the northern coast of the wild and enormous island of Borneo. In the north-east was the colony of North Borneo, with a broken coastline and a mountainous interior; to the south-west, spread along 500 miles of coastline, was the colony of Sarawak, a land remembered by many for its association with Rajah Brooke, and in the centre was Brunei. The remainder of Borneo, which was three times bigger than the British section, belonged to Indonesia, whose President was eager to incorporate the three British territories into his country. His ambitions had been felt in Sarawak where there were restless stirrings among the Chinese population and in North Borneo where there had been an alarming outbreak of murderous piracy. However, it was in Brunei town that open revolt started

when, at 2am on 8 December, with the crashing of gunfire, the rebels seized police stations and the power station. In other parts of Brunei the rebels had even greater success, and when daylight came there were alarming claims of captures they had made and hostages they had seized.

Fortunately, thanks to its SEATO commitments in the area, the British Army was still strongly represented in both Malaya and Singapore, although the dense jungles of Borneo and the primitive conditions made a fast airlift of troops almost impossible. The commando carrier HMS *Albion* had just relieved the *Bulwark* on the Far East Station, but she was in the middle of the Indian Ocean having just carried out exercises with 40 Commando Royal Marines off East Africa. The *Tiger,* however, was due to arrive alongside the naval base at Singapore at 8am on Monday 10 December, and late on Sunday 9 December orders were received on board that the cruiser was urgently required to lift troops to Brunei just as soon as she had secured alongside. The whole ship's company was galvanised into action and the quarterdeck, instead of being prepared for the Admiral's farewell cocktail party, was converted into a canvas-covered marquee-like structure. Red and Green gun decks and O2G decks forward received the same treatment as they were converted into temporary troop accommodation. As it transpired, the *Tiger* arrived at No 8 berth in the naval base at 9am on the Monday morning, and as soon as the final wires were in place all hands were employed in embarking the army equipment. All the ship's boats, except the whalers, were landed and their place was taken by a variety of transport, including nine Land Rovers, ten trailers, four Ferret armoured scout cars, a tractor and two water bowsers. Also embarked were some 40 tons of stores, including ammunition, and preparations were put in hand to feed and accommodate the troops. The first of these, the 1st Battalion of the Royal Green Jackets, HQ Company of 42 Commando, Royal Marines and a small detachment of the Irish Hussars, together with their pet monkey, arrived during the early evening making, with the monkey, a total of 6,343 passengers. The Green Jackets, who were no strangers to the *Tiger,* had been exercising on the Malay-Thai border less than 48 hours previously and had travelled the 640 miles to Singapore by train thinking that they were to 'stand by' on the island. It was, therefore, something of a surprise to find that they were being bundled aboard the *Tiger*. During the day Admiral Frewen was relieved as FO2 FES by Rear-Admiral J. P. Scratchard, and at 10.45pm that evening the *Tiger* slipped her moorings and set course at 27 knots for Sarawak. Fortunately weather conditions were kind, with a smooth sea and a cessation of torrential rainstorms, which had made embarkation day somewhat trying, and it enabled many of the troops to sleep out in the open on their camp beds.

The day at sea on Tuesday 11 December was, much to

the relief of the catering department, flat calm and they were able to serve over 5,000 meals with an almost continuous service from 5.30am to 7pm. At just after 6am on Wednesday 12 December the *Tiger* anchored off Miri in northern Sarawak, close to the border with Brunei, to disembark the Green Jackets. During the four hours at the anchorage the ship's divers observed a full 'Awkward' procedure with regular searches of the underwater hull and the dropping of scare charges before the cruiser weighed anchor at 10.25am and set course for Labuan Island off North Borneo. The passage took just five hours and by 3.25pm the *Tiger* had secured alongside a wooden structure called Liberty Pier in Victoria Harbour, where the remaining troops, 42 Commando and the vehicles were disembarked. The *Tiger's* own Royal Marines Detachment also had to don battledress and they were landed to take over guard duties at the local airport. Admiral Scratchard went ashore for a conference and, upon his return at 7.15pm, the cruiser left Labuan and set course for the return passage to Singapore Naval Base, where she arrived on the morning of Friday 14 December. Although the Brunei rebellion would continue in the form of Confrontation with Indonesia until 1966, the *Tiger's* part in the campaign was over.

After leaving Australia earlier in December, the *Tiger's* ship's company had been looking forward to spending Christmas in Hong Kong, but the trouble in Brunei had put back her schedule and, in the event, the celebrations took place in Singapore instead. The delay also left insufficient time to service the guns and to have the departmental inspections before Christmas, but on the morning of Thursday 27 December, in company with the destroyer *Caesar,* the cruiser eventually left Singapore bound for Hong Kong. Fortunately she arrived alongside the south-west arm of Hong Kong's dockyard at 1pm on New Year's Eve. Following the festivities here the Harbour Inspection was carried out on Tuesday 8 January 1963 and two days later she left for her Sea Inspection and a visit to Subic Bay in the Philippines where she secured stern to at Alava Wharf. After leaving the 'delights' of Olongapo behind the *Tiger* returned to Hong Kong, but by Saturday 9 February she was back in Singapore and ready to leave the Far East and return home via India and Ceylon (Sri Lanka).

The *Tiger* sailed from Singapore at 2pm on Monday 11 February and, in company with the submarine *Ambush* and RFA *Fort Dunvegan,* she set course for Port Blair in South Andaman Island. The Andaman and Nicobar Islands, of which Port Blair is the capital, form a lush tropical archipelago of about 200 islands in the Bay of Bengal, all belonging to India. The *Tiger's* visit to Port Blair coincided with an assembly of Indian Navy ships, including the cruiser *Mysore* (ex-HMS *Nigeria*), wearing the flag of the C-in-C of the Indian Navy, Rear-Admiral A. K. Chatterji. The *Tiger* arrived at Port Blair on the morning of Thursday

14 February, and after firing a gun salute to the Indian C-in-C, she anchored off the town. During the four-day visit the local citizens gave the ship's company a warm welcome, which they concluded with a demonstration of Indian folk dancing, and at 9am on Monday 18 February the cruiser left for Madras. The passage to India's fourth largest city took three days and here too there was a friendly reception for the ship's company, with the sports teams being fully occupied. By now, however, everyone's thoughts were turning to home and on Monday 25 February the *Tiger* left Madras for a 24-hour passage to the former British naval base of Trincomalee with its beautiful natural harbour, where she spent just 48 hours before leaving at 9am on the last day of the month, bound for Aden.

During the afternoon of Friday 1 March, when the *Tiger* was some 240 miles west of Ceylon, she rendezvoused with her sister *Lion* who was taking up her station with the Far East Fleet. The main purpose of the meeting was to transfer the *Tiger's* locally enlisted Chinese laundry crew to the *Lion,* but it also allowed for an interchange of officers and ratings for about an hour, one of whom was Junior Seaman Hickmott who was transferred by jackstay from the *Lion* to visit his older brother, PO W. Hickmott, in the *Tiger.*

The stay in Aden, to everyone's relief, lasted only about eight hours which was just long enough to refuel, before the *Tiger* left for Suez and made her northbound transit of the canal which she made during Sunday 10 March. It had been intended that she steam non-stop from Port Said to Gibraltar, but at 6.05pm on Tuesday 12 March, when she was in a position Lat 35° - 23'N/Long 16° - 43'E, she received a distress call from a Dutch cargo vessel, *Doelwijk,* requesting urgent medical assistance. The *Tiger* was, in fact, the closest vessel and she immediately altered course and increased speed to rendezvous with the Dutch ship. Exactly an hour and a half after receiving the distress call the *Tiger* had closed the *Doelwijk* and the Medical Officer was on his way over to her in the seaboat. At 8.45pm he returned to the *Tiger* with one stretcher patient and the cruiser was under way and bound for Malta where, at 3am the following morning, a tender landed the sick crewman at Bighi Hospital. Two days later there was a stop of just 50 minutes at Gibraltar Bay to embark and land mail, before the *Tiger* set course for Plymouth.

The cruiser arrived in Plymouth Sound at 10am on Monday 18 March and she anchored for the night, completing Customs formalities the next morning. Finally, at 3.30pm, families and friends were embarked for the passage up harbour, and at 5.10pm came the moment for which everyone had been waiting, when she secured alongside No 7 wharf of Devonport Dockyard. It was the end of the *Tiger's* commission, during which she had steamed 72,206 miles and called at 37 different ports, but now it was time for leave and, for most of the ship's company, to join new ships.

Chapter Three

HMS *Tiger* – Third Commission 1963-1964

On 22 March 1963, just three days after returning to Devonport from the Far East, the *Tiger's* new commanding officer, Captain H. L. Lloyd DSC RN, joined the ship and Captain Graham left. However, with the ship in dockyard hands it was on Wednesday 24 April that Captain Lloyd assumed command and the *Tiger* was recommissioned with a new ship's company.

The second week of May saw the *Tiger's* refit completed and the ship ready to leave Devonport for her shakedown and work-up at Portland and when she sailed at 1.30pm on Friday 10 May she was met by some choppy Channel weather. The next five and a half weeks were extremely busy for the ship's company as they were exercised in every possible evolution. Even the Royal Marines lifebuoy sentries were kept busy with numerous man-overboard exercises. One member of the Detachment recalls an occasion when, 'I nearly started a panic when the first thing I saw was what I took to be a lifeless sailor floating past the quarterdeck. After frantically heaving the lifebuoys over the side and pressing the buzzers I realized it was our prize dummy "Albert" who had been flung over for exercise.' There were also daily firings of the main armament and the announcement, '6-inch systems close up for surface firings' was regularly on the tannoy and in

A charming welcome for the *Tiger* on her arrival at the Japanese port of Sasebo. *(Author's collection)*

Daily Orders. At the end of May came a very welcome break when the cruiser went alongside South Railway Jetty at Portsmouth for the Whitsun holiday weekend, and FOF (Home), Vice-Admiral F. R. Twiss, hoisted his flag in the cruiser. Once the holiday weekend was over, the *Tiger* went back to sea to continue her work-up off Portland. The final stage, on 17 June, took the form of a two-day exercise in company with other ships, under wartime conditions, necessitating the ship's company being continually at Action or Defence Stations. As part of the exercise the Royal Marines Detachment was transferred by jackstay to the frigate *Tartar* at midnight on an inky black night with rain, high winds and heavy seas. To everyone's relief however, the work-up was completed on Wednesday 19 June and next morning the cruiser left the Portland area for a six-day visit to the Belgian port of Antwerp which, apart from the ceremonial duties, provided some relaxation for everyone. On leaving Antwerp the *Tiger's* nose was pointed towards 'Guz' and she made the passage at high speed in just 24 hours, arriving in Plymouth Sound at 7am on Thursday 27 June and securing alongside No 7 wharf in Devonport Dockyard just over two hours later, where she was destined to stay until the second week in August.

During her period alongside she was opened to the public for Navy Days and nearly 14,000 visitors walked round during the three days that her gangways were open. It was during the forenoon of Monday 12 August that the *Tiger*, accompanied by the destroyer *Cavendish*, and the frigates *Llandaff* and *Tartar*, left Devonport for 'Exercise Riptide' in the Atlantic Ocean and the Bay of Biscay where they rendezvoused with a US Navy task force which included the cruisers *Long Beach* and *Newport News*. The former was nuclear powered and, having been built without a funnel and with a box-like bridge superstructure, had rather unusual and unsightly lines, but the *Newport News* was a very impressive looking warship. On completion of 'Riptide' the *Tiger* headed back to Devonport where, on Friday 23 August, the 17 warships which made up the Home Fleet assembled, to be joined the following day by the cruiser *Belfast* which was due to decommission and join the Reserve Fleet. The ships of the Home Fleet were to take part in 'Captain of the Fleet Week' which mainly consisted of meetings by specialist officers, and a round of inter-ship sporting contests for the ships' companies. The *Tiger's* next activity was in early September when she was involved in 'Exercise Unison' which took the form of convoy protection at sea and a display of the weapons available. The exercise was split into two parts with high-ranking service officers embarking in Torbay whilst the ship was anchored off Brixham. The other ships taking part were the *Hampshire*, *Decoy* and *Leander*, and in between demonstrations the *Tiger* spent a pleasant weekend anchored off Torquay where the ship's company were able to witness the finish of the Daily

Express Power Boat Race. It was at this time that a change to the ship's future programme was announced whereby, instead of returning to the Far East in the early months of 1965 following a refit, the ship was to remain with the Home Fleet, with just an occasional foray into the Mediterranean. With the end of the 'Unison' exercise and the disembarkation of the final guests off the River Dart during the evening of Wednesday 11 September, the *Tiger* set course for Portsmouth where she spent a popular, and all too short, weekend alongside South Railway Jetty. After leaving Portsmouth the cruiser paid a five-day official visit to Rotterdam where, after making the passage up the picturesque waterway, which gave the guard and band a welcome change of scenery from Portland Harbour, she secured alongside Porthaven in the city. The visit proved to be a busy time for everyone and particularly for the Royal Marines, who had numerous guards and bands paraded on the quarterdeck for VIP visitors. One distinguished visitor to the cruiser was the Commandant of the Netherlands Marine Corps, but the full dignity of the ceremonial on his departure was marred when, after being played over the brow with guard and band and full salutes, he duly positioned himself on a grassy area on the quayside to receive a 15-gun salute. As he came smartly to attention and the first round boomed out across the harbour, up chugged a motor mower driven by a man for whom the solemn ceremonial cut no ice and, almost knocking the commandant over, he proceeded to mow the grass all around him, totally oblivious to the crashing of the saluting guns and the dignity of the occasion! As always the Royal Marines Band gave public performances and Beat Retreat on the quayside whilst the ship was opened to visitors, and the ship's company enjoyed a number of organized trips, the favourites being to the De Kuypers and Heineken breweries.

On leaving Rotterdam during the forenoon of Monday 23 September, the *Tiger* headed north for Rosyth where she arrived the following day and secured in the main basin of the dockyard. Four days later, at 10.35pm, fire broke out in A boiler room which burned for 25 minutes before it was extinguished. Two days later, on the last day of September, whilst tugs were moving the cruiser from the main basin to a berth on the south arm, she collided with the lock wall and was holed on the port side forward. Fortunately the damage was not too serious and at 2.30pm on Tuesday 1 October she was able to leave for Invergordon where she secured alongside the Dockyard Pier 24 hours later. The *Tiger* was the first ship of a combined NATO fleet to arrive and, being the flagship, she occupied the one and only alongside berth. Although Invergordon is a picturesque and charming town it did not offer much in the way of a run ashore, but the ship herself was popular with the locals and over 2,000 people visited her when she was opened to the public. After leaving Invergordon early on Tuesday 15 October, the cruiser rendezvoused with the NATO fleet,

The *Tiger* high and dry in Singapore Dockyard's King George VI dry dock.

(Author's collection)

which included the Dutch aircraft carrier *Karel Doorman* (ex-HMS *Venerable*), for 'Exercise Flat Rock', which took place off the north-west of Scotland around Cape Wrath and Loch Ewe. The exercise was dogged by severe weather in the form of gales, heavy rain and rough seas which, on one occasion, caused the upper decks to be placed out of bounds to those who were not on duty. On completion of the exercise the *Tiger* spent a weekend at Rosyth before she steamed south to Portsmouth, arriving alongside South Railway Jetty on Wednesday 30 October.

During the cruiser's 13-day stay in Portsmouth there was plenty of time to paint the superstructure and to put on a ship's dance at Southsea's South Parade Pier, before the *Tiger* left at 9.30am on Tuesday 12 November bound for Lisbon and Gibraltar. No sooner had she cleared Fort Blockhouse, however, than the tug *Grinder* was summoned alongside to take off a rating who was suffering from appendicitis, after which course was set for Lisbon and the cruiser left the Solent by way of the Needles. After a reasonably flat passage across the Bay of Biscay the *Tiger* arrived alongside Alcantara Wharf at Lisbon at 9am on Friday 15 November. Once again the guard and band were kept busy with ceremonial duties, but there was still time to enjoy Portugal's capital city before, at just after midday on Wednesday 20 November, the ship left for an overnight passage to Gibraltar where, on 22 November, she was joined by the *Lion* and the news of the assassination of President Kennedy was received. Next day FOF (H), Vice-Admiral Twiss, transferred his flag to the *Lion,* which had just returned via Beirut from service on the Far East Station. The two cruisers, together with the destroyer *Decoy* and the frigates *Berwick, Whitby* and *Verulam,* left Gibraltar on Monday 25 November and, after setting course for Devonport, they carried out gunnery exercises en route.

Unloading stores at Brunei.

(Imperial War Museum A34694)

The *Tiger* along-
side at Wellington,
New Zealand.
(Author's collection)

The *Tiger* arrived alongside No 8 berth in Devonport Dockyard on Thursday 28 November, and no sooner were the last mooring ropes secured than dockyard workers swarmed aboard for what was termed a 'clean refit'. This meant, among other things, that all the corticene-covered decks were protected with hardboard and mess deck lockers were boxed in but, despite the precautions, many disputed the term 'clean refit'. However, it marked the end of what had been a short, but busy, commission.

HMS *Tiger* leaves Singapore on 11 February 1964.

(Author's collection)

Chapter Four

HMS *Tiger* – Fourth Commission 1964-1966

During the *Tiger's* refit those members of the ship's company who remained with the ship were accommodated in the now redundant cruiser *Belfast,* which had been decommissioned in August 1963 and was awaiting, it was thought at the time, the breaker's yard. It was at 2.30pm on Friday 22 May 1964 that the *Tiger's* Commissioning Ceremony was held on the jetty alongside the ship, and three days later she left Devonport to undergo trials in the Channel. That summer the *Tiger* underwent her work-up off Portland, during which she towed the RFA *Black Ranger,* and the ship's divers were put through their paces in a night 'Awkward' exercise in Weymouth Bay. The main armament was fired and at the end of July, when it was all over, there were huge sighs of

relief when the cruiser left Portland to return to Devonport for summer leave. Once again she took part in the annual Navy Days, during which she attracted in the region of 20,000 visitors, and she spent just over two weeks in No 9 dry dock. However, by early September normal routine had been restored and on the evening of 8 September the ship's company dance was held at Plymouth's Majestic Ballroom. Next day she and the frigate *Penelope,* together with RFA *Wave Chief,* left Devonport for gunnery exercises before setting course for the Caribbean Sea and Bequia in the Grenadines, where they were to rendezvous with the submarine *Odin* and the frigate *Lynx,* which was wearing the flag of Vice-Admiral Sir Fitzroy Talbot, the C-in-C South Atlantic and South American Station. The squadron,

HMS *Tiger* at sea in 1964, during her South American cruise. *(Imperial War Museum A34875)*

The *Tiger's* open day at La Guira in September 1964.

(Imperial War Museum A34871)

together with the destroyer *London,* which had sailed from the UK to Houston, Texas, for the British Trade Fair in the city, had been formed to undertake an extensive series of goodwill visits to South American ports, during which they would circumnavigate the continent in an anti-clockwise direction calling at 13 ports in eight countries. The purpose of the cruise was to foster the close links which existed between the Royal Navy and South American Navies, and it meant a great deal of hard work by everyone concerned.

The force anchored in Admiralty Bay, Bequia, on the morning of Sunday 20 September and banyan leave was granted. Later that day they were joined by the *Lynx* and *Odin,* and two days later Admiral Talbot transferred his flag to the *Tiger.* The first port of call was La Guira, the port for Caracas, the capital of Venezuela, and they arrived there on Thursday 24 September. Here over 12,000 local people visited the four ships, with the longest queues being for the

Odin. In Caracas itself a Royal Navy guard marched through the streets with bayonets fixed, in exercise of a right granted to British forces by Simon Bolivar, the liberator of the northern part of South America from Spanish rule, with the help of a British Legion which was recruited from veterans of the Napoleonic Wars. The parade was organized as part of a wreath-laying ceremony at Bolivar's tomb in Caracas.

The second port of call was Cartagena in Colombia, where they arrived on the morning of Thursday 1 October, and where in the 19th century, an English naval officer had founded the Naval Academy, which was visited by some of the *Tiger's* officers. After making their westbound transit of the Panama Canal on Tuesday 6 October, the four warships of the squadron and the fleet auxiliary rendezvoused with the destroyer *London,* before all the ships went their separate ways to visit ports on South America's west coast.

The *Tiger's* next stop was Callao in Peru where the resident British community chartered a special train for 300 members of the ship's company who wanted to make the 120 mile journey from Callao to Rio Blanca, 11,500 feet up in the Andes. The party set out at 4 o' clock in the morning for the breathtaking journey as the train zigzagged its way up the steep mountains. Back in Callao the expat 'Brits' held barbecues and dances and organized trips to breweries and oil wells, the former obviously being the most popular. From Callao the cruiser steamed south to Valparaiso which was reached on Monday 19 October. Here, in the main square, the Royal Marines Band Beat Retreat and the Detachment performed a drill demonstration in front of a crowd which was so packed in that those who were at the back could only have heard snatches of the music. Despite this, spectators were still arriving as the Chilean Flag and the White Ensign were being lowered at the end of the ceremony. From Valparaiso the squadron exercised with the Chilean Navy before steaming south to Punta Arenas, stopping on the way to lay a wreath close to the site of the disastrous Battle of Coronel where, just over 50 years previously, Admiral Craddock's squadron had been sunk by the more modern cruisers of Admiral Graf Spee's fleet. They arrived in Punta Arenas for an eight-day visit on Thursday 29 October, and once again the Royal Marines Band Beat Retreat, this time in the Plaza Minoz Gamero.

The final and the most popular port of call in South America was Rio de Janeiro where the local exuberance is well expressed in song and dance rhythms such as the Samba and Rumba. The *Tiger* arrived on Friday 20 November, to moor alongside the Preco Mana Wharf for a week's visit, after which Admiral Talbot transferred his flag to the *London,* while the *Tiger* led the remaining ships across the Atlantic to Dakar for a three-day visit which started on Monday 10 December when they moored alongside the French Naval Jetty in the port. The transatlantic crossing had been uneventful, although they sighted the Brazilian island of Fernando de Norhona which is some 300 miles offshore and, at that time, served as a penal settlement. Another 300 miles beyond that landfall they passed St Paul's Rocks where the *Tiger* stopped and landed the Navigating Officer, the Medical Officer, a midshipman and a photographer to record the event. It was certainly fascinating to see the rocks, which occupy about one eighth of an acre, rising to a height of 60 feet in the vast empty space of the Atlantic Ocean. The short stopover in Dakar was something of a disappointment after the bright lights of Rio, and with prices ashore very high men preferred the French Navy's canteen facilities. After leaving Dakar on 10 December, the *Tiger* and the *Lynx* returned to Portsmouth where seven days later, as soon as the mooring lines were made fast, the families of the ship's company swarmed aboard for some happy reunions. The *Odin* put into Gosport three days after that on Monday 21

December, just in time for Christmas.

For the *Tiger's* ship's company there was seasonal leave to look forward to, but in the second week of February 1965 the ship was ready for sea again and she sailed for Invergordon during the forenoon of Monday 8 February where, three days later, she secured alongside the dockyard pier. From Invergordon the *Tiger* steamed south to Rosyth, where she joined the aircraft carrier *Ark Royal* and other ships of the Home Fleet. A few days later, whilst at sea off the coast of Scotland, FOF (H) hoisted his flag in the cruiser, after being transferred by jackstay from the frigate *Falmouth,* and the end of February saw the cruiser alongside the dockyard pier at Invergordon once again. During the first few days of March the *Tiger* was engaged in anti-submarine exercises off the Dornoch Firth and on Wednesday 3 March she joined a NATO fleet, including the aircraft carriers *Ark Royal* and *Karel Doorman,* the destroyer *Cassandra,* the frigates *Brighton, Falmouth* and *Murray* and units of the Norwegian, American and Canadian Navies, for the NATO exercise 'Pilot Light' which started on Friday 5 March. During the exercise the *Lion* joined the fleet after steaming up from Portsmouth. The weather ranged from flat calm to howling gales and heavy seas during the exercise, which was under the direction of the C-in-C Home Fleet, Admiral Sir Charles Madden, and divided into several phases such as anti-submarine defence, mine clearance and air defence. On conclusion of the manoeuvres, on Wednesday 10 March, the fleet steamed into Bergen Harbour where all the ships, apart from the *Ark Royal,* were able to berth alongside and the *Tiger* actually secured alongside her sister ship *Lion* on the Skorlergrunnskien Jetty. The five days alongside saw daily make and mends being granted and so a good time was had by all. On Monday 15 March the two cruisers, the *Ark Royal, Falmouth* and *Cassandra* left Bergen and the *Tiger* made a 24-hour passage to Rosyth to undergo a nine-day self-maintenance period.

Three days after her arrival alongside the south arm of Rosyth Dockyard, during the morning of Friday 19 March, there was a change of command on board the *Tiger* when Captain G. J. Kirby DSC** RN relieved Captain Lloyd, who left the ship by whaler at 11.15am. Captain Kirby had entered the Navy in 1936 and he had first gone to sea in the battleship *Malaya* in the Mediterranean Fleet. In 1939 he was appointed to the destroyer *Kingston* which had a very active war in the Mediterranean, starting with the capture of an Italian submarine in the Red Sea. She was involved in the evacuations of Greece and Crete and the blockading of the Vichy French port of Beirut, and was also involved in the protection of Malta convoys, during which she was damaged by a 15-inch shell from the Italian battleship *Littorio.* Although the *Kingston* managed to return to Malta, she was destroyed in dock by enemy bombers. In the summer of 1943 Lt Kirby was appointed to the destroyer

HMS *Tiger* at sea in the first week of August 1965 with the ship's company manning ship as a rehearsal for the Clyde Royal
Review.   *(Maritime Photo Library)*

On a very misty August morning in 1965 the royal yacht *Britannia* steams past the *Tiger*
and the aircraft carrier *Centaur* during the Clyde Fleet Review.   *(D. Palmer)*

Melbreak and he took part in frequent actions in the Channel and in the Western Approaches, during which five E-boats and six enemy merchant ships were sunk. By 1945 Lt-Cdr Kirby was in the Far East and was present at Singapore for the surrender of the Japanese forces. His subsequent appointments included the command of the destroyers *Charity, Crossbow* and *Diana,* and he earned a great reputation as a ship handler. Having been promoted to Captain in 1957, he spent two years in Karachi as Naval Adviser to the Pakistani Navy, and after a spell in the Admiralty at Bath he was appointed to command the *Tiger.*

Captain Kirby's first duty in command of the *Tiger* was to take the cruiser on a Home Fleet cruise, which started on Thursday 25 March when, flying the flag of FOF (H), she sailed for Sunderland and secured alongside Corporation Quay in the town's harbour at 10am the next day. The hospitality shown by the townspeople was tremendous and the Wrens of the local RNVR laid on a dance for the ship's company which was very well attended. From home waters the *Tiger* steamed across the North Sea to spend two days at Trondheim, followed by a quick 24-hour stop at Narvik before returning via the North Sea and the Channel to Devonport, where she arrived alongside No 5 wharf at 6.45am on Thursday 15 April. During the six weeks spent in her home port the ship's company were able to take some leave and the ship herself was docked for the scraping and repainting of the underwater hull. It was Thursday 27 May when the cruiser put to sea again and, after carrying out engine trials during the day, she set course for Gibraltar, accompanied by the frigates *Grafton* and *Russell.* They all arrived on the last day of the month and next day the three warships, plus another frigate, the *Yarmouth,* left Gibraltar to steam east for Malta. En route they exercised with the aircraft carrier *Centaur* before anchoring in St Paul's Bay three days later. For the next seven days the *Tiger* exercised in the Mediterranean with a number of frigates, including the *Argonaut, Galatea* and *Yarmouth,* as well as the nuclear-powered submarine *Dreadnought,* and the RFAs *Retainer* and *Tideflow.* By Friday 11 June she had berthed once more at Gibraltar for a long weekend, before departing during the afternoon of Tuesday 15 June for a 39-hour passage to Funchal on the beautiful Atlantic island of Madeira, where she berthed alongside the main mole on the morning of Thursday 17 June. Once again the visit was limited to a long weekend, and by the morning of Friday 25 June she was back alongside Portsmouth Dockyard's Pitch House Jetty. The remainder of June and the first two weeks of July were spent operating from Portsmouth on Sea Days for the various Staff Colleges and for Members of Parliament and Naval Attachés before, on Thursday 15 July, she left Spithead for a Round Britain Home Fleet cruise which was code-named 'Exercise Jack Tar'. The idea was to 'show the flag' in various UK ports during the summer, and at

5.30am on Friday 16 July she embarked the River Humber pilot, before navigating the river itself to enter the King George V Dock at Hull for a five-day visit to the port. From Hull she steamed north again and at 6.15am on Thursday 22 July she entered the River Tyne to steam upriver and secure alongside Corporation Quay at Newcastle upon Tyne. During the visit a ship's dance was laid on by the civic authorities and 4,000 girls applied for the 1,000 tickets which were on sale. However, although there was a great deal of fun, a lot of hard work was also required, with the ship open to visitors, static displays and visits by school parties and local VIPs.

From the River Tyne the *Tiger* steamed north again, and after navigating the Pentland Firth she set course south to arrive alongside Belfast's Victoria Wharf in the middle of Harland & Wolff's shipyard at Queens Island on 30 July, where she joined the destroyer *Kent,* and then an hour later the aircraft carrier *Centaur* arrived. Once again there was the usual round of visiting by groups of schoolchildren and the general public. After leaving Belfast on the morning of Thursday 5 August, the *Tiger* rendezvoused in Bangor Bay with HM Ships *Fearless, Centaur, Kent, Dido, Oracle* and *Brave Borderer,* for joint manoeuvres, before making an overnight passage to the Firth of Clyde where all the ships anchored at the Tail of the Bank to prepare for a Royal Review of the Home Fleet. The previous Royal Review on the Clyde had been in July 1947, when all three Tiger-class cruisers had been laid up in the area, and over 100 ships, including three battleships, had taken part. During the five days at anchor prior to the review there was a great deal of painting and polishing of brightwork, as well as rehearsals for manning and cheering ship. However, there were also lighter moments, one of which was a visit to the ship by 'Miss Great Britain' who spent two hours on board the *Tiger.* By Monday 9 August the fleet of 73 ships, including both the *Tiger* and the *Lion,* had anchored off Greenock. That morning the Royal Family embarked in the royal yacht *Britannia* at Holyhead, after travelling from London by train, and set course for the Clyde. They made a short stop in Kirkudbright Bay where the Queen and Prince Philip visited the nearby lifeboat station. On the morning of Tuesday 10 August, which had dawned a damp and misty day, the *Britannia* arrived on the Clyde to find the assembled warships arrayed in three smart lines and dressed overall. At 8.45am, in true Spithead style, the *Britannia,* preceded by the flagship of the Northern Lighthouse Commissioners, *Pharos,* steamed past the Cloch Lighthouse, escorted by the *Aurora,* which was on station astern of the royal yacht. There was a glimmer of sunshine as the *Britannia* steamed by the lines of warships on the south side of the Clyde, and as she glided along, 15 vessels of the flagship and frigate line fired a royal salute of 21 guns. Helicopters hovered overhead and bands played as the royal yacht dropped anchor. Meanwhile ashore, all

Princess Grace of Monaco visits the *Tiger* on 20 November 1965.
(Imperial War Museum A34994)

River Mersey to secure alongside in Liverpool's Gladstone Dock at midday. After five very hectic days in Liverpool, the *Tiger* left the Mersey on Wednesday 18 August to make a 24-hour passage to Plymouth where she anchored in the Sound. Four days later she steamed up harbour to be docked down in No 9 dry dock for routine maintenance. Despite the fact that the ship was high and dry she took a full part in Devonport's Navy Days at the end of the month when she was as popular as ever with visitors.

It was during the early afternoon of Monday 27 September that the *Tiger* left Devonport and set course for Gibraltar. On the way an SOS message was received from a Liberian freighter saying that she had a casualty on board, and the cruiser then embarked on an eight-hour full-power trial as she raced to reach the cargo vessel. The injured sailor was successfully transferred and eventually landed at Gibraltar where the *Tiger* remained overnight before sailing for Malta on the morning of 1 October. En route she met up with a target-towing tug which allowed the gunners to carry out a noisy bombardment exercise while they knocked large chunks off the target before arrival in Grand Harbour during the afternoon of Monday 4 October. After hoisting the flag of the C-in-C Mediterranean, Admiral Sir John Hamilton, the *Tiger* departed on the morning of Wednesday 6 October and, with the frigate *Rhyl,* set course for the Libyan coast and 'Exercise Dazzle', a joint air-defence exercise with the RAF from the base at El Adem. Five days later the cruiser left the area for the Adriatic and the Yugoslavian (Croatian) port of Split which was an unusual port of call for the Royal Navy in the 1960s. For most of the *Tiger's* ship's company it was their first glimpse of life behind the Iron Curtain and it proved to be a popular run ashore, with a rather potent local brew and a folk dance group who put on a display on the jetty alongside the ship, before being treated to lunch on board. The next port of call was Soudha Bay in Crete where the cruiser moored at a buoy in the harbour. For many visitors this port is memorable for the strength of the ouzo, but several bus loads' of the ship's company spurned the bars in favour of the museum at Heraklion and the Palace of the Minoan Kings at Knossos. From Crete the *Tiger* returned to Malta where the C-in-C was disembarked and the cruiser left an hour later for a fast passage to Gibraltar, where she arrived on Tuesday 26 October, docking alongside. Two days later the *Lion* arrived, leading the rest of the Home Fleet and the C-in-C Home Fleet, Admiral Sir John Frewen, transferred his flag to the *Tiger*. During the stopover the ship's football team had the satisfaction of beating the *Lion's* team 4-0, and the *Tiger's* team won the 'Top of the Rock' race. However, on

along the esplanades of Greenock and Gourock, the local police struggled to cope with the cars which had been parked in every available space as thousands of sightseers flocked in to watch the arrival of the royal party. Next morning, Wednesday 11 August, was as damp and misty as the previous day, but this did not deter the crowds who once again turned out, this time to watch the *Britannia* leave the Clyde as the ships' companies manned the decks to cheer ship as the royal yacht passed by. At 12.50pm, as the *Britannia* left the Tail of the Bank for the Pentland Firth, a signal was received to 'Splice the Main Brace' and to grant a make and mend, both of which were very popular orders. Just over an hour later the flagship *Lion* left the Clyde. Next day at 6.20pm, after six days of paint, bands, guards, boats and barges, the *Tiger* left the Clyde and set course down the Irish Sea.

At 9.50am on Friday 13 August, after embarking the pilot off the Mersey Bar light vessel, the *Tiger* set course up the

Thursday 4 November, with the end of the Home Fleet Assembly, the C-in-C moved back to the *Lion,* and the *Tiger* left for Malta where she arrived four days later to re-embark the C-in-C Mediterranean. Having spent just two hours at anchor in Marsaxlokk Bay, the *Tiger* put to sea again the same day to carry out main armament firings off Filfa, at the conclusion of which an accompanying MFV 1186 caught fire which enabled the firefighting teams to get some real life practice, although they were unable to save the vessel. There then followed two more Mediterranean visits, the first to Genoa and the second to Monaco where the *Tiger* anchored on the morning of Thursday 18 November. It had been decided that the harbour was too small to allow the cruiser in, and so she actually anchored half a mile out, which did allow the ship's floodlighting to be seen by everyone ashore. Unfortunately, owing to the swell, some official functions on board had to be cancelled, but nevertheless Prince Ranier and Princess Grace, together with their children Caroline and Albert, were able to visit the ship for over two hours on Saturday 20 November. After lunching with the C-in-C the family were taken on a tour of the ship by Admiral Hamilton. Because of inclement weather the Royal Marines Band were forced to cancel much of their programme, but they were able to Beat Retreat in front of Monaco's Royal Palace which, as always, was well received.

After leaving Monaco the *Tiger* made a two-day passage back to Malta where the C-in-C once again transferred his flag, this time to HMS *St Angelo,* and on Friday 26 November the cruiser left for Portsmouth with just a 24-hour stop at Gibraltar. The passage through the Bay of Biscay and the Channel was rough, with Force 9 gales and heavy seas, but during the morning of Friday 3 December she arrived alongside Portsmouth's Pitch House Jetty for leave and essential maintenance.

The New Year of 1966 started with a few weeks at Portland carrying out trials and a mini work-up to blow away the cobwebs, but on the evening of Sunday 6 February, with a small detachment of the Royal Irish Fusiliers as passengers, the *Tiger* set sail for Gibraltar, along with HMS *Troubridge* and the French destroyer *Kersaint.* There they took part in joint exercises with Dutch units before, on the first day of March, the *Tiger* berthed at Lisbon on the River Tagus for a four-day visit. After leaving Lisbon course was set across the Atlantic for Bermuda, where she arrived alongside No 6 Wharf at Hamilton, close to the city centre, during the afternoon of Saturday 5 March. This was followed by a visit to Freeport, Grand Bahamas, two days in the US Naval Base at Key West, Florida, and a brief, four-hour stop off Georgetown, Grand Cayman. The latter was just long enough to enable official calls to be made and to remind the local people that the Royal Navy still had a presence in the area, despite a strong American influence. At 8.30am on Saturday 26 March the *Tiger* secured alongside the East Pier at Kingston, Jamaica, for a visit which proved very popular, mainly because prices here were much more reasonable than had been found in Bermuda and in the Bahamas. After leaving Kingston on the morning of Wednesday 30 March the cruiser set course for San Juan, Puerto Rico, where she arrived at 9.30am on

Friday 1 April. That evening the Royal Marines performed their ever-popular ceremony of Beating Retreat for guests at the official reception on the quarterdeck as well as a large crowd of spectators. Next day the children's party was held, and at 10am on Monday 4 April the cruiser left for Portsmouth where she arrived alongside South Railway Jetty at 8.30am on Thursday 14 April.

It was Monday 23 May when the *Tiger,* together with the *Dainty* and the *Lowestoft,* left Portsmouth to steam north through the Irish Sea to the area off Cape Wrath where the gunners were allowed to carry out a very noisy bombardment exercise with the main armament. This was followed by a visit to Glasgow where, at 7am on Friday 27 May, she secured alongside the King George V Dock off the Renfrew Road on the south side of the river and not too far from the city centre. After a very enjoyable long weekend the *Tiger* slipped her moorings at 10am on Tuesday 31 May and set course downriver bound for Portsmouth. Just a quarter of an hour after leaving Glasgow she passed her birthplace, John Brown's shipyard, from where she had been launched almost 21 years before, and where the liner *QE2* was now under construction.

After arriving in Portsmouth on Thursday 2 June there was just one weekend alongside before the cruiser was employed on Sea Days for two weeks, during which, sailing from Spithead each day, she embarked guests from the Service Staff Colleges, groups of schoolchildren and civic dignitaries. These were concluded on Friday 17 June and the *Tiger* left Spithead five days later bound for the North Sea and Middlesbrough where she spent six days before, on the last day of the month, she took the town's Lord Mayor and a number of other guests to sea for the day.

From Middlesbrough the *Tiger* steamed north to Rosyth where the annual Home Fleet Assembly was taking place and where, on Thursday 7 July, Rear-Admiral Pollock, Flag Officer Second in Command, Home Fleet, hosted a dinner on board which was attended by the C-in-C Home Fleet and the First Sea Lord. The deployment came to an end on Monday 11 July when the *Tiger,* accompanied by the *Wakeful* and the *Defender,* left Rosyth for gunnery exercises off Cape Wrath and the passage to Portsmouth where she arrived on Saturday 16 July. After a weekend alongside, the *Tiger* left South Railway Jetty at 8am on Tuesday 19 July and steamed out to Spithead where she embarked the recently retired Prime Minister of Australia, Sir Robert Menzies, and steamed up the Channel to Dover where she anchored to disembark her VIP passenger who was visiting the port in his capacity as Lord Warden of the Cinque Ports. Two days later, after weighing anchor at 9.15am, the *Tiger* set course for Devonport where she arrived the following day for her final refit of the commission.

During the refit she gained a great deal of publicity nationwide when, on Wednesday 10 August, a 6-inch practice shell was accidentally fired from the main armament. Fortunately no one was in its way and the shell embedded itself harmlessly into a dockyard wall. The refit ended on Monday 5 September when the *Tiger* left Devonport for exercises, a two-week stopover in Portsmouth, and a three-day visit to Belfast where she tied up alongside the Aircraft Wharf, in the Sydenham area of the city, on 28 September. This visit was followed by exercises with the Dutch cruiser *De Ruyter* and more Sea Days from Spithead.

On Friday 21 October 1966 the *Tiger* steamed up the Bristol Channel to begin a weekend visit to the city of Cardiff. After entering the entrance lock at 10.30am, she secured alongside the city's Alexandra Docks at just after 11 am that morning. However, unknown to anyone on board at that time, at 9.15am that morning, in the little mining village of Aberfan, just 20 miles from Cardiff, Pontglass Junior School had been engulfed by an avalanche of three million tons of coal slurry when one of the gigantic heaps of waste which towered over the village on the Glamorganshire hillside slipped. This appalling disaster killed 116 young children and 28 adults, and literally wiped out a generation of children. A local Baptist minister who was only a few streets away at the time recalled how he, '...went up the road and turned the bend and could see nothing but a mountain of black waste.' Initially the villagers of Aberfan began digging frantically while a huge workforce was assembled in order to clear the hundreds of thousands of tons of slurry and slag that had engulfed the school and part of the village. Meanwhile, back on the *Tiger* at Cardiff news of the disaster had come in and moves were quickly under way to muster volunteer working parties who left the ship by army truck for the disaster area on Sunday 23 October. One of those who went was Steward Rodger Sloper from Middlesbrough and he recalls those sad days: 'When we got there we stopped on the outskirts of the village between the Miners' Club and Church Hall, where we set up a field kitchen to provide an emergency centre for those who needed it. I remember we used the club's snooker tables in order to lay out the food and whilst we were doing this we couldn't help noticing truck after truck leaving the scene full of coal slag, and lines of empty trucks driving in. We saw bereaved mothers who had lost their children crying desperately and one lady took me into the Church Hall and showed me 100 food boxes that a truck driver had left. She was very upset and she said to me, "We don't want food, we want our children back". It was very upsetting and it made me feel very inadequate. I just couldn't think of anything comforting to say to her. That evening we were invited to the club where the miners provided us with free beer. It was a very emotional time but, in our own small way, we tried to help the bereaved community.'

It was during the afternoon of Monday 24 October that the *Tiger* left Cardiff to steam round into Cardigan Bay to carry out exercises off the Aberporth ranges, and four days later she arrived back at Portsmouth's South Railway Jetty.

On her departure seven days later the cruiser steamed north into Force 10 gales and waves of up to 50 feet in height off the north-west coast of Scotland where she was to take part in her final fleet exercises as a conventional cruiser. Also participating in the exercise were the aircraft carrier *Hermes*, the frigates *Berwick, Dido, Naiad, Phoebe, Russell* and *Salisbury*, and the RFAs *Olna* and *Retainer*. Joining the exercise from the Londonderry area were the Canadian destroyers *Assinibone, Margaree, Chaudiere* and *Ottawa*, together with their tanker *Provider*, while the 'enemy' force consisted of a number of submarines, including HMS *Grampus*. Weather conditions throughout the exercise were atrocious and the *Tiger* had to go to the aid of the *Grampus* to evacuate a cook who had been badly burnt in an accident in the galley. Most of the ships suffered broken crockery and the *Russell* had to withdraw with a fractured mast. On board the *Phoebe* four men were injured during replenishment in heavy seas when an unusually high wave knocked them to the deck. All four were transferred to the sickbay on board the *Hermes*, and there were huge sighs of relief when the exercise ended and, on Friday 17 November, the *Tiger* returned to Portsmouth.

It was on Thursday 24 November that the *Tiger* left Portsmouth for her final foreign visit of the commission, to Casablanca in Morocco. Four days later, at 9am on Monday 28 November, she arrived alongside for what should have been a five-day stopover, but even before the mooring lines were secured political events in Africa were destined to alter her schedule and afford her worldwide publicity. On 11 November 1965 the government of the self-governing colony of Rhodesia, in language which parodied the famous Independence speech of 4 July 1776, issued a Unilateral Declaration of Independence (UDI). This illegal act, which was clearly against the interests and the wishes of the African majority in the country, led to United Nations sponsored sanctions against Rhodesia, while at governmental level Britain and Rhodesia tried to find a settlement. On Wednesday 30 November, just two days into the *Tiger's* Casablanca visit, Captain Kirby was ordered to sail immediately for Gibraltar and at 6.20pm the cruiser slipped her moorings and set course for the colony. After a passage of just over 26 hours, during which time Rear-Admiral Pollock had to vacate his quarters, and the wardroom was converted into a temporary conference

Prime Minister Harold Wilson and delegates to the Rhodesian Talks on board the *Tiger* in December 1966. *(Imperial War Museum A35065)*

51

centre, the *Tiger* anchored in Gibraltar Bay at 8.40pm on Thursday 1 December. Just under three hours later, at 11.30pm, the Prime Minister, Harold Wilson, who had left Heathrow six hours previously, arrived on board with his negotiating party after being brought out by RAF launch. Two hours after his arrival, at 1.35am on 2 December, the legal Governor of Rhodesia, Sir Humphrey Gibb, embarked and the last to arrive at 2.30pm was Ian Smith, the leader of the illegal Rhodesian regime. The purpose of the meeting, which was set out in an official communiqué, was: 'To ascertain whether, within the programme of action to which the British Government is committed by the communiqué issued at the end of the recent meeting of Commonwealth Prime Ministers, a settlement can be reached on the basis of the principles to which they have adhered throughout.' These principles demanded unimpeded progress to majority rule, an immediate improvement in the political status of the African population and progress towards ending racial discrimination with any settlement being acceptable to the people of Rhodesia as a whole. At 3am, half an hour after the Rhodesian delegation had embarked, the *Tiger* weighed anchor and, with the world's press speculating on her whereabouts, she steamed into the Mediterranean Sea whilst on board the politicians prepared to start negotiations. Rodger Sloper, who had been detailed to act as steward to Harold Wilson, recalls the event: 'Mr Wilson wore his famous Gannex raincoat and he had his trusty pipe, both of which had become his hallmark. We had all the daily newspapers delivered to him by helicopter, and I remember one occasion when I was in his dining room

reading them when, very suddenly, he came in and caught me. I was taken by surprise and I jumped up quickly, but he was a very kindly man and he told me not to worry about it. He often stopped to chat with me, not about politics, but just small talk.'

The political discussions started at 9am on Friday 2 December and the two Prime Ministers met face to face, accompanied by only one member of staff on each side for 90 minutes before officials from both sides joined them. However, given the intransigent nature of the Rhodesian leader there was little chance of a settlement, although a working document was produced which had to be agreed by 5 December, and after 41 hours at sea, at 8.15pm on Saturday 3 December, the *Tiger* returned to Gibraltar Bay and dropped anchor. Four and a half hours later, at 12.45am on Sunday 4 December, Sir Humphrey Gibb and Ian Smith disembarked into an RAF launch and were taken ashore, and at 7.30am the *Tiger* weighed anchor to berth alongside in Gibraltar Dockyard. Once the mooring ropes were secured Harold Wilson addressed the ship's company and thanked them for their efforts during the time he had been on board, before he and his staff disembarked to return to London by air.

Two days later the *Tiger* herself left Gibraltar to return to Devonport, where she arrived alongside No 7 wharf at 9.15am on Friday 9 December. Later that day Admiral Pollock lowered his flag and six days later, at 2.30pm on Thursday 15 December, Captain Kirby left the ship. Four days later the *Tiger* was decommissioned. Like her two sister ships, *Lion* and *Blake,* she was to await conversion to a helicopter command cruiser.

A magnificent aerial view of majesty and power at sea. The *Tiger* at speed in 1966. *(Rodger Sloper)*

Chapter Five

HMS *Tiger* – The Ugly Duckling 1967-1975

Plans to convert the Tiger-class cruisers to carry helicopters were first mooted in 1963, when the Admiralty had been considering the deployment of anti-submarine helicopters to meet the growing Soviet submarine threat which had developed in the late 1950s and early 1960s. The Admiralty were particularly worried about the threat which, in the event of a limited war, had increased with the commissioning of fast nuclear-powered attack submarines, and the helicopter played an essential part in the defence against them. The new Wessex III helicopter could quickly reach a submarine datum and its good sonar performance could go below the layer, in addition to which it had the ability to outpace a nuclear submarine and attack it with homing torpedoes. Flights of Wessex II helicopters were carried in aircraft carriers, and it was planned to put a flight in commando ships. However, this scale of deployment was not considered sufficient and as there were too few ships which could deploy anti-submarine helicopters in an emergency the fleet was not in a position to gain enough experience of their potential. If increased operational capability was to be achieved this deficiency had to be remedied, and under plans which were in existence at that time, this was unlikely to happen before a proposed new generation of escort cruisers* joined the fleet in the early 1970s. The 1963 naval long-term costings allowed for the first of these escort cruisers to be ordered in July 1966, but because of the heavy load of design work with the ballistic missile submarine programme (eventually to become the Resolution-class of SSBNs), the building programme would be delayed by at least two years. The Defence Review 'Strategy for the 60s' called for a total strength of seven cruisers, which included the three Tiger-class ships in reserve, and one of the top secret economy measures which had been put forward in the summer of 1962, and which led to much rumour and speculation about the future of the three ships, was the disposal of the Tigers as the new escort cruisers came into service. However, the postponement of the escort cruisers made it necessary to keep the Tiger-class in service into the late 1960s and, therefore, it was essential for them to undergo long refits in order to prolong their lives. In view of these factors the Admiralty came to the conclusion that the best course would be to use these long refits to convert the *Tiger*, *Lion* and *Blake* to carry anti-submarine helicopters.

The main features of the conversion scheme would be to fit a flight deck and hangar to enable each of the three cruisers to operate four Wessex helicopters. This was to be achieved by removing the after 6-inch armament and installing a flight deck which was sufficient in size to range two Wessex IIIs with their rotors spread, together with a hangar for all four machines. It was envisaged that the total cost of each conversion and long refit would be about £5 million, but this figure would become irrelevant as inflation gripped the economy. The limited design work which was necessary could be carried out from resources then in existence at the Admiralty, and there was plenty of capacity available in the Royal Dockyards for the conversion work to be carried out in the period between 1965 and 1967. It was originally envisaged that the three cruisers would recommission in 1966, 1967 and 1968, which was well ahead of the dates for the escort cruiser programme although, once again, the initial plans were somewhat optimistic.

In order to provide the helicopters for the ships it was proposed to form two new flights, one in 1967/68 and a second in 1968/69. For the first converted cruiser, which was to be the *Blake*, improvised arrangements were to be made from the helicopter resources already in existence until the first new flight was available, and once both flights had been formed, it was thought that it would be possible to maintain them for all three cruisers from the total anti-submarine helicopter resources. It was also envisaged that after their conversions and long refits, the three Tigers would have a further eight years of operational life and that the fleet would benefit not only from the valuable contribution they would make to anti-submarine capability, but also from their air-defence and surface gunnery capability. It was anticipated that, equipped with their own helicopters, the three cruisers could be deployed in an emergency with an effective military force on board. The helicopters could also, if necessary, be used for carrying a limited number of passengers or for carrying loads and the flight decks would enable the ships to operate a military lift and reconnaissance or other anti-submarine helicopters. Thus it was thought that at relatively small cost the three Tiger-class cruisers would provide a useful access of strength until the mid-1970s for anti-submarine warfare, for colonial 'brush fire' wars and for general emergencies of the seemingly never-ending Cold War.

*The new anti-submarine escort cruisers which were envisaged in the early 1960s were to have been 13,500-ton, 650ft vessels armed with a twin 4.5-inch gun and Sea Slug missiles, capable of carrying nine anti-submarine helicopters. It was intended that these ships would accompany the fleet carriers on operations, and that the first such vessel would be included in the 1962-63 Naval Estimates. However, with funds being sought for the giant new fleet carrier *CVA 01* it was clear that these smaller, but very expensive, ships were out of the question at that time. In the event, with the demise of the fleet carriers, the basic design was adapted for the 'through deck' cruisers or, as they became, the Invincible-class light fleet carriers.

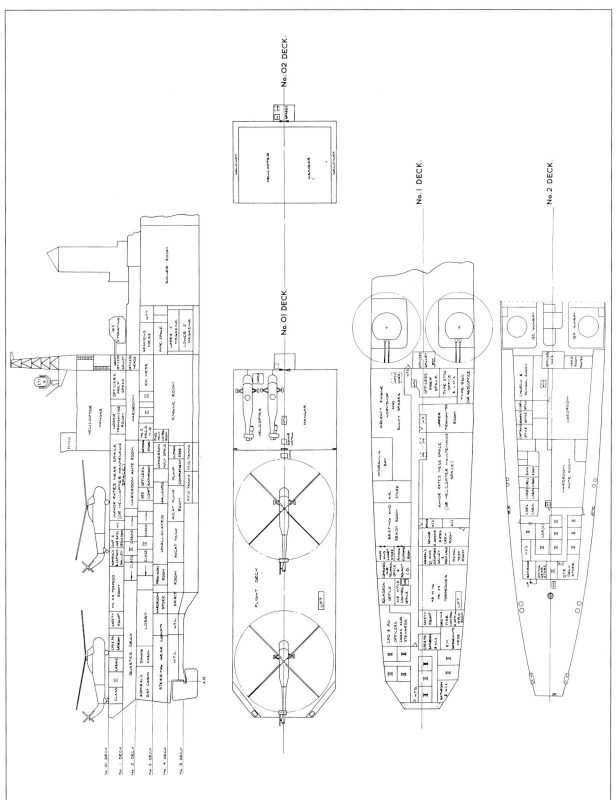

Early Admiralty drawings dating from 1964, showing the proposed changes required to convert the Tiger-class vessels to helicopter cruisers.

(Author's Collection)

55

Escorted by the tug *Sealyman,* the *Tiger* leaves the Solent in the autumn of 1972 to show off her new flight deck for the first time. *(Maritime Photo Library)*

As regards their complement, the cruisers would carry 49 officers and 635 ratings of the ship's company, and 17 officers and 80 ratings of the embarked air squadron. In addition the troop-carrying capacity was put at 50 officers and 500 other ranks, with an increased capacity for periods of less than 24 hours. However, it was not proposed to update their communications equipment and the original Admiralty plans stated: 'A part of their equipment is unavoidably obsolescent and in both scale and quality they will not have the command communications facilities which will be required in the 1970s.' On conversion their displacement tonnage would be increased to 12,080, their maximum speed would be 28 knots, and their endurance at 20 knots would be about 3,550 miles. It was proposed to reduce their armament to one twin 6-inch gun system and three twin 3-inch gun systems but, before the conversions were completed, this would be modified.

The *Tiger* herself was taken in hand for conversion at Devonport Dockyard in early 1968, which meant that the original timetables were already behind schedule and in the meantime, the Defence Reviews of the mid-1960s put paid to the building of any new fleet aircraft carriers for the Royal Navy. They also set the scene for Britain's withdrawal from its military bases east of Suez and, effectively, its final withdrawal from Empire. Although controversial at the time, in retrospect it can be seen that, apart from Hong Kong, the

former colonies of the Far East were all independent countries and bearing in mind the fact that Britain herself was inevitably drawing closer to mainland Europe for both her economical and political future, this retreat from Empire was a logical move. Added to these political moves, in late 1967 came Britain's worst financial crisis for nearly 20 years, which led to the devaluation of sterling, increases in bank interest rates and the inevitable cuts in defence expenditure. In January 1968 it was announced that the aircraft carrier force was to be phased out by 1972, although the *Ark Royal* eventually gained a seven-year reprieve, and, although it was not announced officially, the plans to refit and convert the *Lion* were shelved.

Fortunately, the conversion of the *Tiger* had already started in Devonport Dockyard and although it was well behind schedule the work progressed unimpeded by the defence cuts. As the 1960s drew to a close, the *Tiger* lay alongside the dockyard's No 5 basin, with the spindly profile of a tower crane dominating the skyline above her as the clumsy looking superstructure of the box-like hangar, beneath which were aircraft engine workshops, took the place of Y turret and two of the after 3-inch mountings, completely enclosing the once open quarterdeck. Eventually, as with her sister *Blake,* the firepower of Q2 and Q3 3-inch mountings, which had previously escaped the cutting torches, were replaced by two quadruple Sea Cat missile launchers, and at the same time improvements were made to the living accommodation on board. Kevin Marshall remembers events at that time: 'I joined the *Tiger* in the summer of 1971, whilst she was undergoing her conversion and refit in Devonport Dockyard, and as a member of B Engine Room Unit, I made regular trips to the *Lion* which was moored with the reserve ships in the Tamar. We "salvaged" many of the *Lion's* boiler room valves and machinery parts and took them back to the *Tiger* where they were either fitted or used for spare parts. So frequent became our trips that the *Lion* was eventually towed into the basin alongside us and it became easier to take the spare parts we needed whenever they were required.'

Although in official circles opinions as to whether the conversions should go ahead were mixed, everyone agreed that two good-looking and aesthetically pleasing cruisers had been transformed into a pair of ungainly ugly ducklings, although in an effort to give a more balanced appearance, the *Tiger's* funnels were lengthened. On Tuesday 24 August 1971 the *Tiger's* new commanding officer, Captain D. T. Goodhugh RN, was appointed and ten months later, in June 1972, the *Tiger* completed her preliminary sea trials and returned to Devonport. In the following month, on Thursday 6 July, the first helicopter deck landing took place, when a Sea King of 826 Squadron flew from Culdrose to Devonport. Next day the Commissioning Ceremony took place and it was attended by hundreds of people, including families of the ship's company. The chief guests were Admiral Sir Nigel Henderson, a former C-in-C Plymouth, the Secretary of State for Defence, Lord Carrington and, on loan from 'Tiger Company' of the Royal Anglian Regiment, a Siberian tiger cub, Chara, who was placed in the care of LMEM Faulkner for the day. The ceremony concluded with Lady Henderson cutting the 60lb commissioning cake, before the guests departed and work resumed to prepare the *Tiger* for sea.

It was Friday 17 November before the cruiser left Devonport for sea trials which were to last four weeks in almost continuous gale force winds. One member of the ship's company, Shipwright Fred Green, who had served in the *Tiger* between 1961 and 1963 and who was back in the ship, remembers these trials: 'When I served in the *Tiger* during her 1961 commission, being someone who suffers from seasickness, I considered her to be one of the most comfortable ships I have served in, particularly in a heavy sea. She was also not so big that one became anonymous in a sea of faces. However, following the conversion and alterations to her profile, the huge area of the hangar and flight deck acted almost like a sail. I can remember one night in particular when the whole of the shipwrights' department was called out when we were steering through some pretty rough seas, with gale force winds blowing. The ship had changed course and had immediately developed a list which could not be righted by counterflooding the double bottom tanks. We had the onerous task of checking all the spaces in the double bottom compartments, but we found nothing at all and as soon as the course was changed again the list disappeared just as quickly as it had come.'

Despite the foul weather conditions the trials were remarkably successful, and most of the sea acceptance trials were completed. The main propulsion machinery performed well and even the full-power trial, which was carried out in a howling gale, was a success. All the ship's armament was fired and the radar, radio and ASW equipment was tested. Two Sea King helicopters from 826 Squadron were embarked for a ten-day period and they were operated night and day. Following the trials the *Tiger* returned to Devonport for a break and for seasonal leave to be taken.

The New Year of 1973 saw the *Tiger* at Devonport, and as soon as the leave period was over she sailed for Portland for pre-work-up exercises during which the four Sea Kings of 826 Squadron were embarked. Once again all the armament was fired and the first Sea Cat missile that was fired brought down its target, which was almost unheard of. The work-up itself occupied four extremely busy weeks off Portland, although the landing parties that went ashore to practise riot control had a little relief from the hard grist of continual 24-hour exercising in all aspects of weaponry and ship operations. On Wednesday 18 April, much to everyone's relief, the *Tiger* went alongside at Portsmouth for six weeks of maintenance and leave before she left for her first post-conversion deployment.

On the last day of April there was a change of command when Captain M. L. Stacey RN took over from Captain Goodhugh. Captain Stacey had entered the Royal Navy as a cadet in 1942 and over the following 16 years he served in HM Ships *Hawkins, Rotherham, Cambrian, Shoreham, Hornet, Euryalus, Bermuda* and *Vigilant.* In 1960 he was appointed to command the frigate *Blackpool,* and in 1968 he commanded HMS *Andromeda* as well as being Captain (F) of the Sixth Frigate Squadron. After a spell in the Admiralty he was appointed to the *Tiger.*

The *Tiger* was to be the flagship of a powerful group of warships which included the nuclear-powered submarine *Dreadnought,* the frigates *Dido* and *Hermione,* the RFAs *Regent* and *Tidespring* and the Dutch frigates *Limburg* and *Van Golen.* The squadron was commanded by the Flag Officer, Second Flotilla, Rear-Admiral R. P. Clayton, and the *Tiger* left Portsmouth in the first week of June to rendezvous with the other ships and to set course for Gibraltar, where they called on Friday 8 June, in time for the weekend. With the Suez Canal closed, on leaving Gibraltar for Cape Town the squadron steamed into the Atlantic where intensive exercises were held en route. The crossing of the equator was marked with due ceremony and on the *Tiger* the forecastle became the venue for the arrival of King Neptune and the ensuing celebrations. Despite the

A dramatic aerial view of the *Tiger* at sea with a Sea King helicopter of 826 Squadron on the flight deck.

(Rear-Admiral M. L. Stacey)

HMS *Tiger* alongside at Cape Town during her passage east.

(Fleet Air Arm Museum)

Despite the clumsy box-like structure of her new hangar the *Tiger* still presents a majestic sight at sea.

(Rear-Admiral M. L. Stacey)

July 1973 in the Malacca Strait. The *Tiger* catches the 30,000-ton tanker MV *Anson* bullying the smaller MV *Carnation.*
(F. G. Green)

The *Anson* and *Carnation* are locked together while a Sea King lifts stores onto the latter ship. The *Tiger* and the *Dreadnought* are standing off.
(Fleet Air Arm Museum)

Sea King 144TG lifting stores to the damaged *Carnation*.
(Fleet Air Arm Museum)

old Naval Dockyard on Singapore's north-east coast.

At just after midday on Thursday 26 July, as the force steamed south through the Strait of Malacca, the *Dreadnought* which had been sent on ahead, passed through an intense tropical storm and on emerging from this she came upon the 20,000-ton Cypriot-registered oil tanker, MV *Anson,* with her bow embedded in the side of the 7,000-ton Panamanian-registered freighter, MV *Carnation,* as the result of a dramatic collision. Apparently the *Anson* had been under way with her navigating bridge temporarily unmanned and, in the tropical storm, she had run straight into the port side of the *Carnation,* ramming her bow into the freighter's hull, amidships and just forward of the bridge. Kevin Marshall who was on board the *Tiger* recalls the incident: 'It was a fine, clear day and we were making our way south when the submarine *Dreadnought* passed us at great speed. Only her conning tower was visible above the surface and members of her ship's company were waving at us as they went by.' As the *Dreadnought* closed the scene she saw that the *Carnation's* crew, complete with their suitcases, had already taken to the lifeboats. The submarine's casing officer, Lt Jamie Barr, together with LS Barry Seager, immediately organized the rescue of the 35 men in the lifeboats, bringing one batch over the foreplanes and the others over the casing. When the *Tiger* and *Rhyl* arrived on the scene at 4pm they found the two ships still firmly locked together and the cruiser's boarding officer, Lt Martin Hearn, and her shipwright officer, Lt Peter Tibbenham, who had been flown onto the *Carnation,* were assessing the damage. Lt Tibbenham quickly decided that there was a good chance of saving the freighter as long as the *Anson's* bows remained firmly wedged into her side long enough for temporary repairs to be made, but if she broke free before repairs were completed then the *Carnation* was likely to fill and sink. Meanwhile, the freighter's 35-man crew were disembarked from the *Dreadnought* and transferred to the *Rhyl,* before the submarine resumed her course for Singapore.

Once the necessary Lloyds' forms had been signed a full 40-man damage control team, commanded by Commander John Rose, boarded the stricken and deserted *Carnation* to find the only remaining occupant was a bright orange canary which had been abandoned by the fleeing crew. One of the first on the scene was Chief Shipwright Alfred Patten, who reported only four feet of freeboard in the damaged area, with No 1 hold flooded and beyond

fact that the Royal Navy's warships were regular visitors to Africa's most southerly city, the citizens of Cape Town swamped them with hospitality and a bureau was set up on board the *Tiger* to deal with the numerous invitations of all kinds. In addition there was a heavy sporting fixture list, and the usual full range of official calls and civic functions. The group sailed from Cape Town on Monday 9 July, pleasantly exhausted from their run ashore, and immediately began an intensive period of training with the South African Navy, followed by exercises with the French Navy as passage was made across the Indian Ocean bound for Singapore and an assisted maintenance period in the

The *Tiger's* steaming crew take a break during their voyage south to Singapore in the damaged freighter *Carnation*.

(F. G. Green)

repair, but with the hole in No 2 hold still above water level. There was no doubt in anyone's mind that should this hold flood then the *Carnation* would sink very quickly and it was imperative that repairs were carried out quickly. To start with the boarding party stuffed bags of fertilizer, which formed part of the ship's cargo, into the massive gap and later they shored up damaged bulkheads with timber and cement which had been supplied from the *Tiger*. The first attempts to separate the ships ended in failure, but at 2.30am the next morning, with the *Anson's* engines going full astern, they eventually moved apart and the engineers immediately set about getting the *Carnation's* machinery systems working in the face of many obstacles, not least being the fact that all the machinery instructions were printed in Chinese. At 7am on 27 July, just 15 hours after the *Tiger's* arrival, all the problems had been surmounted and with Commander John Taylor (the *Tiger's* Executive Officer), acting as captain, and his 40-man prize crew at the controls, the *Carnation* set off on the 180-mile voyage

to Singapore. Fred Green's overriding memory of the freighter was the unhygienic state of the galley, which was 'literally infested with cockroaches and was so filthy that we were supplied with food by the *Tiger*.' The *Rhyl* steamed on ahead for Singapore, but the *Tiger* remained in escort until the *Carnation* was in safe waters. Throughout the passage the cruiser's Sea Kings were an invaluable support, flying over food and stores. On board the freighter hourly watches were kept during the voyage and in spite of atrocious weather and a couple of minor breakdowns, the *Carnation*, wearing *Tiger's* 'houseflag' and the Blue Ensign, anchored in a blaze of lights in midstream off the ANZUK Naval Base at 9pm on Saturday 28 July, after a voyage of 38 hours in the busy shipping lanes of the Malacca Strait.

After carrying out maintenance in Singapore the *Tiger* and the other ships of the squadron left for the waters of the South China Sea and the Philippines for an intensive Anglo-American exercise, before steaming north to Hong Kong. With the *Tiger, Rhyl, Dreadnought*, HMAS *Yarra*, six highlight of the deployment was to be a visit to Sydney to represent the Royal Navy at the opening of the city's new Opera House. However, Australia's new Labour Government, which had been elected in December 1972, had strong views on nuclear weapons and they refused to allow the nuclear-powered *Dreadnought* entry. The British Government took the line that it was 'all go' or 'none go' and, with the Australian Government having refused to soften its stance, the Royal Navy's proposed visit was cancelled. In the event the two Dutch frigates did go to Sydney for the ceremony but, sadly, the British ships stayed away, which was disappointing for both the ships' companies and the people of Sydney. Instead, the *Tiger*, the *Dreadnought* and RFA *Regent* made an unscheduled call at the US base in Guam, the only place in that part of the world with the necessary engineering technology for the *Dreadnought's* machinery. As the cost of living on Guam was extremely high, with the main 'industries' being the US military bases and tourism, most of the social and sporting activities took place at the US bases, where the US Navy personnel proved to be excellent hosts. From Guam the three warships moved on to Singapore where they arrived on Friday 5 October for a three-week assisted maintenance period in the much more familiar surroundings of the former naval base.

Joining the *Tiger* in Singapore for her homeward leg of the deployment was Lt-Cdr Richard Baker RNR, the well-known broadcaster, who wrote of the passage home: 'Before I had

Captain Stacey, his officers and men, pose for the traditional photograph during the ship's stay alongside HMS *Tamar* in Hong Kong.

(Kevin Marshall)

Malayan vessels and the ships of the Hong Kong squadron, it was some time since the colony had seen such an impressive line-up. However, no sooner had the ships' companies begun to sample the colony's attractions than a tropical storm called 'Joan' caused a premature departure of the task force which returned to the Philippines. Calling at Manila the *Tiger* hosted a children's party for 70 orphans, and played host to three beauty queens. Another highlight was a dancing display on the flight deck, given by a local dance group. For the *Tiger's* officers and men the real

chance to renew my acquaintance with the dubious delights of Singapore's Bugis Street, the ship sailed for Mauritius and I embarked on a vigorous programme of visits to all the ships in the task group. I travelled in "cabs" kindly provided by the "Airy Fairies" of 826 Squadron, who inhabit the after end of the *Tiger*. It's a vaguely alarming experience the first time you descend on the high wire to the deck of a rolling ship, but when the time came to be lowered into the fin of HMS *Dreadnought* I was getting quite used to it, though I admit there was a nasty

A magnificent aerial view of the *Tiger* at sea during her deployment to the Far East in 1973.   *(Rear-Admiral M. L. Stacey)*

moment when I left the submarine. My flying harness got hitched up on something just as I was about to be hauled aloft, and I had a passing vision of the *Dreadnought* becoming airborne with me as the hoisting shackle. My two days and a night revealed, rather to my surprise, how cheerful life can be several hundred feet below the surface. I soon got used to groping around in dim, red lighting and I even managed to insert myself with middle-aged acrobatics into a bunk above the beer barrels in the fore ends, but it would have taken more than a couple of days to learn how to handle the "planes". I did have a go for a while, but when we got to wavering uncertainly between 50 feet above and 50 feet below set depth, I was, for some reason, relieved. I did rather better, I think, when the *Tiger* was doing an "RAS" with RFA *Regent,* and I conned the ship for some time. By some miracle all went well, and I was able to keep the distance line around the 100 feet mark for about an hour. Then, suddenly, our stern swung in and when someone was seen to fling a packet of fags across to

the *Regent,* the *Tiger's* captain came out with a few sharp words. I don't blame him. For the most part during my visit to the fleet things were pretty friendly. The frigate *Rhyl* reminded me of my days at sea in the Western Approaches on convoy escort duty in the Second World War and I had the pleasure of listening to some of the amusing tapes produced for the ship's "Hello Sailor" show. Wherever I went I was impressed by the amount of hard work being done, on that leg from Singapore to Mauritius, with its constant succession of exercises, there's no doubt the taxpayer was getting value for money. We had a day in Diego Garcia, the isolated Indian Ocean atoll where the American "Seebees" are constructing a communications station. We offloaded large quantities of beer for the lads ashore and some of us onloaded a drop or two as well. Three days after Diego Garcia, and after we'd survived an Admiral's inspection and Divisions, there was Mauritius, which proved to be a better run ashore than we'd been led to expect. Much too soon my time with the *Tiger* expired

The *Tiger* exercising with the Dutch frigate *Van Galen* during the deployment east of Suez. Sea King 43TG is lifting a Wasp helicopter from the frigate's deck.   *(Fleet Air Arm Museum)*

and it was back from Mauritius, 80°F, to the UK, 38°F, and back to the newsdesk.'

The final leg of the deployment was, once again, by way of Cape Town, and as they passed the lonely island of St Helena in the Atlantic Ocean the *Tiger* headed a 'steam past' close to Jamestown, while helicopters of 826 Squadron carried out a fly-past over the town. It was in time for Christmas that the force returned to Portsmouth where, soon after her arrival, she was joined by the *Blake* which secured alongside her. Following Christmas and New Year leave it was time to start work again and at the end of January 1974 the *Tiger* sailed for the Mediterranean for a ten-week deployment. During what was described as her 'spring cruise' she made a visit to Limassol in Cyprus, which was an extremely rare event for the Royal Navy in the 1970s, and in fact the *Tiger* was the first large ship to use the new port. An excellent rapport was struck with the RAF at Akrotiri, who provided all the social and sporting activity, with ski-ing on Mount Olympus being a major attraction. The only casualty on the slopes timed his accident to coincide with the arrival of two Sea Kings from the *Tiger*, which had been sent to collect the C-in-C Fleet, Admiral Sir Terence Lewin, who was touring military establishments. Admiral Lewin flew back onto the *Tiger*

where he visited mess decks and stayed overnight. In company with the frigate *Juno*, the cruiser visited the Italian port of Civitavecchia, close to Rome, before carrying our gunnery exercises with units of the Italian Fleet off the coast of Sardinia at the Cape Teulada Range. A proposed trip to Athens was cancelled and instead the ship carried out an independent exercise off Crete, before steaming into Turkish waters for a joint NATO exercise with the Turkish, Greek, Italian and US Navies. In Turkey visits were made to the city of Izmir and the picturesque town of Marmaris.

Additional passengers on the final stretch from Malta to the UK were six Sea Cadets who had been brought out by the *Hermes*. The engineers of 826 Squadron were faced with the task of changing a Sea King's main gearbox, and by working non-stop in 12-hour shifts, eight ratings completed the task in four and a half days. The last time it had been carried out it had taken nine and a half days, which illustrates the great efforts made. When she arrived in Plymouth Sound on Wednesday 10 April, 19 sons of ship's company members joined the *Tiger* to make an overnight passage to Portsmouth. For Nicholas Pisani, the son of the gunnery officer, there was the added thrill of opening fire with the ship's main armament. Next day the

Tiger arrived in Portsmouth where families were waiting to be reunited, and where LREM Payne met his two-month old daughter, Emma, for the first time.

Following a period of maintenance and Easter leave for the ship's company, the remainder of the *Tiger's* commission would be spent with the Home Fleet, and in July she was off Rockall, the outcrop of rock some 200 miles west of the Isle of Skye and perhaps known to most people as the 'star'of radio gale warnings. This 70ft-high pillar of rock that had been virtually ignored for centuries had, in the early 1970s, with successful oil exploration in the area, assumed a greater significance. In 1972 a beacon was installed at the top of the rock but after much pounding by heavy seas, it had failed. The *Tiger's* task was to examine the navigational beacon and to remove components for detailed inspection by the Board of Trade. A landing party of three led by Lt-Cdr Chilcott, together with the ship's photographer, were winched down by a Sea King of 814 Squadron and, secured by a safety line, they started work on the hazardous summit. After dismantling the light they found that the batteries were highly corroded and decided to remove the lantern for repairs. Before leaving the rock the party left a photograph of the ship and their names on the inside of the beacon's lid. Meanwhile, during the operation, one of the Sea Kings carried out some friendly barter trade with a nearby trawler and in exchange for a bottle of whisky they acquired 350lb of fresh fish.

In early August the *Tiger* berthed at Rosyth for a 'Meet the Navy' visit and, ironically, she secured alongside her redundant sister ship *Lion*. This gave the electrical and engineering departments a field day as they went aboard the deserted cruiser to scrounge as many parts and stores as could be dismantled, in an effort to replenish long-outstanding items of spares. Even the ship's divers were sent down to remove a grill from one of the *Lion's* main circulation inlets, to replace the *Tiger's* broken part. This indignity led to an exchange of signals thus: From *Lion* to *Tiger*, 'Grrr! You've pinched my bottom', to which the *Tiger* replied, 'Thereby hangs a tail'. During her passage from Rosyth back to Portsmouth the *Tiger* embarked 21 boys, the sons of ship's company members, ranging in age from ten to 15 years. They were accommodated in ratings' mess decks and were delegated to help with the ship's duties. When the *Tiger* arrived at Spithead they were joined by 700 wives, sweethearts, mums and dads for a Families Day, at the end of which the *Tiger* finally re-entered harbour.

In the latter half of 1974 there were visits to Hull, where the cruiser spent a week, and to Portugal's capital city of Lisbon where two Allouette helicopters of the Portuguese Air Force visited the ship and treated the aircrew of 826 Squadron to a flight over the city. Meanwhile, the ship's

The ship's company is shown here manning the decks of an extremely smart *Tiger* during the Far East deployment of 1963.
(Rear-Admiral M. L. Stacey)

company enjoyed the hospitality of the resident British Community. Earlier in the month, 826 Squadron's Sea King 145 became the first aircraft of its type to achieve 2,000 flying hours and the event was duly celebrated when Captain Stacey read a citation and presented the four-year-old 'veteran' with a Long Service and Good Conduct Medal.

The early part of 1975 saw the *Tiger* in home waters once again and in early June, together with ten other units of the fleet, 16 aircraft, two hovercraft and numerous VIPs and senior officers of the three Services, the *Tiger* took part in 'Sea Days 75'. Under the command of Flag Officer Second Flotilla, Rear-Admiral J. D. E. Fieldhouse, who was flying his flag in the *Tiger,* all the units gathered to combine a year's quota of exercises into a close action visual spectacular. The Royal Navy's vessels also included the frigates *Londonderry, Plymouth, Rothesay* and *Scylla,* the submarine *Finwhale* and two RFAs, while the RAF and the USAF demonstrated their might with Buccaneers, Phantoms, FIIIs, Nimrods, Shackletons and Victor tankers, involving more than 3,000 men. During the exercises the popular television personality Jimmy Savile 'fixed-it' for a ten-year-old schoolboy, Peter McLeod from Farnborough, to spend a day at sea in a warship, following which the cruiser received some unexpected publicity when the television film of Peter's day at sea was shown as part of the 'Jim'll Fix It' programme.

After Sea Days the *Tiger,* flying the flag of FOF2, took part in a Joint Maritime Course (JMC) off the coast of Scotland. There were also visits to Rosyth and Leith on opposite sides of the Firth of Forth, for a 'Meet the Navy' week. On two open days the ship was visited by 400 schoolchildren in organized groups and by 7,000 members of the public. At a dance a delightful 'Miss Tiger' was elected and the highlight of the stay was a show which was broadcast on local radio while the ship was open to the public. This included competitions between the public and the ship's company in knot tying, using the bosun's call and in donning diving suits, which is an art in itself. After leaving Leith the *Tiger* sailed to Malmo where the ship's company were able to enjoy the delights of sauna baths and Swedish hospitality. This was followed by a visit to the German Naval Base of Kiel where, with the frigate *Zulu* and naval units from the hosting German Navy, Belgium,

Holland, France and the USA, she took part in Kieler Woche, or Kiel Week. This annual event, which is essentially a large sailing regatta with strong international naval contributions, involves the whole city in street parties and concerts in an extremely picturesque setting. Various sports take place throughout the week, with cutter sailing as the main event and involving much prestige. Although the five crews from the *Tiger* and *Zulu* did not win against strong German and Dutch opposition, they set high standards and gained seven trophies. Both British ships were caught up in an overwhelming whirlwind of hospitality and activity which proved a fitting end to the *Tiger's* commission. However, before she returned to Portsmouth she went back to Rockall where another team fitted new equipment to the island's beacon, and a group of the ship's divers collected rock samples from a nearby reef for examination by the Institute for Geological Studies. Twice in two weeks Sea Kings from the *Tiger* scrambled to go to the aid of merchant ships in distress. The first mercy mission on 8 July involved a trawler, *Granton Harrier,* which had suffered a serious fire in which four crew members had died, and a fifth, badly burned, man was airlifted to the *Tiger.* The second incident, eight days later, involved the Belgian ore carrier *Federal Schelde,* which was 210 miles west of Scotland and in need of urgent medical assistance. The *Tiger's* Medical Officer was transferred to the ship to find one crew member had died, and another was seriously ill after breathing toxic fumes. He was transferred to the cruiser for treatment.

For the last few weeks of the commission the *Tiger* shared with the royal yacht the distinction of having an Admiral in command, for Captain Stacey received confirmation of his promotion to Rear-Admiral a few weeks before he was due to leave the ship. It was mid-August when the commission came to an end and, having handed over command to his Executive Officer, Rear-Admiral Stacey left the ship which he had commanded for over two years. His departure was strictly formal and conducted with all the ceremonial due to an officer of flag rank – until he reached his car door when the ship's company gave three cheers for a popular Captain. For the *Tiger* an eight-month refit lay ahead.

Chapter Six

HMS *Tiger* – The Last Commission 1976-1978

For eight months of 1975 and the early part of 1976 the *Tiger* lay in dry dock at Portsmouth dockyard, shrouded in scaffolding and undergoing her first long refit since her conversion, which was also destined to be her last. During this period, as well as assisting the dockyard personnel, the ship's company provided volunteers to help more than 200 elderly residents of Portsmouth as part of a 'good neighbour' scheme organized by the city's Social Services Department. The ship's sports teams flourished with successes at soccer, hockey, boxing, badminton and squash. Meanwhile PO Cook Bradley and Ldg Cook Bridger created a one-hundredth scale model cake of the *Tiger,* complete with Sea King helicopter, and also two smaller cakes depicting the *Tiger* as a ship of the line before her conversion to a helicopter cruiser, ready for the recommissioning ceremony. On Tuesday 27 April 1976, the *Tiger's*

new commanding officer, Captain S. A. C. Cassels CBE RN, was appointed to the ship. Captain Cassels had entered the Navy in 1945 and between 1962 and 1967 he had commanded the frigates *Vigilant, Roebuck, Tenby* and *Eskimo.* In 1972 he had commanded the assault ship HMS *Fearless* and after a spell as the Staff Officer to the Chief of the Defence Staff, he was appointed to command the *Tiger.*

The Recommissioning Ceremony took place on Friday 28 May 1976 and it was attended by the ship's company and many of their relatives and friends, including three men who had served in the battlecruiser *Tiger* in the 1920s. The service was conducted jointly by the Reverends J. T. Beach, P. Brown and J. F. Ellis. The magnificent cake was cut by Mrs Cassels, ably assisted by the youngest rating on board, 16-year-old JMEM Thornley, after which Rear-Admiral J. D. E. Fieldhouse, Flag Officer Second

HMS *Tiger* enters Gibraltar in early 1977. *(Fleet Air Arm Museum)*

An unusual shot of the *Tiger* and the frigate *Jupiter,* taken from RFA *Green Rover* during the Fifth Group Deployment to South America and West Africa.

(Geoffrey Mortimore/ Action Photos)

Frigate Squadron, inspected the Guard of Honour which was commanded by Lt Travis Terrell USN, who was on exchange from the United States Navy. The cruiser's sea trials took place in the summer and in October 1976 the ship underwent four weeks of sea training and work-up at Portland. During these evolutions the *Tiger* practised refuelling at sea by the regular abeam method and by the more unusual astern method from RFA *Green Rover,* when the fuelling parties tested new fluorescent orange foul weather jackets.

The *Tiger's* first major deployment of the commission came in January 1977 when, flying the flag of Rear-Admiral M. La T. Wemyss, Flag Officer Second Flotilla, she led the Fifth Group Deployment. Also taking part were the frigates *Ariadne, Danae, Aurora, Eurylas, Jupiter* and *Antelope,* together with the nuclear-powered submarine *Churchill* and three RFAs. After carrying out four days of weapons training in the South Western Approaches the group sailed to join other NATO forces for 'Exercise Locked Gate' in the Atlantic, off the coast of Portugal. During the exercise they took part in convoy escort duties, carrier support operations, replenishment at sea, and were themselves subjected to all manner of air attacks. They 'sank' several submarines and after ten days of 'war' they emerged victorious. The exercise was followed by a visit to Gibraltar where inter-ship sporting activities were arranged, with the *Tiger* winning the basketball, badminton, volleyball and boxing competitions, but the prestigious 'Top of the Rock' race was won by the *Ariadne.* After leaving Gibraltar there was another session of weapons

training in the Atlantic, before the group set course west for the sunnier climes of the Caribbean. As the Fifth Deployment Group headed across the Atlantic for Puerto Rico, HMS *Antelope* and RFA *Green Rover* detached to Palm Beach, Florida, to fit trials equipment which was to be used on the Autec Range off Andros Island, where there were also perfect banyan beaches. Most of the group's exercises took place in the areas off Puerto Rico, but visits were also made to La Guira, Buenos Aires and Rio de Janeiro. During a visit to St Lucia the *Tiger's* Sea King helicopters airlifted a 200-year-old, 32-pounder cannon to Fort Rodney which is 350 feet above sea level on Pigeon Island. The fort, named after Admiral Lord Rodney, whose fleet defeated the French at the Battle of the Saints in 1782, had had all the cannons removed in the 19th century, and was being restored by the St Lucia Historical and Archaeological Society. The Royal Navy were asked if they could help to replace the fort's guns and the *Tiger* was able to oblige, with the operations being watched by the Prime Minister of St Lucia, Admiral Wemyss and Captain Cassels. Lifting the underslung guns to the fort was an exacting task for the Sea King pilots, and after the installation Lt-Cdr Geoff Harvey, the CO of 826 Squadron, and one of the pilots presented the Historical Society with a commemorative plaque to place in Fort Rodney. With the restoration of the fort to its former glory the Society could make plans for the Battle of the Saints to be celebrated in style at Fort Rodney during the bicentennial in 1982. On the return passage to the UK, ships of the group made calls at Madeira, The Gambia and Dakar in Senegal. On the

The nuclear-powered submarine *Churchill* leads the *Tiger* during the Fifth Group Deployment in April 1977.
(Geoffrey Mortimore/Action Photos)

night of Wednesday 11 May, when the *Tiger* was at Dakar, one of the Sea King helicopters went to the aid of a Polish trawler off the coast which had an injured seaman aboard. Despite being off duty, and with no experience of stretcher lifts at night, POACMN Davies volunteered for the mission which involved being winched down to the trawler in bad weather conditions. Once on board PO Davies prepared the patient before ensuring that the injured man was winched safely to the Sea King and flown back to the *Tiger*. For his dedication to duty in difficult conditions, PO Davies was subsequently awarded the Queen's Commendation for Valuable Service in the Air. It was in late May that the *Tiger* returned to Portsmouth, having participated in the major NATO exercise, 'Locked Gate', and in bilateral exercises with the Venezuelan and Brazilian Navies.

The *Tiger's* next major duty was to take part in The Queen's Silver Jubilee Review of the Fleet at Spithead on Tuesday 28 June 1977, which was the largest since the Coronation Review in 1953 and involved some 180 ships. In addition to units of the Royal Navy and the Royal Fleet Auxiliary there were ships from 17 other countries, representing the Navies of the Commonwealth, NATO, CENTO and EEC countries. The *Tiger*, flying the flag of Rear-Admiral Wemyss, headed the Second Flotilla, which included the 3rd, 7th and 8th Frigate Squadrons. The review was the first held at Spithead in which battleships did not take part, and the C-in-C Fleet, Admiral Sir Henry Leach, was flying his flag in the soon to be withdrawn aircraft carrier, *Ark Royal.* In the final rehearsals for the review on Monday 27 June, RFA *Engadine* took the role of the royal yacht *Britannia,* while overhead 154 aircraft, including 110 from the Fleet Air Arm, rehearsed their fly-past in an 'ER' and anchor formation. Although everyone had hoped for a warm, sunny day, Tuesday 28 June dawned distinctly chilly and blustery, with a wind that at times reached Force 4, but at least the threatened rain held off. Despite the weather the ceremony lacked none of the panache it had acquired since it was first performed in 1773, and it got under way with a salute fired from seven warships as the *Britannia,* led by the Trinity House vessel *Patricia,* left harbour. Unfortunately, the cold blustery weather kept many of the expected crowds away from Southsea seafront, but for two hours the royal yacht, dressed overall, cruised at eight knots along the 15-mile circuit of 180 ships, while 30,000 sailors who were lining the decks snapped to attention, raised their caps and cheered as the *Britannia* passed by. Following the review, 90 helicopters took part in the Fleet Air Arm fly-past led by the Flag Officer Naval Air Command, but the inclement weather conditions prevented all fixed-wing aircraft and some helicopters from taking part.

After taking summer leave and carrying out maintenance, in September 1977 the *Tiger,* flying the flag of Rear-Admiral Wemyss, led a task group from Portsmouth bound for the Mediterranean. The force, which had been designated Task Group Six, included in addition to the *Tiger,* the frigates *Amazon, Cleopatra, Mohawk, Rhyl* and *Zulu,* together with the RFAs *Grey Rover, Regent, Tarbatness* and *Tidepool,* and they were heading for a seven-month deployment to the Mediterranean, Indian Ocean, South-East Asia and Australia. They were to take part, with allied navies, in NATO and CENTO exercises, as well as bilateral and multilateral exercises in the areas visited. With the Suez Canal having been reopened in 1975 after a closure of eight years, the force was able to use the old familiar route once again, something which had not been possible on the 1973 Group Deployment. First on the agenda was the NATO exercise 'Display Determination', which was designed to rehearse the reinforcement and resupply of the organization's southern flank. The exercise started in the Atlantic and progressed into the western Mediterranean,

The *Tiger* in the Kiel Canal, having attended 'Kieler Woche'.
(Michael Cassar)

Here the *Tiger* is looking very smart at her Spithead anchorage for the Queen's Silver Jubilee Review of the Fleet in June 1977.
(Maritime Photo Library)

HMS *Tiger* on passage up the Brisbane River on 27 January 1978.
(Fleet Air Arm Museum)

71

By 1985 the solitary *Tiger* was looking very forlorn as she lay rusting away at her moorings in Portsmouth Harbour.

(Walter Sartori)

moving then via the north of Corsica and the south of Sicily to the Aegean, where the US Marines carried out an amphibious landing near the Dardanelles. Following the exercise the group split up, with the *Tiger* and the *Amazon* visiting Istanbul, while the other ships went to either Varna in Bulgaria, Thessalonika or Piraeus, although the *Tidepool* had to sail to Malta to collect a spare Wasp helicopter for the *Cleopatra* after her original machine crashed on the *Tiger's* flight deck. On Tuesday 11 October, whilst the *Tiger* was at Istanbul, she was joined by the Minister of State for the Navy, Patrick Duffy, who spent six days at sea during which he saw most of the Group's ships which had refuelled in the eastern Mediterranean, following their various official visits. The minister disembarked at Port Said for an official visit to Egypt where he met Government officials and visited a Royal Navy Clearance Diving Team who were assisting the Egyptians to recover ancient monuments which had been submerged by the opening of the Aswan Dam.

Once through the Suez Canal the group split up again, and the *Tiger* and the *Amazon,* together with the RFAs *Regent* and *Tidepool,* visited Aqaba in Jordan. The *Rhyl* and the *Mohawk* put into Jeddah in Saudi Arabia, while the remainder stayed north of the Suez Canal for a little longer to visit Alexandria. During the *Tiger's* stay in Aqaba she received an unexpected and informal visit from King Hussein, who was no stranger to the Royal Navy's warships. After touring the ship and taking a flight in a Sea King helicopter, the King visited the *Amazon* where, once again, he walked informally round the ship. Next on the Group's agenda was an exercise with CENTO maritime forces, before the *Tiger* and RFA *Tidepool* visited Bandar Abbas, the Iranian port in the Strait of Hormuz. It was still six months before violent anti-Shah riots would make the area politically unstable and in late 1977 the country was still very pro-western. Braving temperatures of over 100°F the ships' seven-a-side rugby teams held an inter-ship tournament, and after the visit to the Iranian port the ships went on to call at ports as diverse as Port Sudan, Muscat, Karachi, Bahrain, Abu Dhabi, Doha and Salalah. When Rear-Admiral Wemyss and his staff departed from Bandar Abbas for the UK, command of the group until the end of January 1978 was assumed by Captain Cassels.

Unfortunately, when the time came to leave Bandar Abbas, machinery problems delayed the *Tiger's* departure and the remainder of the group exercised together in the Arabian Sea en route to Sri Lanka, where they split up once again and the frigates *Amazon* and *Cleopatra,* with the *Grey Rover,* departed for Singapore and Hong Kong. The rest of the ships continued south across the Indian Ocean to take part in exercises with the Australian Navy. Meanwhile, the *Tiger,* which had been left behind at Bandar Abbas, was now experiencing one of the quietest times in her commission as a helicopter cruiser, followed by a relatively relaxed transit of the Indian Ocean to Australian waters. As the ship crossed the equator, King Neptune held court and the young first-timers were called forward for their initiation ceremony. When the *Tiger* arrived in Fremantle for a four-day visit, there was a frantic programme of sporting fixtures, open-to-visitors and two-way hospitality, including some never-to-be-forgotten runs ashore.

Much to everyone's delight the *Tiger,* together with RFA *Regent,* spent Christmas and New Year in Sydney, while the *Mohawk, Rhyl* and *Tidepool* spent the seasonal holiday period in Adelaide, the *Zulu* was at Geelong and the *Tarbatness* at Hobart, whilst the *Amazon* and *Cleopatra* were at Hong Kong where they had the honour of being the first visiting Royal Navy warships for two years. The 'Tigers' enjoyed a sunny Christmas in Sydney, with the day itself being spent traditionally on board. Many took advantage of the weather to visit the city's beaches, enjoying the sun and the surf. A team from one of the POs' messes played Santa to children at a local hospital, while volunteers from 826 Squadron helped out in the casualty department at the city's main hospital. Competing in the 109th Sydney 'Highland Gathering', which is Australia's biggest reunion of kilts and cabers, the ship's tug-of-war team found themselves matched against a ten-ton elephant, and they won the contest by two pulls to one, although their opponent never really understood, or played by, the rules. The *Tiger's* New Year of 1978, which was to be her last operational celebration of the event, was rung in with a five-foot bell rope which had been specially made for the occasion, and as the ringing finished the ship's company were treated to a grandstand view of the Sydney Harbour fireworks display, which signalled the opening of the Sydney Festival. The honour of opening the folklore section of the festival fell to the *Tiger's* folk group, Fiddlers Green, who had also made a number of radio, TV and club appearances in the city.

On leaving Sydney, the *Tiger's* ship's company was brought back down to earth very quickly with an inspection by Admiral Wemyss, who had returned to the ship, and exercises with the main body of the deployment which had rendezvoused with them off Sydney. At the end of January 1978, in a farewell to Australia, the *Tiger* and RFA *Regent* paid a visit to Brisbane, Queensland. On the last day of January, with the *Tiger* berthed at Brisbane, the cruiser's last operational commanding officer, Captain G. M. K. Brewer RN, took command.

Captain Brewer had entered the Royal Navy just after the end of the Second World War and in 1964 he commanded the destroyer *Carysfort* in the Far East. Between 1967 and 1974 he commanded the destroyer

Agincourt, as well as the frigates *Grenville* and *Juno,* when he was also Captain Fourth Frigate Squadron.

Meanwhile the *Rhyl* and RFA *Tidepool* went to Townsville, 600 miles up the coast, while the *Mohawk* called at Mackay, south of Townsville, and the *Zulu* and *Tarbatness* visited the northern port of Cairns. For the *Amazon* and the *Cleopatra* there was a totally different scene, with the two frigates receiving an enthusiastic welcome in Tokyo, where they were the first major British warships to visit for ten years. Their very successful Far Eastern visits ended with a call at the US Naval Base at Yokosuku, after which they set course south to the area off the Philippines where they were to rendezvous with the ships of the southern detachment. The main body of the group, on leaving their Australian ports, steamed north through the Coral Sea, following the Second World War route of the Allied forces, and homed in on the Philippines, where all the units came together. A five-day visit to Manila followed and after the cancellation of a multi-national exercise planned for the Subic Bay area, Admiral Wemyss decided to take most of his force to Hong Kong instead. There is no doubt that this was a very popular alternative, although the *Cleopatra* and *Rhyl* were sent to exercise with the Thai Navy before visiting Bangkok. From Hong Kong it was back to the South China Sea and exercises with a US Navy submarine, before the group set course for Singapore.

The long entry through the eastern half of the Johore Strait evoked nostalgic memories for those 'old hands' who remembered the former naval base on Singapore's north coast, just east of the Causeway, and for just a few days the Stores Basin of Sembawang Dockyard took on the familiar look of the 1960s as the *Tiger, Mohawk, Zulu, Amazon* and RFA *Tidepool* lay alongside. There were grey funnels everywhere and the shops and bars of Sembawang Village bustled with business once again, just as they had when the Royal Navy was based there. Once the ships were settled in the Stores Basin a round of inter-ship sporting fixtures got under way and the ships' teams also played local sides. However, after the first weekend the *Amazon* and the *Zulu* left for the island of Penang, while the *Cleopatra* and the *Rhyl* arrived from Bangkok for a fleeting visit before they, the *Tiger* and the rest of the force set sail for some mainland ports in India, Sri Lanka and the Maldive Islands. The *Amazon* even paid a visit to Basra, Iraq, and was the first British warship to do so for many years. By the second week in April, however, the group had steamed north through the Suez Canal once again and on Monday 10 April the *Tiger* led the way into Malta's Grand Harbour for two days' stay before they sailed for home.

The *Tiger* arrived in Portsmouth for the last time on Thursday 20 April 1978 and 14 days later, on Thursday 4 May, she was decommissioned. With the imminent recommissioning of HMS *Bulwark,* which would be followed in the early 1980s by the entry into service of the

On a misty September day in 1986 the *Tiger* was towed from Portsmouth Harbour by the Dutch tug *Smit-Lloyd 25* for her final voyage to the breaker's yard.

(Walter Sartori)

first of the Invincible-class of light fleet carriers, the *Tiger* and the *Blake* were finally redundant. The *Tiger* remained in the non-tidal basin at Portsmouth Dockyard and she went into reserve in a condition described as 'Preservation by Operation'. Her ship's company was reduced to around 150, mainly electrical and engineering ratings, with Cdr M. B. Thomas RN in command. Equipment was installed on her decks while what was known as MDH (massive dehumidification) treatment was carried out. This involved circulating dry air throughout the working spaces and mess decks, which reduced the relative humidity to about 50 per cent and inhibited corrosion. However, it was clear that she would never go to sea under her own power again, and by 1980 she had been placed on the disposal list and moored at a buoy in Fareham Creek where, for a time, she lay alongside

the destroyer *Devonshire*. Finally, on 15 April 1986 the Ministry of Defence sent out a letter to prospective purchasers which began: 'The Director of Contracts/Refits and Equipment hereby invites you to tender for the purchase of HMS *Tiger* "as lying" at HM Naval Base, Portsmouth, for breaking up for the recovery of scrap.' Tenders for the *Tiger* were required at the Ministry of Defence by Tuesday 20 May 1986, and in the event she was sold to the Spanish shipbreakers, Desquaces Valera, who chartered the Dutch tug *Smit-Lloyd 25* to tow her from Portsmouth Harbour on Tuesday 23 September that year to begin the journey to Spain for demolition. She was the last of the three sisters to be scrapped and it was a condition of the sale that the cruiser was not 're-exported before breaking up'.

Previous Ships

The first recorded *Tyger* was a galleas of 200 tons, which was built at Deptford in 1546. She had a crew of 120, and was armed with four brass and 39 iron guns. In 1588 she was part of Lord Henry Seymour's squadron which pursued the Armada, a chase which took her as far north as Newcastle where the pursuit was abandoned because of unfavourable winds. Her master was Captain William Caesar and the ship herself was broken up in 1605. There was another *Tyger* at sea during this period, one of four privateers under John Hawkins which sailed for Africa and the West Indies. Sadly, it is thought that this vessel took part in the slave trade. In 1585 a hired ship, the *Tyger*, in company with the *Lion, Elizabeth, Dorothy* and *Roebuck* sailed under Sir Richard Grenville for Virginia where members of the ship's company, together with soldiers, were landed in an effort to colonise the area. It was whilst she was in these waters that she boarded and captured a Spanish ship, the boarding parties, having no boats, making their way alongside the Spanish ship on rafts made out of ship's chests. One of the earliest recorded Arctic expeditions was that of 1613 when a *Tyger* of 260 tons, with William Baffin as pilot, took Captain Joseph on a voyage of exploration.

In 1647 a new *Tiger* of 38 guns was completed at Deptford and she served with the fleet for almost 100 years, during which time she saw varied and active service. Her first captain, James Peacock, brought her fame when, during the Civil War, he commanded her during the siege of Colchester. She was with Admiral Blake in his pursuit of Prince Rupert in 1650, when he took Rupert's *Guinea* and *Charles* as prizes. In 1652 she took a Dutch ship, the *Morganstar* without a single British casualty. After taking part in the battle of the North Foreland under a new captain, Gabriel Sanders, she recommissioned for service in the Mediterranean. In 1666, early in the Second Dutch War, the *Tiger*, under the command of Phineas Pett, met a Zeeland privateer of 40 guns and although Pett was killed by the enemy's first broadside, his Lieutenant continued the fight for a further six hours, by which time the *Tiger* was too heavily damaged to catch the escaping enemy ship. Later that year Sir Robert Holmes flew his flag in the *Tiger* and sailed into the Terschelling Roads. With fire ships and a number of smaller vessels he raided the Dutch Fleet, destroying 170 vessels and severely damaging some shore installations. In 1672 Captain Thomas Harman took over the *Tiger* from John Turner under whom she had fought in the Battle of Solebay, and Captain Harman's first action was in defence of a fleet of colliers he was escorting along the east coast to the Thames during which he fought off eight Dutch privateers.

On 22 February 1674 the *Tiger* entered Cadiz Harbour close on the heels of a Dutch ship, the *Shakerloo* (Captain De Witte). Having been criticised for not having attacked the *Tiger*, De Witte borrowed 70 officers and men from his flagship and set sail, and soon he was engaged by Harman at close quarters. Each ship repelled boarders and after a long battle the *Shakerloo* was boarded by the victorious 'Tigers' as she began to sink. The Dutch had suffered 50 killed and 70 wounded, while the British suffered nine killed and 15 wounded, including Captain Harman who was hit below his left eye by a musket ball.

Records show that another *Tiger* was in commission in 1678; an Algerine prize captured by the *Rupert* and the *Mary*, but she was subsequently sunk at Sheerness. The *Tiger* of 1647 was rebuilt four times, the first in 1681 before operations against Guadeloupe and Martinique. The second time in 1701, before sailing for the Mediterranean and assisting in the defence of Gibraltar and the third time in 1705 when, commanded by Captain Charles Fotherby, she played her part in the destruction of de Pointi's squadron near Gibraltar. In 1721 she was rebuilt for the last time and she subsequently saw service in the defence of Gibraltar and, in 1726, with Admiral Francis Hosier, she served in the West Indies and took part in the blockade of Cartagena.

In 1743, under Captain Edward Herbert, this ship ended her long career by foundering off Tortugas in the West Indies, but her crew managed to make the shore in boats having loaded stores and 20 of the ship's guns to fortify the island. The Spaniards sent a 60-gun ship, the *Fuerte,* to capture the crew but she was lost in bad weather and in the event the *Tiger's* crew captured a Spanish sloop and sailed their prize to Jamaica.

The next *Tiger* was launched on the Thames in 1747, and she was a 60-gun ship commanded by Captain Thomas Latham. She sailed out to India where she remained throughout her service, playing a part in the capture of Calcutta, and in actions at Cuddalore, Negapatam and Pondichery. She was made a hulk in 1761 and sold in Bombay four years later.

In 1762 the Spanish ship *Tigre* was captured at the surrender of Havana, but little is known of her subsequent career except that she was a hospital ship at Plymouth from 1783 until she was sold in 1788. Another vessel, the *Ardent,* was captured by British forces at the Battle of the Saintes and she was renamed *Tiger,* but she was sold in the following year. In 1794 an 80-ton gunboat was named *Tiger* and she was used as part of the anti-invasion flotilla, but was sold in 1816. In 1795 a second *Tigre* was taken from the French and she became the flagship of Sir William Sydney Smith, and was present at the bombardment of Alexandria. In 1799, with the French forces being held down in the Nile Delta, a delegation boarded the *Tigre* to conclude a treaty, but bad weather forced the ship to sea with the delegation still on board and the treaty was not

The magnificent 35,160-ton battlecruiser *Tiger* of 1914 is shown here in 1925 whilst serving as a seagoing gunnery training ship. It was once said that, 'Speed and beauty were welded into every line of her.' *(Maritime Photo Library)*

concluded until she returned to Alexandria a month later. In 1805 the *Tigre* was blockading Cadiz under Nelson, but she missed the Battle of Trafalgar in October that year because she was taking on stores at Gibraltar. Her captain at this time was Benjamin Hallowell who, with HMS *Cumberland*, lay off Rosas Bay and sent in a force of brigs under the command of the *Tigre's* First Lieutenant. They destroyed 11 French men-of-war.

A small tender of 31 tons which was built in 1808 and named *Tiger* was employed on the south coast until 1829, when she was broken up. By 1849 another *Tiger* had been launched and fitted out at Chatham. She was a sloop of 1,221 tons, and armed with 16 guns and a number of 24-pounder rockets she sailed for the Mediterranean three years later, commanded by Captain Henry Gifford. Together with HM Ships *Sampson, Furious, Terrible, Retribution* and *Arethusa,* she bombarded Odessa in 1854. One shot from the *Terrible* blew up a magazine on the Imperial Mole and the resulting fire destroyed several Russian ships. In the subsequent confusion a number of captured British merchantmen were able to escape to sea. Later, on patrol off Odessa in thick fog, the *Tiger* lost contact with her consorts and ran aground five miles southeast of the port. When the fog cleared the shore batteries opened fire and within minutes the ship was ablaze. Having dumped most of the guns in an effort to lighten the ship only one gun could return the fire and her captain

was killed in the action. The ship was eventually blown up by Russian gunfire. The next *Tiger* was launched at Clydebank in 1900, a torpedo boat of 383 tons, but she was lost after a collision with the cruiser HMS *Berwick* off St Catherine's Point in 1908.

The most famous *Tiger* of all was the 35,160-ton battlecruiser which was launched from John Brown's Clydebank shipyard in 1912. She was completed in October 1914, and with eight 13.5-inch and 12, 6-inch guns, she was the largest and fastest capital ship in the fleet. She was the only battlecruiser to mount 6-inch guns, and she was also the last coal-burning capital ship. She served throughout the Great War of 1914-18 and saw action at the Battle of Dogger Bank and Jutland. In the latter battle she received 17 hits. The 6-inch magazine had to be flooded after the action when a shell was found to be jammed between the barrels of X turret. It was said of her, 'Speed and beauty were welded into every line of her. Wherever she went she satisfied the eye of the sailorman and I have known them to pull miles just that the sweetness of her lines might delight the eye. Besides any other ship she made them look like floating factories.' From 1919 to 1922 she served in the Atlantic Fleet Battlecruiser Squadron, and from 1924 to 1929 she was employed as a sea-going gunnery training ship. She finally paid off at Devonport on 30 March 1931 and in the following year she was sold for breaking up.

Battle Honours
HMS *Tiger*

Quis Eripet Dentes (Who Will Draw My Teeth)

Armada 1588	Marbella 1705
Portland 1653	Sandras 1758
Gabbard 1653	Negapatam 1758
Scheveningen 1653	Porto Novo 1759
Lowestoft 1665	Egypt 1801
Orfordness 1666	Dogger Bank 1915
Solebay 1672	Jutland 1916

HMS *Tiger*
Commanding Officers

Name:	Date Appointed:
Captain R. E. Hutchins RN	21 July 1959
Captain P. W. W. Graham DSC RN	22 April 1961
Captain H. L. Lloyd DSC RN	24 April 1963
Captain G. J. Kirby DSC RN	19 March 1965
Captain D. T. Goodhugh RN	24 August 1971
Captain M. L. Stacey RN	30 April 1973
Captain S. A. C. Cassels CBE RN	27 April 1976
Captain G. M. K. Brewer RN	31 January 1978

Part Two
HMS *LION* 1960-1975

Chapter Seven

HMS *Lion* - First Commission 1960-1962

In early 1960, whilst the *Tiger* was showing the flag in the Mediterranean, the second of the three Tiger-class cruisers was nearing completion on the River Tyne, and on Monday 22 February 1960, at 9.35am, HMS *Lion* was pulled from her fitting-out berth by four tugs to begin her first passage downriver to Tynemouth and the North Sea for her Contractor's Sea Trials. At 10.50am that morning she passed Tynemouth Pier and anchored just one and a half miles offshore. Next day, after an early start at 6.40am, the *Lion* steamed north for engine trials, but by 5.50pm she was back alongside Swan Hunter's quay on the Tyne after problems had been found with her steam turbines. Two days later she left the River Tyne again for a further two days of trials, but by 5pm on Friday 26 February she was back alongside once again for further rectifications to her turbines. The *Lion's* next foray into the North Sea took place on Monday 29 February and once again she was at sea for just over 24 hours before she returned to her fitting-out berth. On Tuesday 1 March she steamed downriver

once more, this time to carry out a number of speed runs at full power over the St Abb's measured mile. The trials continued into the second week of March and they included gun-firing tests with both main and secondary armament. The initial trials finally ended on Friday 11 March when the *Lion* secured alongside her berth for her fitting out to be completed. It would be over four months before she set sail again.

Some months later, in the summer of 1960, the Member of Parliament for The Hartlepools, Commander J. S. Kerans DSO RN (Retd), of Yangtse River and *Amethyst* fame, no doubt concerned about rumours which were circulating to the effect that the second and third cruisers of the Tiger-class would not be completed, asked the Government for a statement about the completion of HMS *Lion*. The reply he received must have set his mind at rest for it was unequivocal: 'HMS *Lion* will be commissioned on 20 July, and accepted from the shipbuilder on 22 July.' Sure enough the necessary

HMS *Lion* in the early weeks of 1960 as she neared completion on the River Tyne.
(Scottish Record Office)

preparations were going ahead as planned and on 24 April 1960 the *Lion's* first commanding officer, Captain J. E. Scotland DSC RN, was appointed to the ship. By mid-July members of the ship's company were assembling at the naval barracks in Portsmouth and on Monday 18 July an advance party joined the ship at Wallsend on Tyne. Next day the main body of the new ship's company boarded an 'RN Special' train at Portsmouth & Southsea railway station, and this is remembered by a member of the Royal Marines Detachment: 'Unfortunately there was nothing very special about this train and true to music hall fashion it delivered us to the ship as darkness fell, over three and a half hours late. We took a belated meal and then commenced unloading all the kitbags, before starting preparations for the Commissioning Ceremony which was due to start the next morning. Thankfully 20 July was a fine day which began with cleaning and preparing the ship for an open day, and we even managed a rehearsal of the ceremony.'

The guest of honour at the ceremony was to be Admiral of the Fleet Lord Mountbatten, who was the only member of the ship's company of the previous *Lion* who was still serving in the Royal Navy, and the ceremony itself was conducted by the *Lion's* commanding officer, Captain J. E. Scotland DSC RN. Having been born and brought up in Sydney, Australia, he joined the Navy as a cadet at the Royal Naval College, Dartmouth, in 1927. He went to sea in 1929 and qualified as a gunnery officer in 1938. During the Second World War he served in the ill-fated cruisers *Dunedin* and *Curacao,* the brand new cruiser *Jamaica* and the battleship *King George V.* After the war he commanded the destroyers *Gravelines* and *Vigilant,* and he was the Naval Attaché in Rome before being appointed to the *Lion.*

The ceremony itself was attended by hundreds of shipyard workers who had virtually rebuilt the ship, as well as members of the *Lion's* ship's company and many of their wives and families. Amongst the VIP guests was Lord Beatty, the son of Admiral Beatty. At 11am Admiral of the Fleet Lord Mountbatten arrived at the shipyard to inspect the Guard and Band and this was followed by the reading of the Commissioning Warrant by Captain Scotland, the raising of the Commissioning Pendant and the White Ensign and a short religious service by the ship's padre. Following this there were short addresses by Captain Scotland and by Lord Mountbatten who told the assembled guests: 'Yesterday, 19 July, was the forty-fourth anniversary of my joining the old *Lion* at Rosyth. I am sure of that date because some years after, when I was at Rosyth when the old *Lion* was being broken up, I pinched the gun room name tally and put the date on it. I have brought it here today and am handing it over to the new *Lion,* together with a small picture of the old ship and a picture of a group of officers of 1916. I am sure it is no exaggeration to say that the *Lion* coupled with the name of Beatty, was the most famous combination of Admiral and flagship

since Nelson and the *Victory.*' He went on to tell the ship's company, 'I think you are inheriting the proudest name of the Navy List, but I hope you will never have to emulate the *Lion's* battle honours.' At last, some 18 years after her keel had been laid, another old Jutland name was back in service in the Royal Navy.

In general appearance the *Lion* resembled her sister ship *Tiger,* but there were some refinements. Her masts were more squat, the enclosed navigation bridge had been modified and the captain's sea cabin, which looked out onto the bridge, had one-way glass which enabled him to look out, but no one could see in. Following the ceremony a further 48 hours were spent at Wallsend with the ship's company embarking stores before, at 8.41am on Friday 22 July 1960, the *Lion* slipped her moorings and, with the tug *George V* secured forward and the tug *Marsden* standing by, set course downriver for Tynemouth and the North Sea. On the quayside over 2,000 dockyard workers had gathered to cheer her off, the ship's company lined the deck and the Royal Marines Band played some appropriate north country music. At 9.30am the ship passed Tynemouth Piers and during the day she carried out pre-acceptance trials. That afternoon, at 5pm, the *Lion* stopped off the River Tyne where an acceptance conference was held between the ship's senior officers, Admiralty officials and representatives of Swan Hunter, which culminated, at 5.25pm, with the *Lion* being accepted by the Admiralty and the White Ensign being broken at the masthead. Unfortunately, by the time the conference ended, high winds and heavy seas prevented the trials team from disembarking into tugs and the cruiser had to return to the sheltered waters of the River Tyne where they and the Tyne Pilot could leave the ship.

That evening the *Lion* set course north and at midnight she was off St Abbs Head. Next day, off the north-east coast of Scotland, she carried out speed and manoeuvring trials, combined with initial gunnery trials, and on Sunday 24 July she went alongside the Dockyard Pier at Invergordon and the ship's company got their first run ashore. At 9.10am on Sunday 31 July she left her mooring at Invergordon and set course down the North Sea for Portsmouth. The water was obviously warm that summer, for two hours after getting under way 'Hands to Bathe' was piped and some hardy souls took advantage of a 30-minute dip in the North Sea. It was on this journey that the cruiser's first major defect came to light when, off the east coast, very intense vibrations suddenly indicated that all was not well with the starboard forward turbine. Although the engine was stopped immediately, it was soon discovered that it was in fact seriously damaged and that it would have far-reaching consequences for the ship's future programme. During the passage preparations were made for a ceremonial entry into Portsmouth Harbour and in order to steal a lead of his rivals in A turret, the GI of Y turret

Still wearing the Red Ensign, the *Lion* leaves the River Tyne for the first time on Monday 22 February 1960 for her Contractor's Sea Trials. *(Maritime Photo Library)*

The *Lion's* ship's company mustered on the quarterdeck for the cruiser's Commissioning Service. *(R. Jerrard)*

scrounged some paint to buff up the after 6-inch mounting, and one night the crew of the turret gave it a good coat of fresh paint. However, as daylight dawned on Tuesday 2 August and the ship anchored in Sandown Bay, to his horror, the paint turned out to be duck-egg blue and not grey. What was said by Captain Scotland is not recorded, but for several hours prior to entering Portsmouth the Royal Marines of Y turret were seen with paint brushes in both hands repainting their gun turret and bringing it back to its normal grey colour. At just after midday the *Lion* weighed anchor and, with full ceremony, steamed up harbour to secure alongside North Corner Jetty where a crowd of wives and families welcomed her. Speaking at a press conference that afternoon Captain Scotland, not mentioning the engine problems, said of his ship: 'We have no complaints at all. The outstanding aspect is the accommodation for the ratings, and the eating facilities are as good as anyone could wish for.' He went on

to tell those present that the *Lion* would remain at Portsmouth for about a month before carrying out gunnery trials in the Channel and in the Atlantic Ocean.

Whilst the ship was in Portsmouth Harbour leave was given to both watches and on completion of this preparations were made for a visit to the *Lion* by the Commandant-General, Royal Marines to present a silver plaque to the ship. The ceremony took place on Saturday 3 September and Lt-General Sir Ian Riches KCB DSO arrived on board at 11.30am, with the presentation taking place 15 minutes later. Framed in silver the plaque was a copy of the citation of the award of the posthumous Victoria Cross to Major F. J. W. Harvey RMLI, for gallantry on board HMS *Lion* at the Battle of Jutland in 1916. The citation read: 'Major Francis John William Harvey RMLI, Officer Commanding Royal Marines Detachment, HMS *Lion*, Battle of Jutland, 31 May 1916. Whilst mortally wounded and almost the only survivor

At 5.25pm on Friday 22 July 1960, with the *Lion* stopped off the mouth of the River Tyne, Captain Scotland accepted the cruiser into Her Majesty's Service. *(R. Jerrard)*

after the explosion of an enemy shell in Q gun house, with great presence of mind and devotion to duty ordered the magazine to be flooded, thereby saving the ship. He died shortly afterwards.' Major Harvey had joined the Royal Marines Light Infantry in 1892, and had joined the battlecruiser HMS *Lion* on 12 February 1913. After the outbreak of war in August 1914, the *Lion* took part in actions at Heligoland Bight on 28 August 1914 and Dogger Bank on 24 January 1915. Then on 31 May 1916 came Jutland with the British and German battlecruisers opening fire on each other at 3.47pm. Major Harvey was commanding Q turret, containing two 13.5-inch guns, which was placed between the second and third funnels of the ship. Within ten minutes HMS *Lion* had been hit and Q turret had just fired its 12th round when a 12-inch shell from the *Lutzow* penetrated at the junction of the roof plates and detonated in the gun house. The explosion killed or wounded the occupants, blew the front plate out, the front roof plate off, and started a fire in the wreckage. Although severely injured, Major Harvey got to the voice pipe and ordered the magazine doors below to be closed and the magazine itself to be flooded. He then sent a wounded sergeant to the bridge to inform the captain that Q turret was out of action and on fire. At the time the shell hit the turret, the guns had just been loaded for the next

salvo; the detonation had also blown the breech lever of the left gun to the 'open' position. The shell and its cordite had slid down and fallen into the well, igniting in the fire, and the resulting flash fire ignited all the cordite charges in the hoists and handling room, down to the magazine doors which, thanks to Major Harvey, had been shut. Only three of the 60 or so people serving in this part of the ship survived; the wounded sergeant, a sick berth attendant and one of the chamber crew. Major Harvey's body was found badly burnt later that night and he was buried at sea. The plaque, which was presented to the new *Lion,* was mounted above the instrument showcase at the after end of the wardroom flat.

On Monday 5 September the *Lion* left harbour to anchor at Spithead for compass adjustments, but the following afternoon she returned to secure at Middle Slip Jetty. Later that month, on Sunday 25 September, the Chaplain of the Fleet dedicated the ship's chapel, and the *Lion's* sponsor, Lady J. H. Edelston, who had actually launched the cruiser as HMS *Defence,* unveiled a stained-glass window depicting a six-winged lion which was designed and made by L. C. Evetts of the Faculty of Art, Kings College, Newcastle upon Tyne. Lady Edelston dedicated the window to the memory of all officers and men who had served in ships called *Lion.*

As the end of the month approached, the enormous amount of publicity which the *Lion* had received on radio, television and in the press was felt on board by the huge amount of mail received by Captain Scotland with offers of bronze, brass and plaster lions weighing anything from two to 200lbs, but much to his relief, nobody offered the real thing. Finally, at 7.20am on Thursday 29 September, after taking on stores, ammunition and fuel, the *Lion* was ready to leave harbour to undergo her trials, but unfortunately she would be sailing into a new storm of controversy.

After only three days at sea in October 1960 it was apparent that the starboard forward turbine was still defective and during that month she was in and out of Portsmouth Harbour carrying out trials. Unfortunately, on each occasion faults developed in one or more of the main bearings and, in spite of the best efforts of the engine room department, the cause of the problem could not be found, and by 15 October she was alongside North Corner Jetty and in dockyard hands. By early November it was clear that efforts to rectify the trouble were getting nowhere fast and it was decided that the damaged turbine rotor should be replaced. The size of the rotor meant that a large hole had to be cut through the boat deck and the galley flat, down into the starboard engine room. The hole became, for a time, one of the show pieces of the ship and as it completely cut off the sickbay passage, it meant that the ship's company had to make long roundabout treks over the boat deck in order to move from one end of the ship to the other during a very cold winter. The problems had, by this time, come to

On Tuesday 2 August 1960, with her decks manned for a full Procedure 'Alpha', the *Lion* arrived in Portsmouth from Scotland for the first time.
(Maritime Photo Library)

the notice of the media and once again there was a great deal of press coverage, with rumours of the *Lion's* early demise having to be denied once again by the Admiralty.

Meanwhile, there were other events to keep the ship's company busy, such as the Ship's Company Dance which was held at Southsea's South Parade Pier. Among the VIPs to visit the ship at this time was Prince Chula of Thailand who, as an old Harrovian, had lived in England for many years and who held a great regard for the Royal Navy. So much so that he had actually written a book on the life of Lord Nelson which had been printed in Thai and distributed in that country. On board the *Lion* he was received with the appropriate honour by the Royal Marines Guard and Band and, having inspected the guard, he then toured the galleys, dining halls, junior ratings' and chief petty officers' messes, taking care, of course, to avoid the hole down into the starboard engine room. The New Year of 1961 was rung in with due ceremony and with it, the *Lion* started on a more active and successful year with work under way to fill in 'the hole' and by the end of the month the job had almost been completed. On Friday 10 February the C-in-C Portsmouth, Admiral Sir Manley Power, inspected Divisions on the jetty and toured the ship before tugs towed the cruiser round to South Railway Jetty where preparations were made to get her ready for sea again.

It was at 7.30am on Thursday 16 February that the *Lion* left Portsmouth Harbour and put to sea for her trials, and as these progressed in the Channel it became apparent that the problems with the faulty turbine had been overcome. Once this had been established, the *Lion's* scene of operations switched to Plymouth and the Western Approaches where they were carried out in cold, damp, foggy and miserable weather. The fog was the greatest hazard and on one occasion, with visibility down to just 20 yards in Plymouth Sound, the ship had to secure to a buoy

that could not even be seen from the bridge. During this session of her trials, on Saturday 11 March 1961, the *Lion* put into Devonport Dockyard where she secured alongside No 5 wharf, close to her sister *Tiger,* which was under refit in No 5 basin. It was the first meeting of the two ships and Captain Hutchins from the *Tiger* visited the *Lion* for a tour of the ship. The trials period ended on Monday 20 March when, at 8am, the cruiser anchored at Spithead and after firing a salute to the C-in-C, a 'Families Day' was held when about 400 wives, children and girlfriends came to meet the ship at Spithead to sail up harbour before securing alongside South Railway Jetty later that afternoon. Despite the cold weather the day was a great success and once alongside a week was spent storing ship, followed by one week's general service leave.

After putting a few finishing touches to the ship's paintwork, at noon on Friday 14 April the *Lion* left South Railway Jetty and set course for the Mediterranean and her first real duty, which was to act as the flagship to the escort of the royal yacht *Britannia* as she carried the Queen and Prince Philip to Naples for the start of a state visit to Italy. First of all, however, the *Lion* stopped off at Gibraltar for an eight-day visit where the ship was painted and the Flag Officer (Flotillas) Mediterranean, Rear-Admiral J. F. D. Bush DSC, hoisted his flag. So, at 4pm on Friday 28 April, as flagship of the Mediterranean Fleet, the *Lion* left Gibraltar and steamed to her rendezvous with the royal yacht and the destroyers *Saintes* and *Solebay* off the Lipari Islands, where she arrived at just after 9pm on Monday 1 May and took station ahead of the destroyers. Next morning they were joined by an Italian naval force and together the whole squadron steamed into the Bay of Naples where all the escorts manned ship and one by one steamed past the royal yacht, before firing a 21-gun national salute and setting courses and speeds to enter

The *Lion's* first official duty after joining the Mediterranean Fleet was to act as the flagship to the *Britannia* for the Queen's visit to Naples. Here, with the ship's company manning the starboard side, the cruiser steams past the royal yacht.

(G. T. Nunn)

Naples Harbour. The royal visitors received a tumultuous welcome from the citizens of Naples, and several organized tours were available for the ship's company, including one to Rome where, at the Vatican, a 70-strong contingent from the *Lion* were able to attend an audience with Pope John XXIX. Leaving the ship at dawn the party travelled via the Appian Way to Rome and after a conducted tour of the Vatican they were placed at the front of an audience several thousand strong waiting for the Pope to appear in the courtyard of St Peter's Basilica. In his address, which was translated into four languages, the Pope gave a personal welcome to, 'the visiting personnel from HMS *Lion*'. For others there were numerous boat trips and sailing expeditions in Naples Bay, while an intrepid few tackled a 5,000 feet hill climb up Mount St Angelo, some 20 miles south of Naples, with magnificent views over the Bay of Naples. Numerous parties managed to visit Pompeii, but by the very nature of the cruiser's visit there was a great deal of ceremonial and one member of the Royal Marines recalls one such event: 'On the evening of 4 May, at the conclusion of FO(F) Med's reception, the Band, by floodlight, Beat Retreat and played 'Sunset' on the Molo Argionio. About 350 people watched this, our first big ceremonial function, and in this delightful setting on the waterfront, it could not have been better. During "Crimond" it was surprising to see a large number of female spectators dabbing away tears. Hours of rehearsal at Gib paid dividends for the *Lion* that night.'

Leaving Naples at 8.30am on Sunday 7 May everyone was expecting a quiet passage south to Malta, but that afternoon, as the ship steamed past Stromboli, Admiral Bush exercised 'General Drills' which kept everyone on their toes. Next day, at 10.15am, the *Lion* made her debut at Malta when she moored at No 2 buoy in Pieta Creek, part of Marsamxett Harbour, north-west of Valletta. Over the next nine days the *Lion* worked out of Pieta Creek and Marsaxlokk Bay carrying out gunnery trials and work-up exercises. On Thursday 18 May she left Malta to steam west to Gibraltar where she arrived two days later to be docked down for her annual overhaul, and after almost three weeks in the King George V dry dock and a few days alongside the detached mole, the *Lion* left Gibraltar on Monday 12 June to return to Malta where her work-up was to begin in earnest. For five weeks, with weekends at Pieta Creek, the whole ship's company was tested to the limit as they proved themselves to be a very efficient fighting unit. There were just a few hiccups, one of which was on Thursday 22 June during a towing exercise with the destroyer *Finisterre*, when the two ships collided. Fortunately, with little way on the vessels the damage was only superficial. Finally, the day of judgement arrived on 19 July when FO(F) Med carried out his Sea Inspection to a cacophony of guns, rockets, boarding parties and air attacks but finally, at noon on 21 July, Admiral Bush signalled: '*Lion* has shown that she has grown claws and teeth. I rehoist my flag with much pleasure.' There then

The *Lion*, foreground, and the *Tiger*, anchored off Port Larnaka, Leros, on 2 October 1961.

(G. T. Nunn)

HMS *Lion* moored at Flagship buoy, Grand Harbour.

(*G. A. Henderson & G. T. Nunn*)

followed ten days of maintenance at Parlatorio Wharf in Grand Harbour before, on Wednesday 9 August, the *Lion* left for a cruise to Ancona in the Adriatic, where many took the opportunity to visit Venice, before returning to Malta for FO(F) Med's Harbour Inspection. As soon as this was completed, on 29 August, she sailed for Tripoli where she secured alongside the Karaminili Oil Berth for a four-day 'jolly', which ended at 3pm on Monday 4 September. It was noted that during this stay the visitors to the ship included several million flies that were attracted, not by the ship, but by a cattle hut on the jetty. However, the local British Army garrison, which was manned by the 1st Battalion Royal Irish Fusiliers, looked after the ship's company well, with nothing being too much trouble and transport being produced for every function which had been laid on. On leaving the port about 70 Army families lined the point of the jetty to cheer the cruiser off and the *Lion* returned once again to Maltese waters where she anchored in Marsaxlokk Bay next day, prior to mooring in Pieta Bay. After just four days in Malta, the *Lion* left during the morning of Sunday 10 September to carry out exercises with the *Battleaxe* and *Diamond,* although the former returned to Malta with engine trouble, leaving the *Diamond* and *Lion* to set course for Beirut. The *Lion* secured alongside the eastern mole of Beirut Harbour at 8.30am on Thursday 14 September and the British residents, not having seen a Royal Navy warship for over two years, vied with each other to take members of the ship's company out for a day. Even the British Embassy ran out of beer on what was unanimously agreed to be the best run ashore in the Mediterranean. After leaving Beirut on 19 September the *Lion* steamed to Akrotiri Bay, Cyprus, and on to Rhodes where she anchored in Rhodes Bay on the morning of Tuesday 26 September. After three days there

the *Lion* steamed north-west to anchor off the island of Leros at 8am on Saturday 30 September where, just 40 minutes later, she was joined by her sister *Tiger,* and units of the 5th Destroyer Squadron. During the two days spent here the ships' companies of the two cruisers did friendly battle at aquatics, uckers and even all-night fishing before they left, with the *Tiger* bound for Salonika and the *Lion* for the northern Greek port of Kavalla. Although it was picturesque, the town itself had little to offer liberty men and so many went hiking and camping in the surrounding hills. After leaving Kavalla the *Lion* and *Tiger* rendezvoused for 'Exercise Aegex', during which Admiral Bush transferred his flag to the *Tiger* and the *Lion* returned to Malta.

It was at 9am on Monday 16 October 1961 that the *Lion* left Malta to steam via Gibraltar, where she paid a brief visit, to Portsmouth. On leaving Gibraltar on Saturday 21 October, the 156th anniversary of Nelson's great victory, it was fitting that a memorial service and wreath-laying ceremony was held off Cape Trafalgar. The ship's company assembled on the quarterdeck, Nelson's famous signal was hoisted and the Chaplain gave a short talk on the events of that day in 1805, concluding with Nelson's last prayer. Then the alert was sounded, Captain Scotland cast a wreath, and the memory of the gallant officers and men who had died during the Battle of Trafalgar was saluted. Three days later the *Lion* anchored at Spithead for Customs clearance and next morning, at 8.10am on Wednesday 25 October, she secured alongside Portsmouth's Middle Slip Jetty, the Mediterranean leg of her first General Service Commission completed.

Following her return to Portsmouth there was just time for a week's leave for each watch before, at 1pm on Friday 24 November 1961, the *Lion* slipped her moorings and set

A very smart Royal Marines Guard standing to attention on the quarterdeck, and...

...Relaxing in 16 Mess, the Royal Marines Barracks, at tot time.

(R. Jerrard & G. A. Henderson)

HMS *Lion* leaving Malta for Gibraltar.   (*G. T. Nunn*)

sail for an eagerly awaited visit to South America. The *Lion* was to be the flagship of a special squadron commanded by the C-in-C South Atlantic and South America Station, Vice-Admiral Sir Nicholas Copeman. It was to be the first major cruise by the Royal Navy in South American waters since before the Second World War and its purpose was twofold: to 'show the flag' in a part of the world which, in the early 1960s, was seldom visited by British tourists, and to renew long-standing ties with the navies of the South American nations which, in many cases, had been founded by Royal Navy officers. Accompanying the *Lion* was the destroyer *Dunkirk,* the frigates *Leopard* and *Londonderry* and the RFA *Wave Prince,* although she would not rendezvous with the two frigates until she reached South American waters. On the passage to Freetown the *Lion* was carrying as a passenger the Bishop of St Helena, the Rt Revd Harold Beardmore, who had been visiting the UK to raise awareness of the hardship caused to the islanders by the fact that fewer and fewer ships were visiting St Helena. During the voyage the Bishop held a Confirmation Service for several members of the ship's company, and as the chapel was not big enough to accommodate the congregation, the service was held on the quarterdeck while the cruiser was under way on a sunny day off the West African coast. Bishop Beardmore was no stranger to the Royal Navy, for he had been the Chaplain in the ill-fated battlecruiser *Hood* from 1939 to 1941, leaving her shortly before her loss in May that year. Having made only a short 48-hour stopover in Gibraltar, the *Lion* arrived in Freetown, Sierra Leone, on the morning of Monday 4 December for a stay of just 24 hours, which was long enough for most members of the ship's company, while

Vice-Admiral Copeman hoisted his flag, having travelled up from Cape Town, and Bishop Beardmore disembarked. After leaving Freetown the cruiser set course for Rio de Janeiro, and at 8.55am on Thursday 7 December she crossed the equator. Just over an hour later speed was reduced to 12 knots and for the next hour and a half most of the ship's company assembled on the quarterdeck to meet King Neptune, his royal court, guard, police, bears, heralds and, of course, the all-important barber. Amongst those to be 'called' to the royal presence was the Principal Medical Officer who was amply rewarded for all the injections and medicine he had administered in preparation for the cruise. He was followed by a variety of junior seamen and midshipmen, but the final ducking was reserved for the ever-popular Master-at-Arms. Six days later, at just after 8am on Wednesday 13 December, the *Lion* fired a 21-gun national salute before securing alongside the Praca Mava Pier of Rio de Janeiro's harbour. Within three hours of tying up alongside, the Guard and Band had paraded and the official calls had started. For the ship's company work ceased at 12.30pm each day when an open gangway operated and the social life began, with a whirl of tours and dances, with Copacabana and Sugar Loaf Mountain dominating the scene.

After leaving Rio at 6pm on Sunday 17 December the British squadron, which had all come together for the first time, rendezvoused with the Brazilian aircraft carrier *Minas Gerais* (ex-HMS *Vengeance*), the cruiser *Tamandare* and the destroyer *Parana* for joint exercises. Then at 1.15pm on Wednesday 20 December, with the squadron at the mouth of the River Plate, special sea dutymen were piped to their stations for the long passage upriver to Buenos Aires. This took over 17 hours, which included seven hours at anchor

On Thursday 19 October 1961, whilst at Gibraltar, Captain Scotland, his officers and men, posed for a traditional photograph. *(R. Jerrard)*

outside the Argentinian capital city, and it was 9am on Thursday 21 December when the cruiser secured alongside her berth and more rounds of official visits began. Being Christmas the hospitality was even more lavish than that at Rio, with most members of the ship's company finding plenty of entertainment in the city although a few explored inland areas. On 27 December the *Lion* steamed back downriver for a 24-hour passage to Montevideo where the New Year celebrations heralded yet another round of socializing with little or no sleep.

Just before leaving Montevideo on 2 January 1962, Admiral Copeman transferred his flag to the frigate *Leopard* and the squadron steamed south to the Argentinian port of Puerto Madryn in the Golfo Nuevo which, 20 years later, would be in the spotlight of the world's media when the defeated Argentinian Army was repatriated by the P&O liner turned troopship, SS *Canberra*. The squadron anchored off Puerto Madryn Pier, which meant a boat routine for liberty men, but some of those who did venture ashore received a warm welcome from a Welsh colony at Gaiman in the Chubut Valley, about 40 miles south of Puerto Madryn. The valley spreads over an

area of about 150 square miles with green fields, poplar trees, farms and small Welsh chapels. The settlers arrived there from Wales in the 1870s and, despite the passage of time, Welsh is still spoken in many homes by people who have a curious mix of Welsh-Spanish names.

After three days anchored in the Golfo Nuevo the British squadron weighed anchor early on the morning of Sunday 7 January and set course south for the Magellan Strait and then north for Valparaiso. During the passage there were exercises with the Chilean cruisers *O'Higgins* and *Prat,* the latter being the flagship of the Chilean Navy. Six days after leaving Puerto Madryn the British ships put into Valparaiso, with the *Lion* securing alongside A Pier in the port. Within an hour of tying up, a large contingent of the ship's company was departing for Santiago to be entertained by the expatriate British community there. However, most found their entertainment in the city itself which was voted second in popularity to Rio. Fifty members of the ship's company volunteered to give up their spare time to completely repaint a ward at a local children's hospital, which specialized in treating polio. In addition they took a hefty parcel of sweets and chocolate for the youngsters.

During the *Lion's* passage to Freetown the Bishop of St Helena held a Confirmation Service on the quarterdeck.

(R. Jerrard)

Christmas at Buenos Aires and Captain Scotland stirs the Christmas pudding.

(R. Jerrard)

HMS *Lion* negotiates the Gatun Locks in the Panama Canal. *(G. A. Henderson)*

Meanwhile, the *Leopard,* which had called at Concepcion, held a special memorial service in the English church in the city to the memory of Admiral Craddock and all those who perished in the Battle of Coronel, which took place off the coast on 1 November 1914.

On Wednesday 17 January the *Lion* left Valparaiso and set course for Callao, Peru, where she arrived four days later. An editorial in the Peruvian newspaper *El Commercio* reported the event thus: 'Today three ships of the Royal Navy, *Lion, Dunkirk* and *Leopard,* arrived in our principal port. Their mission is one of goodwill, to strengthen the ties between the people of England and Peru. The arrival of these ships is a happy occasion for this country and is worth a particular mention.' From Callao the *Lion* and her squadron steamed north for the Panama Canal which was reached on the morning of 29 January and which proved to be a busy time for special sea dutymen, but a goofer's paradise, as the cruiser negotiated the locks and lakes of the waterway. However, by 5.20pm that evening the *Lion* had cleared the canal and was heading across the Caribbean bound for the final South American port of call, Cartagena, Colombia, where she arrived on the last day of the month. Once again the visit was a great success and shortly before she left, on Sunday 4 February, Vice-Admiral Copeman finally transferred his flag back to the *Leopard.* Shortly after leaving he sent the following signal to the *Lion*: 'Before we break up and go our separate ways I want to "wash up" the cruise and let you know what we have achieved. First of all from the naval viewpoint we have now exercised on five occasions with a foreign navy. These exercises, in fact, probably made little impact on the majority of your lives, but the effect they had on the prestige of the Royal Navy has been greatly to our advantage. These modern ships

manoeuvring with dash and purpose, showing off their new weapons, have made their mark. The Argentinian Navy has, in fact, purchased four Leanders, and other navies have shown definite interest in our ships. Secondly, your conduct ashore has done nothing but impress; there have been few exceptions, very few, and while greatly disappointed by these instances of gross stupidity, I am more than deeply impressed by the good work that has been done all round. So great has been the success of our cruise that there has been a noticeable increase in goodwill towards Great Britain. His Royal Highness the Duke of Edinburgh will shortly be touring the South American countries as well. A most important benefit, which derives from this most friendly atmosphere, is that businessmen from England find a good market for British goods; the country's trade and export increases, and in the end the whole country reaps the benefit of the seed we have sown.'

After Cartagena the *Lion* hoisted the flag of the Senior Naval Officer West Indies and after a short visit to San Juan, she left the Caribbean on Friday 9 February and accompanied by the *Dunkirk,* set course for Ponta Delgada in the Azores for a short stay of just 44 hours before heading home to Devonport. At 7am on Wednesday 21 February the *Lion* arrived in Plymouth Sound. After clearing Customs in record time, at just after midday she slipped C buoy to steam up harbour and finally secured alongside No 7 wharf at 1pm, where she was greeted enthusiastically by wives and families. Twelve days later, on Monday 5 March, the ship was taken over by the Dockyard for a long refit, and three days later the ship's company moved into shore accommodation. After a faltering and shaky start it was the end of an eventful and successful commission.

Chapter Eight

HMS *Lion* - Second Commission 1962-1964

Following her return from South America and the end of the first commission, the *Lion* underwent an eight-month refit at Devonport. On 25 April her new commanding officer, Captain I. L. M. McGeoch DSO DSC RN, was appointed to the ship. Captain McGeoch had entered the Navy in 1932, and much of his early service was in submarines. During the Second World War he had commanded the submarine HMS *Splendid,* and in the post-war years he commanded the 3rd and 4th Submarine Squadrons. In 1961 he served on the staff of the Imperial Defence College and it was from there that he was appointed to the *Lion.*

The ship's company spent the first months of 1962 making what soon became the familiar twice daily journey between the naval barracks and the ship, come hail or snow, while the emergency parties found life on board grim with 'meals on wheels' rattling down to the ship from HMS *Drake's* galley. Of course there was always Friday to look forward to and a weekend at home, which for many meant a trip on the 'Pompey Flyer', along one of British Railways'

more tortuous routes. A sports day was held and a swimming gala, and on Monday 18 June steam was raised once more, which at least gave the ship an appearance of life. Ten days later the *Lion* was moved out of the basin to No 6 wharf and by this stage vigorous efforts were being made to prepare for recommissioning. The ship's side received the first of many coats of paint and the dockyard work continued apace, with new jobs invariably being started where brand new corticene had been laid or where painting had been completed. In July the tempo of work increased as a sense of urgency started to permeate all departments, with basin trials being conducted, accommodation ladders being rigged and seemingly endless piles of stores being embarked. On one occasion that month the towering superstructure of a new American guided missile destroyer, the USS *Dahlgren,* appeared alongside for a week. Her Terrier missiles made the *Lion's* 6-inch guns look rather archaic. By the end of that month the worst of the ordeal was over, and if any machinery or equipment was still in small pieces then it was well hidden away.

A fine view of the *Lion* as she leaves Portsmouth Harbour. Spitbank Fort is directly behind the ship, and in the background are Gilkicker Point and the Isle of Wight.   *(FotoFlite)*

The Commissioning Ceremony was held during the afternoon of Thursday 2 August 1962. It had been intended to hold it on the jetty alongside the ship, but unfortunately torrential rain caused a last-minute change of plan and it was held on the quarterdeck instead, where there was some shelter from the elements. The guest of honour was the C-in-C Plymouth, Admiral Sir Charles Madden, and the large number of relatives and friends of the ship's company who attended were all squeezed onto the quarterdeck. This lack of space meant that only a small proportion of the ship's company could attend and so the ceremony was relayed by tannoy to everyone who had to remain between decks. Captain McGeoch read the Commissioning Warrant and this was followed by a short religious service. In his address Admiral Madden outlined the exploits of the previous *Lion* and he predicted that the present ship's programme was likely to include visits to Far Eastern ports and the antipodes. After the ceremony the guests were entertained to tea, which included three special commissioning cakes. One cake in the wardroom was cut by the Captain and Mrs McGeoch, another in the CPO's mess was cut by Chief Petty Officer Roskilly and Mrs Wood, the wife of the Chief Boatswains Mate, while the cake in the junior ratings' dining hall was cut by Lt-Cdr Reding and Mrs Davies, the wife of LS Davies. Meanwhile, behind the scenes, the dining hall working party toiled magnificently, washing up countless hundreds of cups, saucers, plates and glasses.

Commissioning Day was followed closely by Navy Days at Devonport where over 18,000 people queued to get a look over the cruiser. The next event in the calendar was the 'Old Lions' Day', which took place on Wednesday 19 September when 50 'Old Lions' from the battlecruiser which had been in commission between 1912 and 1924 were welcomed aboard. It was a memorable occasion for all concerned, with the guests arriving for tea followed by a conducted tour of the cruiser. There were some happy reunions, such as that between two Admirals of the Fleet who had served in the old *Lion,* Lord Chatfield and Lord Mountbatten. Lord Chatfield addressed both the 'Old Lions' and the ship's company and that evening there was a display of physical training by Junior Seamen, and the Royal Marines Band Beat Retreat on the jetty. After the formalities the guests were entertained on board and Lord Chatfield was able to reminisce with ex-Stoker Petty Officer Albert Humphries, both of whom had served in the old *Lion* together, and the latter then spent four days on board the cruiser as a guest of the CPO's mess. Five days later the *Lion,* which had become almost a landmark at Devonport, finally put to sea for her post-refit trials. Unfortunately foggy conditions delayed her departure, but once under way the week was occupied with gun functioning trials, during which Y turret proved extremely troublesome. The weekend which followed saw the *Lion*

securely moored at C buoy in the Sound, whilst tremendous gales raged in the Channel, but happily they did not disrupt the liberty boats. During October and November gunnery and sea acceptance trials were carried out during stormy periods at sea, and a proposed visit to Torquay for 10 and 11 November had to be cancelled because of severe weather conditions in the Channel and Torbay. On Wednesday 28 November, with the ship back at No 7 wharf in Devonport Dockyard, a Families Day was held, combined with another, more informal, 'Old Lions' Day' for those who had not been able to get to the first reunion. For a whole day wives, sweethearts, mums and dads had the run of the ship, with the ship's divers giving a demonstration and at least ten children helping to stir the Christmas pudding. Everyone agreed that it was a happy day, but two days later it was time to start work in earnest and at 1pm on Friday 30 November 1962, with Guard and Band paraded and with full ceremony, the *Lion* left Devonport for a 12-month deployment to the Mediterranean and the Far East.

It was a fine autumn day with blue skies and sunshine as the Royal Marines Band played her out and, off Mount Wise, a crashing 17-gun salute was fired to the C-in-C. Once into the Channel course was set for Gibraltar, with a choppy passage through the Bay of Biscay and the Atlantic Ocean. With a heavily overcast sky even Gibraltar looked bleak, and between two short stays alongside the South Mole, the *Lion* went to sea in order to complete the gunnery acceptance trials and she also assisted in a fruitless search for an aircraft which had crashed in Gibraltar Bay. On Monday 10 December the *Lion* left Gibraltar and set course into the Mediterranean to begin the serious business of her work-up. For the rest of the month the RAS teams had plenty of practice, and the steady increase in loads transferred per hour was a measure of the progress made. There were seaboat evolutions and Officer of the Watch manoeuvres, which made life very awkward as the ship heeled over at every tight turn, and towing exercises were undertaken from both forward and aft. Finally, having been in the vicinity of Malta for several days, on Saturday 15 December the *Lion* entered Grand Harbour to berth at No 8 buoy for a weekend breather. After the welcome break it was back to work again, and with the weather having taken a turn for the worse many in the ship's company were introduced to the vessel's long ponderous roll. Green was now the predominant colour, with green seas breaking over the bows and many green faces between decks. The work-up exercises were carried out in company with the destroyers *Corunna* and *Dunkirk,* and on one occasion a distress signal was received from an Italian coaster, the *Cavouri,* but on the *Lion's* arrival the crew had sorted out the problem and merely wished to know their position. By the afternoon of Friday 21 December it was time to stop for Christmas and the cruiser returned to the calm of

Grand Harbour, although some people found the festivities in Strait Street more exhausting than the work-up. Before they got down to their own celebrations the ship's company gave a party for 200 orphans who were welcomed on board by their 'pirate' hosts. There were games and slides to play on, with tea in the main dining hall, and towards the end of the party the ship's divers 'volunteered' to walk the plank and be pushed overboard. The afternoon ended with the children entertaining their hosts by singing carols. On Christmas Day the celebrations got under way swiftly, with JM(E) Inch and JS Kelly revelling in their roles of Captain and Master-at-Arms. Captain McGeoch and the Commander did their rounds of the mess decks and visited the various parties that were in full swing prior to the turkey dinner. On Boxing Day dghaisa races were held up and down the length of the ship, but on Thursday 27 December work resumed with the *Lion* putting to sea for two days of exercises before returning to Malta for the New Year celebrations.

The morning of Wednesday 2 January 1963 saw the ship's company back at work, with the *Lion* departing at 7.30am to continue her work-up. Next day she was joined by the destroyers *Aisne*, *Scorpion* and *Corunna* for bombardment firings and that evening they anchored in Marsaxlokk Bay. Next morning, Friday 4 January, the four warships again made an early start, but at just after midday a signal was received from the P&O passenger liner, SS *Canberra*, saying that she had been crippled by fire in her main generator room and, being a turbo-electric ship, she had lost all power to her main engines. In those early days of her career before air travel had become so widely available, the *Canberra* carried passengers on line voyages to and from Australia. She had left Southampton bound for Sydney, via Suez, on 30 December 1962 and at noon on 3 January she had called at Naples for just four hours. She left the Italian port at 4pm that afternoon and set course through the Tyrrhenian Sea. At midnight on the 3rd/4th January she passed through the Strait of Messina, and four hours later she was in a position Lat 37° - 18'N/Long 17° - 20'E, which was approximately 160 miles north-east of Malta in the Ionian Sea. She was steaming at 27 knots on a calm, clear night and she was due in Port Said on Saturday 5 January. At that time of the morning the passengers were asleep in their cabins and only the watchkeepers were up and about. This was the situation when, down in the engine room, one of the officers on watch mistakenly broke an electrical circuit which caused an electrical arc of great severity, resulting in a serious fire that quickly engulfed the main switchboard. Although the blaze was brought under control and extinguished within an hour, the *Canberra* lay helpless in the water with over 1,000 passengers on board and with no power on her main engines. The C-in-C Mediterranean quickly dispatched the *Lion,* together with the destroyers *Aisne* and *Scorpion,* and for almost two hours

the three warships steamed at full power into a heavy head sea which broke over their bows, bringing down tons of sea water and spray onto their forecastles and superstructures. When they had covered 50 miles a further signal was received from the *Canberra* stating that she was under power again and proceeding slowly to Malta. Happily, the immediate crisis was over and the three warships were able to return to the Malta exercise areas.

On Saturday 19 January, as a break from the exercises, the *Lion* paid a weekend visit to Taranto where the rain fell continuously, and it even snowed at one stage. So bad was the weather that when the ship was opened to visitors, only 180 hardy souls ventured to come on board. However, the work-up was almost over and after the C-in-C Mediterranean, Admiral Sir Deric Holland-Martin, had inspected the ship on Wednesday 13 February, the *Lion* left Malta for Port Said and warmer waters. With the engine room department carrying out a full-power trial, which achieved well over 30 knots, the cruiser arrived off Port Said during the evening of Saturday 16 February and anchored until just after midnight the following morning when she moved into Port Said Harbour. At just after 7am that morning, Sunday 17 February, the *Lion* led the southbound convoy down the Suez Canal, and after stopping for six and a half hours in the West Branch Cut, she finally cleared Port Suez at 1am on Monday 18 February and set course for Aden.

At just before 4pm on Wednesday 20 February, as the *Lion* was steaming down the Red Sea, about 480 miles from Aden, she overhauled a small Indonesian merchantman, the MV *Blewah.* The cargo vessel was lying hove to and in answer to the *Lion's* queries it turned out that she was on her maiden voyage from the builder's yard in Yugoslavia to Jakarta and that she had been floating for three days with engine failure, but did not require assistance. Following this exchange of signals the *Lion* continued her passage to Aden, but a few hours later a distress call was received from the *Blewah* asking for assistance. Captain McGeoch immediately turned round and returned to the Indonesian freighter and sent over a party of three officers and nine ratings led by the First Lieutenant, Lt-Cdr N. J. D. Walter. Once on board the engineers went below to find that the *Blewah's* engineer spoke no English at all, and that he had stripped vital parts from the machinery so that there was little prospect of getting the vessel under way again. It was clear that the cruiser would have to take the *Blewah* in tow and two further boat trips were made to transfer equipment and extra clothing to the boarding party. The *Lion's* engineers laboured tirelessly and well into the night in atrocious conditions in an attempt to disconnect the freighter's propeller shaft but they were unsuccessful and, in spite of Force 7 winds which had blown up, the tow got under way. The boarding party found that the equipment and food on board the Indonesian vessel was scarcely adequate, with rice being the main course for breakfast, lunch and dinner, so a stretcher loaded with stores and provisions was floated over from the *Lion* each day. During the second night the weather deteriorated still further and in the early hours of the morning the towing shackle parted, under the battering of the high winds and heavy seas. Fortunately a new tow was soon passed and the slow passage southwards resumed at a reduced speed. During the passage the boarding party set about clearing up the *Blewah* and the bathroom was made fit for use, a laundry was set up and PO Elwyn Jones managed to provide a programme of entertainment on the ship's internal broadcasting system. The *Lion,* together with her charge, finally reached Aden at just after 10am on Sunday 24 February after a tow which had lasted over three and a half days. It was one of the Royal Navy's longest peacetime tows.

The arrival in Aden was for some their first glimpse of the East, although the barren rocks of this former colony are hardly inviting, and Steamer Point itself is even less exciting. The 34 hours in harbour enabled everyone to get ashore at least once, which for most was quite enough, and on the evening of Monday 25 February the *Lion* set course at 22 knots for the much more hospitable naval base at Trincomalee in Ceylon (Sri Lanka). On Friday 1 March, as the *Lion* steamed south-east through the Arabian Sea, a small blip showed on her radar screens which turned out to be the *Tiger* on her way home to Devonport. The two sisters rendezvoused about 240 miles west of Ceylon, and although the main purpose of the meeting was to transfer the Chinese laundry crew to the *Lion,* the opportunity for the latter to transfer the parcel mail to the homeward bound cruiser was too good to miss. The transfer was also an excuse for a 'friendly' pitched battle between the two ships with potatoes and firehoses providing the ammunition, but on completion of the transfer the *Lion* officially relieved her sister on the Far East Station. As the two ships parted company the *Lion* piped the *Tiger* and there was loud cheering from both ships as 'Auld Lang Syne' was played over the broadcast system. By late afternoon on Saturday 2 March the *Lion* had anchored in the beautiful natural harbour of Trincomalee, where the tropical greenery was a welcome contrast to the arid brown rocks of Aden. Ashore the fine old former British naval base, which had been so familiar to members of the wartime East Indies Fleet, was now crumbling and the relentless spread of the jungle was taking over the once spick and span buildings. In the small ghost town outside the main gate shopkeepers were selling trinkets and there were small, friendly children everywhere, with mischievous grins, who loved being photographed. Some of the ship's company took the bus journey through the rainforest and tea plantations to Kandy, while back in the harbour a sailing regatta was organized. During the nine days in harbour, units of the Far East Fleet and the Australian Navy gathered for

'Exercise Jet 63', which started on Sunday 10 March and took the combined fleet, via the Nicobar Islands, into the Strait of Malacca. Monday 18 March will be remembered by most Lions from that commission as the day that best white uniforms were worn all morning and well into the afternoon for two Procedure Alphas. The first that morning took place when the *Lion* led the 'Jet' fleet through the densely packed shipping lanes of Singapore's Keppel Harbour on 'Operation Flagwave', and the second, later in the day, was for the cruiser's arrival at the Singapore Naval Base. It was the first of the *Lion's* many visits, and the day after her arrival, Rear-Admiral J. P. Scratchard, Flag Officer, Second in Command, Far East Station, hoisted his flag in the cruiser.

After a week alongside the *Lion* sailed, together with HMNZS *Royalist* and HMAS *Voyager,* for a bombardment exercise followed by a visit to Hong Kong. The first views of the Chinese coast came on the morning of Friday 29 March as the *Lion* threaded her way through the islands of the former colony and headed for her berth on the West Arm alongside HMS *Tamar*. As she steamed through the Lei Yue Mun Narrows she passed the runway of Kai Tak Airport to starboard, beyond which was the city of Kowloon, while ahead lay the merchant ships at anchor. To port were the hundreds of junks with their patched sails and beyond them the impressive modern buildings which dominated the city of Victoria and which, in turn, were overlooked by Victoria Peak. With only four days alongside the runs ashore were fast and furious, and they usually started at the China Fleet Club on the waterfront adjoining the suburb of Wanchai. It was at 5pm on Tuesday 2 April that the *Lion* left Hong Kong and no sooner had she cleared the harbour than a signal was received stating that a Panamanian-registered ship, *National Glory,* had caught fire about 200 miles away and had been abandoned by her crew, all of whom had been rescued apart from six Chinese seamen aboard a whaler. A number of ships and aircraft were already searching for the boat and the *Lion* joined them. Next morning, at 11am, Able Seaman Raymond Smith, who was keeping lookout, with binoculars, sighted a white speck in the sea about six miles away. The *Lion* altered course immediately and the speck gradually began to take shape, becoming larger until it could clearly be seen that it was the missing lifeboat. It was thanks to the alert lookout that the boat was spotted at all, since it was too low in the water to be detected by radar and too small to be seen with the naked eye. When the *Lion* came alongside it became apparent that the boat was waterlogged and the occupants, who were baling out with a small tin can, were suffering from exhaustion and exposure. However, they were soon brought on board the cruiser and considering that they had been drifting for three days without food or water they were in good shape. The Royal Marines Detachment was given the task of sinking the whaler using their light machine-guns. Unfortunately, despite riddling it with well-aimed bullets, the boat refused to sink, so then it was up to the Navigating Officer who, by aiming the *Lion* well, succeeded in smashing the small boat to smithereens, while its former occupants enjoyed a much more comfortable passage to the cruiser's next destination, Saigon.

At 7am on the morning of Friday 5 April the *Lion* embarked a pilot off the mouth of the Mekong River and commenced the long, slow passage up the muddy, twisting waterway, before arriving alongside B Pier at just before noon. The ship's national salute to the President of South Vietnam was returned by the shore battery of ancient cannon, which gave an impressive display of smoke and flame from both ends. Since 1950, when it was divided, Saigon had been in a state of civil war, with the US backed south fighting the North Vietnamese rebels (later dubbed the Vietcong by US Army personnel). Although President Kennedy had taken some measures to shore up the South Vietnamese Government, the aid was very limited and at the time of the *Lion's* visit in March 1963 there was a night-time grenade throwing phase, which meant that shore leave for the ship's company was curtailed at dusk. During their stay the Royal Marines were kept busy with numerous ceremonial Guards and Bands for visiting dignitaries and military officers. The most distinguished guest was the then President of South Vietnam, Ngo Dinh Diem, who spent an hour and a half walking round the ship on the morning of Tuesday 9 April.* Despite their problems, everyone in the city offered much hospitality during the cruiser's stay, and the ship's company's children's party was as popular as ever. The afternoon of 9 April saw the *Lion* leave her berth on Saigon's river and set course for the open sea and the 48-hour passage to Singapore where she arrived at the naval base during the afternoon of 11 April. Once alongside the *Lion* began two weeks of self-maintenance during which everyone made a tremendous effort in the hot, humid climate to complete the programme.

At 6pm on Sunday 28 April the *Lion* departed from Singapore and set course across the South China Sea bound for the US Navy's exercise areas off the Philippines and the major annual SEATO exercise which was code-named 'Sea Serpent'. Fifty-four ships from the SEATO nations were involved, with the Royal Navy providing the *Lion* and the aircraft carrier *Hermes,* together with destroyers and frigates. The world's press covered the event in great detail and the exercise was concluded on the morning of Wednesday 8 May, when the fleet anchored in Manila Bay and an official reception was held aboard the *Hermes* for all the ships involved. The *Lion's* ship's company were allowed a 48-hour breather in Manila before the cruiser weighed anchor during the evening of Friday 10 May and set course

for Hong Kong again. During the seven-day stay alongside HMS *Tamar's* West Arm the Managing Director of the National Shipping Company, which owned the freighter *National Glory,* presented a suitably inscribed silver cup to Captain McGeoch to mark the rescue of the six members of her crew. Finally, before leaving for an eagerly awaited visit to Japan, FO2 FES, Rear-Admiral Scratchard, transferred his flag to the *Hermes* and the C-in-C FES, Vice-Admiral Sir Desmond Dreyer, hoisted his flag in the *Lion.* Next day, with full ceremony, the cruiser left Hong Kong and set course for Nagasaki. After a passage of four days the *Lion* arrived alongside the Dijima Jetty, Nagasaki, at 9am on Friday 24 May for a five-day visit during which the hospitality shown by the residents was described by one of the Royal Marines as, 'truly fantastic'. This was the first visit to Japan for the vast majority of the ship's company, and they were pleased to find good bars and nightclubs and a friendly atmosphere. When the ship was opened to visitors nearly 6,000 people arrived on board, many of them eager to practise their English. There were a number of bus trips, and one tour was to the sobering and thought-provoking monument and museum in memory of the victims of the atomic bomb dropped in August 1945. Two days into the visit Admiral Dreyer inspected Ceremonial Divisions on the jetty alongside the ship, and the Royal Marines Band Beat Retreat. They also played at an old people's home where, in line with Japanese custom, they were required to remove their boots before they went in. Much to the Sergeant Major's relief everyone was wearing the regulation socks, without any holes. Needless to say the concert was much appreciated by the old folk. Towards the end of the visit many new-found friends brought along presents as small mementoes of the visit and when, at 3pm on Wednesday 29 May, the *Lion* left for Osaka, a huge crowd gathered to watch the ship depart. A tannoy system on the jetty played a Japanese version of 'Auld Lang Syne' at full blast, to which the Royal Marines Band duly responded. One Marine made the 300-mile journey to Osaka overland on his racing cycle, while another group used the ship's Land Rover.

After a fogbound passage from Nagasaki, the *Lion* arrived in Osaka on the morning of Friday 31 May, but there was not quite the same thrill as on the previous Friday for the weather was overcast and Osaka, being an industrial city, lacked the charm of Nagasaki. The harbour was some 15 miles from the city centre and this tended to curtail activities somewhat, but once again the ship was a popular venue for the local people with almost 10,500 taking the opportunity to look her over. As before there were swarms of schoolchildren, all eager to try out their English.

The *Lion* left Osaka on Wednesday 5 June and immediately rendezvoused with the *Hermes* to hurriedly

*Ngo Dinh Diem had become President of South Vietnam in October 1955, but the army finally overthrew his increasingly corrupt and unpopular regime on 1 November 1963, and he was murdered.

The *Lion* enters Grand Harbour, Malta, in December 1962.
(Michael Cassar)

January 1963 and the *Lion* pays a visit to the Italian Naval Base at Taranto.
(Author's Collection)

The Singapore Naval Base in the early 1960s. The *Lion* can be seen alongside in the Stores Basin, together with the aircraft carrier *Victorious*, the frigate *Loch Killisport*, the RFAs *Reliant* and *Tideflow*, the ill-fated Australian destroyer *Vendetta*, the new Zealand frigate *Otago* and the Australian destroyer *Quiberon*.
(Imperial War Museum HU 73152)

transfer FO2 FES before the carrier returned to Singapore with unserviceable catapults. An hour later, at 9.30am, the cruiser secured alongside No 5 Pier at Kobe where one of the most popular attractions, after the local bars, were the Japanese bath houses, which included steam baths, deep water baths and even a massage. At Kobe over 13,000 people visited the ship, but all too soon for most the spell in Japan was over and at 9am on Monday 10 June the *Lion* set course for Singapore once more. The passage back was rather hectic with the units of the Far East Fleet taking part in 'Exercise Homerun', with gunnery, nuclear fallout, and RAS exercises to keep them busy. It was with some relief, therefore, that on the morning of Monday 24 June the *Lion* arrived in Singapore Dockyard to begin a two-week maintenance period.

Four days after her arrival in Singapore the cruiser entered the King George VI dry dock and the ship's company moved into the comparative luxury of the shore accommodation at HMS *Terror*. The move into barracks provided a welcome rest and with tropical routine being worked everyone soon began to feel the benefit of the fresh air and sun. On Thursday 11 July the ship was moved out of dry dock and five days later the ship's company moved back on board. Work began in earnest to prepare the *Lion* for FO2's Harbour and Sea Inspections, with the seamen and Marines complaining about the huge quantities of paint which had to be applied to the hull and superstructure. Finally, on the morning of Thursday 25 July the *Lion* put to sea to take part in the annual 'Fotex' (Flag Officers Tactical Exercise). All went well for six days, with two days of intensive exercises, followed by two very popular days anchored off Pulau Tioman and two more days of exercising. On the evening of Tuesday 30 July the fleet again anchored off Tioman, but at 8.30am next morning, as the *Lion* was preparing for sea, there was a serious fire in X boiler room (aft). Fire parties were quickly mustered, but it was an hour before it was brought under control and it was clear that, for the *Lion*, 'Fotex' was most definitely over. By 10am normal power supplies had been restored and although repair parties had started work, it was apparent that the cruiser would have to return to Singapore Dockyard. That afternoon FO2 transferred his flag to the *Albion*, and at 9.30pm the cruiser weighed anchor to return to Singapore where she arrived on the morning of Thursday 1 August. However, although the *Lion* earned the nickname of HMS *Wallflower* for her early return to the dockyard, five days later the *Ark Royal* also withdrew from 'Fotex' with machinery problems. This left the *Albion* with both the C-in-C and his deputy on board for the remainder of the exercise. It was on Friday 9 August that Rear-Admiral Scratchard returned to the *Lion* and five days later he was promoted to Vice-Admiral. His Harbour Inspection took place on Friday 23 August, and the efforts of the ship's company were obviously appreciated for

immediately afterwards he congratulated them thus: 'My Harbour Inspection of *Lion* and her company gave me real pleasure. The standard you have achieved is outstanding.' Preparations were then made for his Sea Inspection, which included the embarkation of two target aircraft in readiness for the gunnery firings.

It was on the morning of Monday 26 August that the *Lion* sailed from Singapore and, with the Australian destroyer *Vendetta* and the New Zealand frigate *Otago*, she set course for the exercise areas off the island of Tioman. The Sea Inspection took place on Friday 30 August and it got under way as soon as FO2 and his staff had been winched down to the cruiser by helicopter. Throughout the day the ship was fully exercised in all aspects of its wartime and peacetime roles, as well as several minor drills that had to be carried out. Admiral Scratchard was satisfied with everything he had seen and after being lifted off the cruiser by helicopter he signalled: 'You can be well pleased, as I was, with your performance at the Sea Inspection today. Though I shall obviously have minor criticisms, today was a worthy sequel to your Harbour Inspection.' That evening the *Lion* anchored off Tioman and next morning she weighed anchor and set course for Hong Kong for her third and final visit to the colony. She arrived alongside the South Arm at HMS *Tamar* at 4.15pm on Wednesday 4 September, but with Typhoon Faye rapidly approaching the colony, at 5pm the next day all liberty men were recalled and the *Lion* put to sea in an attempt to avoid the storm. Although she steamed 250 miles southwards she still encountered some severe weather, but she was able to circumnavigate the worst of it and at 7pm on Saturday 7 September she returned to her berth alongside HMS *Tamar*. With only two full days of the visit left the nightclubs of Wanchai did a roaring trade, but on the morning of Tuesday 10 September, to the sound of a noisy firecracker farewell from the side party, she left for Jesselton (Kota Kinabalu) in North Borneo.

The *Lion*, together with the fast minelayer *Manxman*, arrived at Jesselton on the morning of Friday 13 September, according to some not a good day to arrive anywhere, but fortunately nothing went wrong. The *Manxman* berthed alongside the jetty, but the *Lion* anchored about a mile offshore which meant a long boat ride for liberty men. Jesselton had been the capital of North Borneo since 1946 and it was a small town in what was still a largely wild and unexploited country. It consisted of two main streets of shops, two cinemas and some very attractive tropical beaches. North Borneo itself was also coveted by President Sukarno of Indonesia and as early as April 1963 'volunteers' from that country had made their first incursions by attacking frontier police stations in the colony, sparking the start of the long Confrontation which was to keep a large proportion of the British Army occupied for over two years. The purpose of the *Lion's* visit was to withdraw the last British Governor of the colony, Sir William Goode, for on 16 September North Borneo was to become the independent state of Sabah and was also to join the newly formed Federation of Malaysia, which comprised Malaya, Singapore, Sarawak and Sabah. The Federation was to have come into being on 31 August, but it had been deferred until mid-September because of the objections of President Sukarno who viewed the amalgamation of the former British territories in South-East Asia as a threat to the area. In fact his objections were, in reality, about Indonesian ambitions for gaining control of North Borneo and Sarawak. Fortunately there were no security problems during the *Lion's* visit and on Sunday 15 September, the day that the Governor was due to depart, the cruiser moved to a berth alongside the jetty. At 9am, when the *Lion* secured alongside, preparations were well under way, although that afternoon the cruiser was opened to the public for two hours. A Guard and Band arrived on the jetty at 5.15pm and 20 minutes later the Governor arrived by car with a mounted escort provided by the town's polo club. After inspecting Scout and Guide groups, and the ceremonial guard, he embarked in the *Lion,* which, to the accompaniment of a 17-gun salute from shore batteries, slipped her berth and, escorted by small boats and yachts, set course for Singapore.

On her arrival at the Singapore Naval Base during the afternoon of Tuesday 17 September, and after disembarking the VIP passengers, the ship's company again moved into HMS *Terror* for two weeks while the *Lion* underwent a maintenance programme alongside No 1 berth. Although the discovery of steam leaks in the engine and boiler rooms extended the stay alongside, the cruiser left Singapore for the last time at 10am on Wednesday 9 October 1963, bound for Fremantle. Her departure was marked by a musical accompaniment from the Royal Marines Band on board, and by bands on the jetty and on board HMS *Victorious*. After embarking ammunition from RFA *Retainer* gunnery firings were carried out, before the ship's company went to Defence Stations for the passage through the hostile Sunda Strait, not far from the Indonesian capital of Jakarta. In everyone's mind was the fact that, in September 1962, the Indonesian Navy had acquired the ex-Soviet Sverdlov-class cruiser, *Ordzhonikidze**, which had been renamed *Irian*. She was a powerful cruiser and with the armed Confrontation in full swing it was not known how President Sukarno would react to the *Lion's* passage through the Sunda Strait. Fortunately everything passed off without incident and at 1.28am on Thursday 10 October the ship crossed the equator at Long 107° - 03'E. King Neptune's representatives had arrived on the forecastle the evening before and at 9.30am members of the ship's company were called before the Court to pay their respects

and to receive their duckings. Four days later, at 9am on Tuesday 15 October, the *Lion* arrived in Fremantle and, as always, memories of the six-day visit will be of the traditional friendliness and hospitality encountered in both Fremantle and Perth. Visits were arranged to local breweries, and the ship attracted a large number of visitors when she was opened to the public. On the last day of their stay the ship's company gave a party for 100 disabled children and judging by the noise levels, they thoroughly enjoyed themselves. The *Lion* left Fremantle at 10am on Tuesday 22 October and set course across the Indian Ocean bound for the remote island of Gan in Addu Atoll. During the long run across the Indian Ocean the *Lion* rolled heavily through an apparently calm sea, and the sun worshippers were able to acquire deep suntans. Arriving alongside RFA *Wave Victor* at Gan, the cruiser spent eight hours alongside refuelling before leaving for the 1,900-mile passage to Aden, where she arrived on the morning of 4 November. After firing a salute to the flag of her old commanding officer, Rear-Admiral Scotland, who was now C-in-C Middle East, she berthed off Steamer Point. The forty-eight hours spent in Aden were quite enough for everyone, particularly as they were now homeward bound, and there were sighs of relief when the *Lion* left at 8.30am on Wednesday 6 November; as one member of the ship's company commented, 'As we left we probably had one of the best views of Aden, from astern.' The *Lion* was followed out of harbour by a Soviet ocean-going tug which had attached itself to the cruiser a few days before her arrival in Aden.

After an uneventful passage north through the Red Sea the *Lion* joined a northbound convoy for her transit of the Suez Canal at 7.30am on Sunday 10 November, and she cleared Port Said just over 12 hours later. Shortly after leaving the Egyptian harbour she rendezvoused with the destroyer *Diamond* and embarked Flag Officer Flotillas (Med), Rear-Admiral J. H. Walwyn, who was to remain with the cruiser until after her next port of call, Beirut. It was at 8.40am on Monday 11 November that the *Lion* secured alongside the Eastern Mole of Beirut Harbour, and for most of the ship's company their introduction to the city came via the taxis at the end of the jetty. However, after one terrifying ride in one of these, most people preferred to take the long walk into the city. These were the years before the terrible civil war wrought the country asunder and many will remember the exotic, but very expensive, nightclubs, the sophisticated shops and restaurants, and the fascinating mixture of Eastern and Western influences. To everyone's relief, however, on the morning of Saturday 16 November the cruiser, together with the *Diamond* and the RFA *Brown Ranger,* left Beirut and the *Lion* set course for Gibraltar. With cooler weather soon upon them the ship's company changed from white to

*The *Ordzhonikidze* is better known as the cruiser which visited Portsmouth in May 1956 and under which the naval diver, Commander Lionel 'Buster' Crabbe RN lost his life, causing a diplomatic row between Britain and the Soviet Union.

HMS *Lion* (foreground) and her sister ship *Tiger* in the Arabian Sea on 1 March 1963.
(Royal Navy)

blue uniforms and Admiral Walwyn returned to the *Diamond*. By the time the *Lion* arrived in Gibraltar on Friday 22 November, the hot sunshine was just a distant memory and even the most ardent sun worshippers were fast losing the suntans they had worked so hard to acquire. In Gibraltar the *Lion* secured alongside No 47 berth astern of the *Tiger*, which had arrived from Lisbon the previous day, and during the stay Flag Officer Flotillas (Home), Vice-Admiral F. R. Twiss, transferred his flag from the *Tiger* to the *Lion*. As a parting shot the *Lion's* soccer and hockey teams scored convincing wins over their sister ship's sides.

At 7.45am on Monday 25 November, the *Lion*, accompanied by the *Tiger, Berwick, Whitby, Decoy* and *Verulam*, left Gibraltar to carry out exercises and manoeuvres off the Spanish coast, before the escorts detached and the cruisers steamed on to Plymouth. The *Lion* anchored in the Sound at 8am on Thursday 28 November to await Customs clearance, which wiped the smiles off many faces, whilst the *Tiger* steamed straight into Devonport Dockyard. Then, at 6pm that evening the *Lion* weighed anchor and set course for an overnight passage to Portsmouth, anchoring at Spithead next morning. A few hours later, at 9.30am, two tugs drew alongside loaded with very cold, but happy, wives, families and friends who were quickly embarked and revived with hot tea and coffee. Twenty-five minutes later the cruiser weighed anchor and steamed up harbour to secure alongside Pitch House Jetty at 10.30am. Thus ended the foreign leg of the commission.

In early December the *Lion* was moved into No 14 dry dock in order that repairs could be carried out to the stern glands and rudder posts and on Friday 13 December Flag Officer Flotillas (Home) hoisted his flag in the cruiser. By Monday 6 January 1964 all Christmas and New Year leave had been completed and next day the cruiser was back alongside Pitch House Jetty. It was on Thursday 23 January

that she put to sea once again, this time to join up with the aircraft carrier *Hermes* and the escorts *Berwick, Cassandra, Devonshire* and *Llandaff* for 'Exercise Phoenix' in the cold and rough Western Approaches. There was great relief all round when, on the last day of January, the *Lion* returned to Portsmouth for a long weekend, but this was followed by a spell of gunnery weapon training, and a weekend swinging on C buoy in Plymouth Sound. At 10am on Monday 10 February the *Lion* left Plymouth for Cadiz in Spain and she secured alongside the Muelle Le Ra Reina exactly 72 hours later. Despite the wet and cold weather, the Royal Marines were as always kept busy with ceremonial duties, but most did get time to sample the beer in the Spanish Navy's club. After four days alongside the *Lion* left Cadiz to make the six-hour passage to Gibraltar, where she arrived at 3.30pm on Monday 17 February. In Gibraltar were units from various NATO navies, including French, Dutch and Canadian ships, all gathering for 'Exercise Magic Lantern', which occupied the final days of February. On Monday 2 March the *Lion* put to sea with the Governor of Gibraltar embarked for a day of gunnery exercises and manoeuvres, and after disembarking him in Algeciras Bay that evening she sailed out into the Atlantic for exercises, in company with the frigates *Murray* and *Pellow*. Thursday 12 March saw the final visit of the commission, to the city of Lisbon, where the *Lion* spent five days alongside and on leaving the Portuguese capital she set course for Devonport. At 2.30pm on Thursday 19 March, after clearing Customs, she weighed anchor and with full ceremony she steamed into Devonport to secure alongside No 8 wharf. Once alongside the ship paid off and was soon moved into the North Lock where Devonport Dockyard took her over to carry out a 46-day refit. It had been a very full, and successful, commission.

Chapter Nine

HMS *Lion* - The Final Commission 1964-1965

Following her arrival in Devonport from Lisbon in March 1964, the *Lion* went into dockyard hands and just over two weeks later, at 9am on Monday 6 April, her third, and last, commanding officer, Captain E. F. Hamilton-Meikle MBE RN, joined her. He assumed command at midday and two hours later Captain McGeoch left to take up a post at the Ministry of Defence. For the ship's company it could be said that the commission started 11 days later on Friday 17 April when, against the sombre background of Devonport's North Lock, the Commissioning Ceremony took place. There were no guests and it was a low-key affair, starting at 2pm with Divisions on the dockside, which were inspected by the Captain. The ceremony then continued on the quarterdeck where the Commissioning Warrant was read and there was a short religious service which concluded at 3pm. Three days later Flag Officer Flotillas (Home) hoisted his flag in the cruiser, and by the first week of May 1964 she was ready for sea.

At 1pm on Tuesday 5 May the *Lion* slipped her berth at Devonport and steamed out into the Channel for her post-refit trials, and six days later she set course for the Mediterranean. After a brief stop in Gibraltar on 15 May, she arrived in Malta's Grand Harbour at midday on Tuesday 19 May. It was from Malta that the *Lion* would carry out her work-up and the following 30 days were to prove extremely busy for the ship's company. In the last week of June there was a pleasant interlude when the cruiser anchored off Argostoli on the Greek island of Cephalonia. Having left Vice-Admiral Twiss back in the UK, the cruiser was now wearing the flag of Flag Officer Flotillas (Med), Rear-Admiral J. H. Walwyn, who was the last flag officer to hold the post. The occasion was the Mediterranean Fleet Assembly which was to be the last of these traditional gatherings and, although it was small by pre-war standards, a reasonable fleet was mustered which evoked some nostalgic echoes of the past for the older members of the ship's company. Present along with the *Lion* were the destroyers *Aisne* and *Cassandra*, the frigate *Falmouth*, the dispatch vessel *Surprise*, flying the flag of the C-in-C Mediterranean, two submarines and RFA *Wave Baron*. Soon everyone was caught up in the general drills and the sailing regatta while meanwhile, ashore, a working party from the *Lion* had built a theatre complete with seating, for a memorable joint concert party. One of the 'turns' was the C-in-C himself, who regaled the audience with the wonders of 'Paddy MacGinty's Goat'. The gathering was followed, on Monday 29 June, by a short and stormy visit to Corfu where gale force winds necessitated a change of anchorage, then a defect in the *Lion's* forward boiler room forced a change of itinerary, with Venice being crossed off the calling list and a return to Malta replacing it. In the event the *Lion* arrived in Grand Harbour on Saturday 4 July and within three days the Malta Drydock Company had repaired the defective boiler casings. Leaving Malta again on Wednesday 15 July, the *Lion* underwent her Sea Inspection by Rear-Admiral Walwyn, which included one surprise item. During the afternoon of 16 July the cruiser was ordered into Grand Harbour where she had to embark 200 men of the Royal Sussex Regiment and their Land Rovers, and land them in Marsaxlokk Bay

The *Lion* enters Portsmouth Harbour in July 1964.
(Maritime Photo Library)

The fleet lit up during the evening of 10 August 1965. From left to right HM Ships *Maidstone, Centaur, Tiger* and *Lion* with the royal yacht just visible to the right of the picture. *(D. Palmer)*

early the next morning. In a bid to make the reluctant passengers feel at home the Royal Marines Band took up station on the quay and played 'Sussex by the Sea' as they trudged up the gangway in full battledress and weighed down by kit. Having embarked the 'squaddies' without incident the *Lion* sailed at 8pm, and after steaming off the coast of Malta for over seven hours, she finally anchored in Marsaxlokk Bay at 4am the next morning. Shortly afterwards the tired, and rather 'cheesed-off', soldiers were successfully landed in less than an hour. That morning Rear-Admiral Walwyn congratulated the ship's company on their creditable performance before taking his leave, and at midday the *Lion* weighed anchor and set course for Portsmouth, where she arrived alongside Pitch House Jetty at 8am on Friday 24 July.

Following summer leave and Portsmouth's Navy Days, during which 21,691 people visited the cruiser, the *Lion* left Portsmouth at 11am on Monday 31 August and rendezvoused with the destroyers *Agincourt, Carysfort* and *Diamond,* and the frigates *Eskimo, Galatea, Londonderry, Pellow, Relentless, Rhyl* and *Salisbury.* Once clear of the Solent the force set course for the Firth of Forth where the new suspension bridge, just upstream of the majestic railway bridge, was to be opened on 4 September by the Queen. The new road bridge would replace the old Queensferry crossing, the final journey being made by the elderly paddle steamer *Queen Margaret.* The *Lion,* together with the other units, anchored off Rosyth on Thursday 3 September to await the opening ceremony which was scheduled to take place the next day. Unfortunately, Friday 4 September dawned with a thick sea mist hanging over the Firth of Forth and ironically, although the royal car was to have been the first to cross, because of the poor visibility the ferries below the bridge were unable to sail and so many of the invited guests were allowed to drive across from the north to the southern approaches where the ceremony was to take place. The Queen and Prince Philip drove to the

bridge from Dalmery Railway Station, but very little of the structure could be seen through the mist, and although it cleared a little, nothing of the north tower was visible from start to finish. At 11.15am, on completion of the Queen's speech declaring the bridge open, the *Lion* and seven other ships fired a 21-gun salute. Following the opening ceremony the Queen and Prince Philip drove across the bridge and embarked in the ferry *Queen Margaret* to make the final river crossing and to review the assembled fleet of 25 warships. Charles Davis who was serving in the *Lion* takes up the story: 'We all manned the decks ready to give three cheers as she sailed by. Unfortunately, the morning of the big day saw the Firth of Forth blanketed by a thick sea mist and when we went on deck for a rehearsal we could hear the large crowds on the bridge, but we couldn't see them and in fact we couldn't see anything. It must have been very eerie for them to hear all the ships' companies cheering somewhere in the mist below them, as we practised for the big event. Everything went well for the opening of the bridge, and when the Queen embarked in the ferry to review the assembled warships, as if by magic, the mist cleared to reveal a lovely sunny day. The review was perfect and we all cheered loudly, with us in *Lion* being the last in the line, and as soon as the Queen reached the river bank again the sea mist fell over the area like a grey shroud, but not before we had spliced the main brace.'

With the bridge now open the remorseless tide of road traffic began to flow across in both directions and it seemed that all remained was for the assembled fleet to weigh anchor and put to sea again. At about 4.15pm, with all ships sounding fog signals, the frigates, which were upstream of the cruiser, began to get under way. At 4.30pm the *Lion's* special sea dutymen closed up, all scuttles and screen doors were closed, and on the forecastle the seamen began shortening in the anchors in preparation for her departure. However, as the frigate *Lowestoft* got under way she did not clear the space between the bridge and the *Lion* and at

4.36pm the cruiser's alarm bells rang while an urgent voice rang out over the ship's tannoy, 'Close all Red Openings. Clear the Forecastle. Hands to Emergency Stations.' No sooner had the warning been given than the stem of the *Lowestoft* crashed into the *Lion's* port bow right on the hawse pipe, tearing a gash 24 feet by 10 feet in the cruiser's side, buckling the deck plates above, shearing the port anchor in two and depositing the larger piece on the *Lowestoft's* forecastle. Charles Davis remembers the incident well: 'We were due to return to the Mediterranean just as soon as the review was over, so that we could be in Malta for the island's Independence celebrations. In those days there were still many senior ratings who had served during the Second World War, and I was closed up at my station for leaving harbour with an EA1 who was of wartime vintage. Suddenly, out of the blue, the ship's alarms rang which, to say the least, made me jump and this was followed closely by a terrific bang which was heard throughout the ship as she rolled heavily over to starboard. My colleague's thoughts obviously went back to his wartime service for he grabbed my arm tightly and blurted out, "I think the forward boiler room has just gone up." Being very young at the time, and as we were in a compartment which was between the boiler rooms, I was very concerned and wondered what had happened. In fact it was the frigate *Lowestoft* that had ploughed into us and embedded herself in our port bow. She had actually smashed into our side about six feet away from the cells where a rating was "banged up" for some misdemeanour.'

Once it was realized that neither ship was in any immediate danger, and that nobody had been injured, the *Lowestoft* was secured alongside the *Lion.* At about 6.15pm the frigate was manoeuvred alongside Rosyth's Middle Jetty, and two hours later the cruiser was secured alongside the South Arm, where temporary repairs could be carried out. By the early afternoon of Wednesday 9 September the *Lion* was seaworthy again and the cruiser belatedly left the Firth of Forth, to make a fast passage to Malta, pausing briefly at Spithead in the early hours of Friday 11 September to hoist in a spare hawse pipe. She eventually arrived in Grand Harbour at 9am on Friday 18 September, Independence Day, and as the celebrations had already started she had to prepare immediately for her part in them. The official ceremony passed off without a hitch with the Constitutional Instruments being handed over to the island's Prime Minister, Dr Borg Olivier, by Prince Philip. There followed a day of pageantry during which the massed bands of the Royal Marines Beat Retreat on Palace Square in front of a huge crowd. That evening, after dark, the *Lion* darkened and manned ship all within a few minutes and put on a very effective display with the ship's company stretched along the whole of the port side, revolving hand-held flares in unison. The climax of the Navy's part in the proceedings was signalled by an excellent

fireworks display from HMS *St Angelo* which, combined with that of the city's display over Valletta, lit up Grand Harbour until the early hours of the following morning. Once the Independence celebrations were over the cruiser moved alongside Parlatorio Wharf to undergo more permanent repairs to her damaged bow, and on Friday 25 September the cruiser spent a day in the Admiralty Floating Dock 35. During the long period alongside sporting fixtures and 'expeds' became the order of the day, with one party even taking an MFV to Sicily and climbing Mount Etna.

The *Lion's* repairs were completed on Monday 19 October, and she left the same day bound for Marseilles where, on 22 October, she secured alongside a wharf in the President Wilson Basin. For some the visit was seen as a compensation for ports which had been missed because of the collision, and the Royal Marines Band raised tears of emotion when they Beat Retreat on the jetty during the official cocktail party. There is no doubt that the visit enlivened the passage home, and after calling at Gibraltar the *Lion* berthed alongside Portsmouth's South Railway Jetty on the morning of Friday 6 November, for a long weekend break. After exercising in the Channel with the *Diamond, Rhyl* and *Troubridge,* and spending two weeks alongside in Portsmouth, the *Lion* steamed north for 'Exercise Limejug', which was held in Force 10 gales in the area between the north coast of Ireland and Rockall. On the last day of November the weather conditions became so severe that the cruiser and her escorts were forced to seek shelter for 12 hours in Loch Boisdale off South Uist's east coast. Although no shore leave was granted, the respite from the stormy weather seemed to be a heaven-sent blessing. The exercise ended on the evening of Friday 4 December, and next day at just after midday the *Lion* secured alongside Devonport's No 8 wharf.

The New Year of 1965 commenced for the cruiser with a midday departure on Monday 18 January, to carry out gun functioning trials and a four-day passage to Gibraltar where she arrived on the morning of Friday 22 January. Once alongside she hoisted the flag of Admiral Sir John Hamilton, the C-in-C Mediterranean, and at 3.30pm, just six hours after her arrival, she left for Toulon. The five-day visit to the French naval base was followed by a passage to Malta for six days of exercises, and for Admiral Hamilton to disembark before the *Lion* set course west for Gibraltar and the Atlantic Ocean on Saturday 6 February. Her destination this time was the West African colony of Gambia, which was about to gain its Independence, and the *Lion* arrived alongside the Government Wharf in Bathurst (Banjul) at 9.30am on Sunday 14 February. The Flag Raising Ceremony took place four days later at midday on Thursday 18 February, in the presence of the Duke and Duchess of Kent, and Captain Hamilton-Meikle also attended to watch the handing over of the Constitutional Instruments, whilst

The frigate HMS *Lowestoft* picks a fight with the *Lion*. (C. Davis)

The *Lion's* port anchor is firmly embedded in the *Lowestoft's* stem following the collision in the Firth of Forth. (C. Davis)

hour visit from King Olav of Norway during which the Norwegian Royal Standard was flown at the mainmast. Later that afternoon, at 3.30pm, the *Lion* slipped her moorings to join the NATO fleet before setting course for Portsmouth to disembark the C-in-C. For the Portsmouth members of the ship's company the 29 hours alongside were all too brief, and at 5pm on Thursday 18 March she left for an overnight passage to Devonport and docking down in No 9 dry dock for essential maintenance to be carried out.

It was in the last week of April that the *Lion* moved back alongside the sea wall, and on the first day of May she hoisted the flag of the C-in-C Home Fleet, Admiral Madden, once again. In the first week of May there were inter-ship sports between units of the Home Fleet, when the *Lion's* ship's company acquitted themselves well with the whaler's crew winning the pulling regatta, while the athletics team

on board a 21-gun salute was fired. That evening the Royal Marines Beat Retreat on the jetty and the Captain attended a State Ball at Government House. Next day, at 11am, the Royal Standard was broken at the *Lion's* masthead and 15 minutes later the Duke and Duchess of Kent embarked for the passage to nearby St James Island, where they spent half an hour ashore before re-embarking and returning to Bathurst. This time the cruiser anchored off the port and the royal passengers were ferried ashore by tender after which, at 5.40pm, the *Lion* weighed anchor and set course for Portsmouth, where she arrived alongside South Railway Jetty at 9am on Friday 26 February.

The *Lion's* next sortie began on the morning of Saturday 6 March when she unobtrusively left Portsmouth Harbour, to steam by way of the North Sea to join a NATO fleet for the final stages of 'Exercise Pilot Light' and, more popularly, a visit to Bergen in Norway where, at 1.30pm on Wednesday 10 March, she secured alongside the Skorlergrunnskien Jetty. Just under three hours later she was joined by her 'sister cat' the *Tiger.* That afternoon the *Lion* hoisted the flag of the C-in-C Home Fleet, Admiral Sir Charles Madden, and on the afternoon of 15 March, shortly before sailing, she received a two-

As the *Lowestoft* is towed clear of the *Lion* the damage to her stem is plain to see, as is the *Lion's* anchor. The mist has cleared and the Forth Bridge can be seen in the background. *(C. Davis)*

This picture shows the damage to the *Lion's* bow. Note the absence of the anchor and the 'No Entry' sign which some wag has put up. *(C. Davis)*

Casablanca, for the C-in-C's last cruise before his retirement. Gibraltar was reached on Sunday 23 May and after an overnight stay alongside the familiar South Mole, the *Lion* left for the Moroccan port and arrived alongside at 9.30am on Tuesday 25 May. With high prices in the shops and bars, most of the ship's company found their entertainment in the excellent swimming pools that lined the coast, where the water was warm and the sun scorching. Entertainment for the officers varied from the Governor's reception, where only mint tea was served and little English was spoken, to the Moroccan Naval reception where, although little English was spoken, at least the whisky flowed freely. After leaving the warmth of Casablanca, the cruiser returned to Portsmouth on the first day of June for 14 days, and after the Whitsun holiday she sailed for the highlight of the commission, 'Kieler Woche',

came runners up to the mighty *Ark Royal*. During the afternoon of Monday 10 May the *Lion* left Devonport, and after disembarking Admiral Madden by helicopter in Plymouth Sound, she set course for Spithead. Next morning she embarked the Admiral Commanding Reserves, Rear-Admiral Carew-Hunt, and set course for the Dutch City of Amsterdam for 'British Week', which was opened by Princess Margaret. During the visit, on the evening of 15 May, Princess Margaret and her husband, Lord Snowdon, visited the cruiser for an hour. By 19 May the *Lion* was back alongside Portsmouth's South Railway Jetty and next day saw the ever-popular Families Day, when, with families and press representatives embarked, the *Lion* put to sea at 10.15am in beautiful calm weather for five hours of gunnery, and helicopters hovering over the quarterdeck, with lunch being served halfway through the proceedings. All too soon, at 3.15pm, the *Lion* anchored at Spithead to disembark the families and to embark the C-in-C Home Fleet once again. No sooner was he on board than the cruiser set course for

A final view of the *Lion* under way, with both the ship and her complement looking extremely smart. *(Maritime Photo Library)*

or Kiel Week. This renowned occasion has no real equivalent in the UK, but it could be likened to the Edinburgh Festival, Cowes Week and a major NATO visit, all rolled into one. The event has its origin in a sailing race which took place off Kiel in 1882 and it has grown ever since. The city of Kiel itself which, like Plymouth, was grievously damaged during the Second World War, was rebuilt into a fine modern port with the spire of its ancient church of St Nicholas, the patron saint of seafarers, dominating the skyline. In its beautiful setting of Kiel Bay, it seems to spell out the message of the futility of Europe's two destructive 'civil wars' fought in the 20th century. As soon as the ship was berthed alongside the Tirpitz Mole, opposite the USS *Claude V. Ricketts,* the ship's company was launched into an incredibly hectic eight days of all kinds of sport, but principally sailing, and numerous personal invitations from the citizens of the city, as well as tea dances, brewery visits and various banyans. The official reception held on the quarterdeck was a great success, and Beating Retreat by the Royal Marines band was very much appreciated by the 300 official guests. As always there was a children's party on board and this gave much pleasure to both the guests and to the hosts. All in all 'Kieler Woche' was voted a great success but, on Saturday 26 June, when the *Lion* left Kiel to the strains of 'The Happy Wanderer' played by a German Naval band, the ship's company braced themselves for the rigours of 'Scapa Woche', which was not nearly so popular.

The *Lion's* 12-hour passage through the Kiel Canal kept the cable party on their toes, but by Saturday she had reached the North Sea, and two days later she had secured alongside Golden Wharf, Lyness, on the island of Hay, close to the desolate wartime anchorage of Scapa Flow. As she steamed through the Flow she piped a salute to the ill-fated

battleship, *Royal Oak*, as she passed by her resting-place, so very close to the shore. Having berthed alongside, the ship's company commenced two days of 'exped' training in mist and rain. There were sighs of relief when this was over, and on the last day of June the *Lion* left Scapa Flow to steam south for Portsmouth, where she arrived alongside Middle Slip Jetty at 8.30am on Friday 2 July.

The remainder of July 1965 was spent alongside while summer leave was taken and preparations were made for the cruiser's next task, the Royal Review of the Fleet on the River Clyde. The *Lion* left Portsmouth on the morning of 4 August, this time flying the flag of the new C-in-C Home Fleet, Admiral Sir John Frewen, and set course north for the Clyde. During the passage the ship's company exercised manning and cheering ship, and at 9am on Friday 6 August she dropped anchor off Greenock, almost opposite her birthplace at Scotts Shipyard. By the end of the day the Tail of the Bank was a splendid sight of grey hulls surrounded by green hills. On Tuesday 10 August the royal yacht *Britannia* arrived and that evening, at 8pm, the Queen and Prince Philip visited the *Lion* to dine with the C-in-C and the commanding officers of the visiting warships. On arrival the Queen was met by Admiral Frewen and she was then led to the wardroom by the Master-at-Arms, who carried the traditional Lord High Admiral's 'Verge', and there she dined with the captains of her ships. Next day the royal party left the Clyde in the *Britannia,* and later that afternoon, with full ceremony, the *Lion* departed, leading the frigates *Grafton, Keppel, Palliser* and *Rhyl,* before proceeding independently for the Dutch city of Rotterdam, where she arrived two days later to secure alongside the Parkkade, in the shadow of the Euromast. The weekend visit to Rotterdam was followed

The *Lion* at the shipbreaker's yard, Inverkeithing, in June 1975, four months after her arrival.
(Maritime Photo Library)

closely by calls at Brest, for just 24 hours, and Lisbon from where, on 23 August, the C-in-C left the ship to fly back to the UK. Next day the *Lion* herself left harbour to return to Portsmouth where she arrived in time for Navy Days at the end of the month.

After leaving Portsmouth on Monday 6 September, flying the flag of Vice-Admiral J. O. C. Hayes, FO2 Home Fleet, the *Lion* steamed to Devonport for five days before heading north to the Cape Wrath area to exercise with the *Dido, Salisbury* and RFA *Wave Prince,* followed by a five-day visit to the Swedish port city of Stockholm. For those who could afford it the Swedish capital was a popular run ashore, but by Wednesday 29 September the *Lion* was secured port side alongside HMS *Belfast* at Devonport. The commission was drawing to a close and the *Lion* was to be the first of the three sisters to be paid off to await, it was thought, conversion to a helicopter command cruiser. However, before that there were yet more exercises, and on Monday 4 October she sailed for the Channel and the area off Lizard Point where she spent four days, before anchoring for 19 hours in Falmouth Bay. This was followed by a long weekend in Devonport, before she left with the *Agincourt,* the *Galatea* and RFA *Tidepool,* to rendezvous with the Dutch aircraft carrier *Karel Doorman* (ex-HMS *Venerable*), the destroyer *Amsterdam* and the Canadian aircraft carrier *Bonaventure* (ex-HMS *Powerful*), for 'Exercise Totem Pole' in what turned out to be a very stormy Atlantic Ocean. During the exercise the *Lion* acted as planeguard to the *Karel Doorman* and on conclusion of the exercise she returned to Devonport on 21 October for a long weekend. After leaving Plymouth Sound during the afternoon of Monday 25 October, the *Lion* steamed south to Gibraltar for the Home Fleet Assembly and during the seven-day stopover in the colony the ship was painted and

the Second Sea Lord paid her a visit. After leaving Gibraltar there was a four-day visit to Lisbon after which she returned to Portsmouth on Thursday 11 November.

On Thursday 25 November came the final 'Old Lions' day, for those who had served in the battlecruiser of that name, and 60 veterans, including Lord Mountbatten, attended. It was the 47th anniversary of the *Lion* leading the German High Seas Fleet into Scapa Flow at the end of the First World War, but unfortunately Lord Chatfield regretted that, at 92 years of age, he had to miss the gathering. The visitors arrived on board at 3pm, and after touring the ship a reception was held, followed by the ceremony of Beating Retreat on the jetty. At 6pm the 'Old Lions' left the ship at the end of the last such gathering. During her stay in Portsmouth farewells were made to the various children's charities which the ship's company had supported, including the Dorton House School for the blind. Finally, during the afternoon of Monday 29 November, the *Lion* slipped her moorings and put to sea to cross swords with the elements for the last time. After leaving Spithead she steamed at full power down the Channel and into the Irish Sea, to anchor off Lough Foyle, Londonderry, on the afternoon of Wednesday 1 December. That night the *Lion,* together with the destroyers *Agincourt* and *Carysfort,* and the frigates *Penelope* and *Troubridge,* took part in her final fleet exercise, code-named 'Calpurnia', before steaming south to Portsmouth and berthing alongside the *Tiger* at Pitch House Jetty. On Monday 13 December, Vice-Admiral Hayes addressed the ship's company and thanked them for the hard work they had put in during the commission, before he lowered his flag and disembarked. Three hours later the *Lion* left Portsmouth and set course for Devonport, where she arrived alongside No 5 wharf at 9.30am the next day. That afternoon destoring and deammunitioning got under way, and for most of the ship's company Christmas leave began. Three days later, at 11.30am on Friday 17 December 1965, those members of the ship's company who were left on board marched to shore accommodation in the Royal Naval Barracks. At midday the *Lion* paid off for the last time.

It had always been intended that the *Lion,* like her two sisters, would be converted into a helicopter command cruiser and, indeed, her commission book for 1964-1965 ends thus: 'On the back cover is a representation of things to come. After a drastic and, from an aesthetic viewpoint, cruel transformation, *Lion* will emerge from Devonport Dockyard with an improved effectiveness in Global and Bushfire war conditions. The after 6-inch mounting will give place to a hangar and flight deck and four Wessex helicopters will be carried, equipped with detector gear and anti-submarine torpedoes. She will then be able to offer potent protection against submarines to any group of which she is part. The anti-submarine helicopters could be replaced by those designed to carry troops, adding significantly to her ability in supporting an amphibious assault landing. Despite these alterations in appearance and function, *Lion* will still be a cruiser.'

Sadly it was not to be and it was not long before she was towed from the non-tidal basin out to the reserve ships' trot in the River Tamar. In 1970, with the announcement that the *Ark Royal* was to be retained until the end of the decade, came the news that the *Lion* would not be converted to a helicopter cruiser. However, she could still be of use to the Royal Navy and in the summer of 1971 Kevin Marshall, who was serving in the *Tiger,* recalls that he and his colleagues made frequent trips out to the *Lion* in order to take machinery parts for their ship's boiler rooms. So frequent did the trips become that eventually the *Lion* was towed back to the dockyard and moored alongside the *Tiger,* where it became easier to strip out the parts required. In May 1973 the *Lion* was towed to Rosyth to be stripped of reusable equipment, and in the summer of 1974 the *Tiger* berthed alongside her which was another opportunity for the *Tiger's* electrical and engineering departments to raid the derelict *Lion* for more spares.

However, in early 1975 all the petty indignities came to an end and the *Lion* suffered the ultimate humiliation when she was sold for scrap. Her final voyage lasted only a few hours when, on Monday 24 February 1975, she was towed the short distance from Rosyth to Inverkeithing for delivery to T. W. Ward's shipbreaking yard. She was the first of the three sisters to depart the scene.

The battlecruiser HMS *Lion* in 1919, shortly after the end of the Great War.   *(Maritime Photo Library)*

Previous Ships

The first *Lion* about which there is any firm information was captured in 1511 from a Scottish privateer and little is known of the second and third *Lions* which entered service in 1536 and 1549 respectively. However, records show that the fourth ship of the name was built in 1557 and she helped to defeat the Spanish Armada. She was also the flagship of Vice-Admiral Borough during the sacking of Cadiz in 1596, and she was eventually scrapped in 1609. The fifth *Lion* was built in 1585, and she formed part of Sir Walter Raleigh's second expedition to the West Indies. The sixth ship of the name was built at Chatham in 1640 and she took part in the Anglo-Dutch Wars of 1652-74. In 1667 she was the flagship of Rear-Admiral Sir John Harman at Martinique. The seventh *Lion* was a fourth-rate (frigate) built at Chatham in 1709, and in 1745 she fought an engagement with the French ship *Elizabeth* which was one of two ships escorting the 'Young Pretender', Charles Edward. The *Elizabeth,* which was a larger and more powerful ship, was forced to return to Brest, but the *Lion* lost 107 crew members killed or wounded. The eighth *Lion* was a surveying sloop which was built at Portsmouth in 1753, and the ninth was a third-rate (frigate) built at Portsmouth in 1777. In 1780 she carried Captain Horatio Nelson home from Port Royal after he had been taken seriously ill directing the expedition against St Juan's. He maintained that it was due to the care and attention which he received on board the *Lion* that his life was saved. In 1800 this *Lion* took part in the blockade of Malta. The tenth *Lion* was a second-rate built in Pembroke in 1847 and she was designed to take her place in the Battle Fleet. In 1859 she was converted to screw propulsion and until 1868 she was in Coastguard service at Greenock. In 1881 she became part of the *Implacable* training establishment at Devonport, and she was sold in 1906.

The eleventh, and probably the most famous ship of the name, was a 29,680-ton battlecruiser which was completed at the Devonport Royal Dockyard in May 1912. She was the first warship to cost more than £2 million, and at the time of building she was larger and faster than any other in the world. Her armour at the waterline and around the barbettes and turrets was nine inches thick. Her Parsons steam turbines developed 70,000 SHP, giving her a speed of 28 knots, and at full power her boilers consumed 950 tons of coal a day. Her massive array of armament included eight, 13.5-inch, and 16, 4-inch guns. The *Lion* was the flagship of the 1st Battlecruiser Squadron throughout her career, and she flew the flag of Admiral Sir David Beatty from January 1913 until November 1916. She took part in the Battle of Heligoland Bight, the first general action of the Great War, when the 1st Battlecruiser Squadron arrived on the scene of battle as the crippled cruiser HMS *Arethusa,* protected by destroyers, was being engaged by the German cruisers *Strasburg* and *Cöln.* The former disappeared into the mist, while the latter fought a brave,

but hopeless, battle against Beatty's squadron. There was a brief respite when the German cruiser *Ariadne* appeared on the scene, but she was hit by the *Lion's* second salvo and she disappeared, blazing furiously, into the mist, sinking two hours later. Meanwhile the *Lion* soon caught up with the *Cöln* once more and she too was sunk. With the second German cruiser having been destroyed, Beatty decided to retire from the area before stronger German forces arrived.

In January 1915, the Naval Intelligence Division forecast a German sortie into the North Sea, and this enabled our forces to be near the crucial spot at the right moment. The enemy forces, which consisted of a Battlecruiser Squadron, with light cruisers and destroyers in company, were chased by the 1st Battlecruiser Squadron and the *Lion* landed a salvo on the after turret of the *Seydlitz*; the resulting explosion started a cordite fire which put both of the German's turrets out of action. As Beatty's ships turned to avoid a torpedo attack, the *Lion* was hit by a salvo from the forward guns of the *Seydlitz* and she sustained serious damage. She was hit again near the waterline by a salvo from the *Derfflinger,* causing her speed to be considerably reduced, and the other battlecruisers steamed past her as she slowed right down. Beatty transferred his flag to HMS *Princess Royal,* and the *Lion* limped home to the Tyne with A magazine flooded and a 10° list to port.

At Jutland on 31 May 1916 the *Lion* was the first ship to open fire in the battle when the 1st Battlecruiser Squadron engaged their German counterparts. The *Lion* received a hit on Q turret which pierced the armour and burst over the left gun. Every man inside was killed and a fierce fire ensued. The officer of the turret, Major Harvey RMLI, although mortally wounded with both legs shot off, passed the order to close the doors and flood the magazine. A few minutes later a cordite charge slid back from the damaged gun into the fire, and in an instant a vivid sheet of flame passed right down the ammunition trunk, killing all who were within range. If the magazine doors had not been closed the *Lion* would no doubt have suffered the fate of the *Queen Mary, Indefatigable* and *Invincible,* which blew up after hits in the region of Q turret. For his action of selfless devotion, Major Harvey was posthumously awarded the Victoria Cross. During the action the *Lion* sustained 101 killed and 44 wounded. She fired 326 rounds of 13.5-inch ammunition and seven torpedoes.

Repairs to the ship were completed in July 1916, although Q turret had to be removed and she went to sea without it from 20 July to 23 September. In November 1916 she became the flagship of Rear-Admiral Pakenham and she remained with the Battlecruiser Squadron to lead a number of sorties. In 1923, under the terms of the Washington Naval Treaty, she was paid off and in the following year she was sold for breaking up.

Battle Honours
HMS *Lion*

Concordant Nomine Facta
(The Facts Agree With The Name)

Armada 1588	Barfleur 1692
Cadiz 1596	Finisterre 1747
Portland 1653	*Santa Dorotea* 1798
Gabbard 1653	*Guillaume Tell* 1800
Lowestoft 1665	Java 1811
Orfordness 1666	Heligoland 1914
Schooneveld 1673	Dogger Bank 1915
Texel 1673	Jutland 1916

HMS *Lion*
Commanding Officers

Name:	Date Appointed:
Captain J. E. Scotland DSC RN	24 April 1960
Captain I. L. M. McGeoch DSO DSC RN	25 April 1962
Captain E. F. Hamilton-Meikle MBE RN	3 April 1964

Part Three
HMS *BLAKE* 1961-1983

Chapter Ten

HMS *Blake* - First Commission 1961-1962

The third and last cruiser of the *Tiger* class, HMS *Blake*, had been launched in December 1945 and at that time only one of the three cruisers had been given the name of a 'big cat', so after the *Defence* had been renamed *Lion* it left the *Blake* as rather the odd one out. She was, in fact, named after Admiral Robert Blake, 1599-1657, who was a notable scholar of his time and a famous Parliamentary Admiral of the Cromwellian Navy in the Civil War and later in the Dutch and Spanish Wars. The *Blake* was the fifth ship of the name and over the years, having been laid up in Gareloch and firmly tied up alongside Fairfield's fitting-out berth for over 15 years, she had been dubbed 'Old Immovable' by the popular press, but in early 1961 the *Blake's* fortunes appeared to have changed for the better.

In early March that year the majority of the ship's company had joined the cruiser at Fairfield's Govan shipyard and her first commanding officer, Captain D. G. Clutterbuck RN, had been appointed two months earlier.

Captain Clutterbuck had entered the Navy in 1929 and had served as a junior officer in the cruisers *Sussex* and *Dunedin*. He was the First Lieutenant of the destroyer *Acheron* and in 1938 he qualified as a navigation specialist. During the Second World War he was the Navigating Officer of the sloop *Deptford* and following that he was appointed to the same position in the cruiser *Ajax,* taking part in actions in the Mediterranean, including those off Crete, Matapan, Greece and North Africa. Between 1942 and 1946 he was the Navigating Officer of the cruiser *Newfoundland,* in which he served in the Mediterranean, the Atlantic and the Far East, and he was present in Tokyo Bay for the Japanese surrender. During the war he was twice Mentioned in Dispatches. After the war he was ashore for a few years carrying out instructional and intelligence duties, before being appointed as the commanding officer of the destroyer *Sluys* followed by the *Cadiz*. After a spell as the Naval Attaché at Bonn, he was appointed Captain (D) of the Third Training Squadron in

HMS *Blake* at Fairfield's shipyard in July 1960.

(Maritime Photo Library)

The *Blake* at Fairfield's fitting-out yard on the Clyde. The three ships in the foreground are the Turkish ferries *Karlica,*
Pendik and *A. Kavagi,* which are fitting out for service on the Bosphorus at Istanbul. *(Glasgow City Library)*

HMS *Zest* at Londonderry. From there, on 17 January 1961, he was appointed to the *Blake* at Govan.

The Commissioning Service for the *Blake* took place on the jetty at Fairfield's yard, alongside the ship, on Wednesday 8 March 1961 and the ship's Chaplain, The Revd C. Prior RN, conducted the service. The Royal Marines Detachment paraded the Guard of Honour and the builders presented the ship with a magnificent silver model of Admiral Blake's flagship the *George,* on which he had died in 1657 as he was approaching Plymouth on his return from a successful campaign. Next day, guided by tugs, the *Blake* steamed downriver to anchor off Greenock whilst stores and ammunition were embarked, although on Saturday 11 March she left the anchorage for 12 hours to carry out engine trials. Finally, at 9am on Saturday 18 March, with all hands manning the decks, she left Greenock to carry out her acceptance trials and at 4.57pm that day in the Firth of Forth, in a position Lat 55° - 40'N/Long 04° - 59'W, with the main engines stopped, Captain Clutterbuck accepted the *Blake* into service with the Royal Navy. With his signature on the acceptance

documents the Red Ensign was struck, and the White Ensign was hoisted at the masthead. Just over an hour later the *Blake* anchored off Princes Pier, Greenock, where Fairfield's trials party was disembarked, and at 7.35pm she weighed anchor and put to sea as a unit of the Royal Navy for the first time. Next day, with the ship off Fastnet Rock, gunnery trials were held and these continued for four days between Fastnet and the Old Head of Kinsale. At 2.38am on the morning of Thursday 23 March, a distress signal was received from the French trawler *Aimejean Louis,* which was in trouble north of the Longships Light and about 90 miles from the *Blake's* position. Captain Clutterbuck altered course and increased speed as the cruiser set course for the trawler's last known position, but an hour later the alarm was over when an Admiralty tug arrived on the scene and was able to assist the trawler. The *Blake* was then able to reduce speed as she continued her course towards Land's End and at 10.30am on Friday 24 March she passed Plymouth breakwater for the first time to secure on D buoy in the Sound. Next day all hands were mustered for Divisions, and on the morning of Tuesday 28

March, the C-in-C Plymouth, Admiral Sir Charles Madden, paid a short visit to the cruiser. Later that afternoon the *Blake* slipped her moorings and steamed up harbour to secure alongside No 8 wharf, where she met her older sister *Tiger,* which was alongside the east wall of No 5 basin, under refit. During her stay alongside, the ship's chapel saw its first baptisms when Stephen Roy Hartshorne, the son of Marine R. Hartshorne, and Joanna Kathryn Green, the daughter of Lt D. N. Green RN, were christened. At this time a number of senior officers, including the Third Sea Lord, Admiral Sir John Reid, and the C-in-C Plymouth's Chief Technical Officer, Rear-Admiral Desmond Hoare, and Captain P. W. W. Graham, who had just taken over as the *Tiger's* commanding officer, visited the ship. The *Blake* also played host to the West German destroyers *Z1* and *Z2,* which tied up alongside her for several days.

On Monday 1 May, the *Blake* left harbour to carry out a series of trials which were to last for 12 days, with weekend breaks at anchor in Plymouth Sound, and finally at 4.30pm on Friday 12 May she steamed into Portsmouth Harbour where she secured alongside North Corner Jetty. During her 13 days alongside, Vice-Admiral Sir Geoffrey Blake, whose wife had launched the cruiser over 15 years earlier, paid a visit to the ship, and the ship's boats rescued the crew of a capsized dinghy. On 25 May the *Blake* left harbour to carry out further trials of all descriptions, but the routine was broken on Friday 2 June with a weekend visit to Guernsey where local hospitality was quite exceptional and the sight of many members of the ship's company 'swaying' smartly down the jetty after sampling the local 'brew' was not unusual. By mid-June the *Blake* was back alongside at Portsmouth where the ship's chapel was dedicated in a service conducted by the Chaplain of the Fleet and the Royal Marines Band joined the ship for her first 'foreign' visit.

At 3.30pm on Monday 26 June, with the Guard and Band paraded and the ship's company manning the decks, the *Blake* left Portsmouth and set course for Rotterdam where she arrived next morning to berth alongside Parkkade East in the city's docks for a six-day visit. After what was a very enjoyable week the *Blake* left the Dutch port to return to Spithead to disembark the band who had still to complete their pre-embarkation training, before the cruiser left to carry out yet more initial sea trials, including a day at sea with the C-in-C Home Fleet, Admiral Sir Wilfred Woods. However, by the afternoon of Friday 7 July the *Blake* was alongside at Devonport where she was to remain for the rest of the month. On Saturday 29 July the Mayor, Mayoress and Town Councillors of Bridgwater, Somerset, which was the birthplace of Admiral Robert Blake, visited the ship to unveil a plaque which commemorated his victories over the Dutch in the first Anglo-Dutch War of 1652-54. On Thursday 3 August the

Blake left Devonport and secured alongside Portsmouth's Pitch House Jetty the next morning, in time for the city's Navy Days which took place over the holiday weekend. There were 17 ships in harbour for the event and 23,000 people visited the *Blake,* which was a testimony to the popularity of the cruiser with the public. She remained alongside at Portsmouth until Monday 11 September, when she sailed on a goodwill cruise to Barrow-in-Furness and Newcastle upon Tyne.

The passage north through the Irish Sea was extremely bumpy, with severe Force 10 gales blowing and heavy tumbling seas. Because of the weather conditions *Blake's* entry into Barrow's Ramsden Dock was delayed and she spent two days at anchor off Queen's Pier in Ramsey Bay, Isle of Man, until the winds decreased. Eventually she arrived in Barrow at 5pm on Sunday 17 September and she stayed for just four days before sailing for Newcastle upon Tyne where she arrived alongside the Walker Navy Yard on the afternoon of Friday 22 September. During the visit to the River Tyne some 5,000 people visited the ship which, at low tide, was sitting on the bottom of the dock. After leaving Newcastle during the afternoon of Tuesday 26 September she steamed south through the North Sea, arriving in Devonport two days later. Most of October was spent alongside, with just four days spent at sea before finally, at 7.30pm on Saturday 28 October, she left Plymouth Sound, bound for Gibraltar and the Mediterranean.

The *Blake* arrived in Gibraltar on the first day of November and after just two days alongside she set sail for Malta in company with the destroyer *Diana* and the frigates *Plymouth* and *Rhyl.* At 10.30am on Monday 6 November, when the force was in a position Lat 38° - 02'N/Long 08° - 36'E, about 55 miles due south of Cape Teulada, Sardinia, ploughing through heavy seas and gale force winds, they took part in a search for survivors from a cargo ship, MV *Durham Trader,* which had foundered in the area. In the event the merchantman SS *Clan Keith* had rescued five survivors, and at 11.33pm the *Blake* picked up the body of a South African seaman, E. J. Pollscut, from the sea, and at the same time an empty and waterlogged lifeboat was sighted. Glen Beck, who was a Junior Seaman on board the *Blake* remembers the incident: 'Whilst on passage from Gibraltar to Malta in November 1961 we ran into severe storm force winds and mountainous seas, which for me as a young Junior Seaman was no joke. I was too worried to be seasick, and at times it seemed as if the *Blake* would roll right over. All the inflatable life-rafts that were stowed aft on the quarterdeck wings were washed away, and it was said at the time that a ship later sighted them and thought that we had foundered in the storm. That morning we received an SOS from a merchantman called the *Durham Trader* which had sunk with all hands quite close to our position, and we altered course to search for survivors. It was due to Captain Clutterbuck's seamanship

The *Blake* at sea on her Contractor's Sea Trials. She is still flying the Red Ensign.   *(Glasgow City Libraries)*

skills in the heavy seas that we found anything at all. Soon afterwards the lookouts spotted a body in the water and the Captain was able to manoeuvre the ship alongside the person who showed no signs of life. I was part of the forenoon watch on deck at the time and I recall the First Lieutenant shouting at the top of his voice, "Ahoy there! Are you all right?" and almost immediately a burly able seaman threw a line with a large grappling hook which actually bounced off the man's head. We all agreed that if he had been all right, then he certainly wouldn't be after that and we soon hauled him on board where it was confirmed that he was indeed dead. He turned out to be one of the *Durham Trader's* officers and he was armed with a pistol and had documents wrapped in a plastic bag and taped to his leg. The body was carried down to the Royal Marines' bathroom where, after downing a tot of rum, the sailmaker sewed it up in canvas. Later that afternoon the man was buried at sea.' The search was eventually called off at 11.30pm that evening and next day the cruiser arrived off Malta where, after two days of exercises, she moored at No 3 buoy in Grand Harbour at 4.30pm on 9 November. Two days after arriving in Malta she was joined by her sister *Tiger* which, flying the flag of FOF (Med), Rear-Admiral J. Bush, had returned from a visit to Taranto.

During the week of Monday 13 November 1961 the *Blake* and *Tiger* were operating from Marsaxlokk Bay on exercises together and on their conclusion the C-in-C Mediterranean, Admiral Sir Deric Holland-Martin, inspected Divisions. In early December both the *Blake* and

the *Tiger* took part in major fleet exercises with the Mediterranean Fleet and the aircraft carrier *Victorious* which was passing through the area on her way home from a deployment east of Suez, and in the days before Christmas Admiral Bush carried out the *Blake's* Operational Readiness Inspection. The extremely hectic round of exercises and manoeuvres was finally completed on Christmas Eve when FOF (Med) took the salute at Divisions on Parlatorio Wharf, after which everyone was able to relax.

The New Year of 1962 saw some exceptionally stormy weather in Malta and on Monday 15 January the *Blake* left harbour to carry out goodwill visits to Toulon and Leghorn (Livorno). She arrived alongside the Quai d'Honneur at the French naval base on the morning of Thursday 18 January for a six-day visit, and a week later she tied up alongside No 1 Jetty in the northern Italian port of Leghorn. On departure from there on 30 January the *Blake* rendezvoused with the destroyers *Crossbow, Diamond* and *Duchess* and the frigates *Berwick* and *Scarborough*. During the gunnery exercises that followed, the *Scarborough* was streaming a splash target for the *Blake's* 3-inch guns' crews who were carrying out a rapid-fire exercise using practice shells. The story is taken up by Mr A. Saunders, who was the *Scarborough's* Ch M(E): 'I was having a cuppa in the forward Chief's mess when the Coxswain knocked on the door and said, "Chief Stoker, have you seen the hole in our bows?". I told him not to be so daft, but soon realized he wasn't joking so I went up to the forecastle and looked over

HMS *Blake* commissions at the shipbuilder's yard.   *(Author's collection)*

the port side to see a hole about 36 inches in diameter, just above the waterline. There was a corresponding hole on the starboard side where a shell had gone straight through. It seems that one shell went astern of us, one went over the funnel and the third went straight through the stem. The ship's carpenter patched them up with timber and grommets, and when we entered Grand Harbour we got a signal from the C-in-C congratulating us on our patchwork. We went into Malta dockyard where a team of local cleaners went into the forepeak to clean up prior to repairs. They had just started work when they suddenly came rushing out shouting, "Bomb! Bomb!". I went in there to find the remains of one of the *Blake*'s 3-inch shells.' Mr Saunders recalls that during the following weekend he and others from the *Scarborough* met members of the *Blake*'s ship's company who, during the ensuing party, sang to the tune of a popular song of the time, 'There's a Hole in your Bows, Dear *Scarborough*, Dear *Scarborough*'. He also remembers that the remains of the 3-inch shell were carefully mounted on a mahogany base by the *Scarborough*'s shipwright and presented to the *Blake*'s wardroom by the

frigate's officers.

The two vessels spent the remainder of February 1962 in Grand Harbour undergoing maintenance and, in the *Scarborough*'s case, repairs. It was on Saturday 3 March that the *Blake* left Malta for her second flag-showing cruise of the Mediterranean deployment, and two days later she anchored at Suda Bay in Crete for a visit of just 30 hours. This was followed by a six-day stopover at Piraeus, during which Crown Prince Constantine, accompanied by Princesses Sophia and Irene, paid a short visit to the ship, as did several thousand of his countrymen when the gangway was opened to visitors. The cruise was followed by another short stay in Malta following which, on Monday 26 March, in company with the destroyer *Diamond,* she sailed for Gibraltar from where she was to make her next goodwill cruise. This started on Wednesday 4 April when she left for Valencia, Ajaccio and the lovely town of Villefranche, but the end of the month saw the *Blake* back in Malta and moored to No 2 buoy in Pieta Creek, where she underwent a seven-day maintenance period.

On Thursday 3 May the cruiser left Malta to rendezvous with the aircraft carrier *Centaur*, the destroyer *Broadsword* and her old friend *Scarborough* for anti-submarine exercises. During the manoeuvres one of the *Centaur*'s Whirlwind helicopters landed on the cruiser's quarterdeck and another crashed into the sea, but fortunately the crew were rescued safely. The *Blake*'s 6-inch guns of Y turret gave some very impressive bombardment firings before she secured alongside Grand Harbour's Parlatorio Wharf at 3.25pm on Saturday 5 May. The *Blake* sailed again on 29 May with the *Trafalgar, Lowestoft* and *Scarborough* to rendezvous with the C-in-C's yacht, HMS *Surprise,* and on the morning of Friday 8 June they steamed past in salute to the C-in-C Mediterranean, Admiral Sir Deric Holland-Martin. Following this the C-in-C was transferred to the *Blake* by jackstay and he hoisted his flag in the cruiser for three hours before he left for the *Trafalgar.* Next day, Saturday 9 June, the squadron steamed into Palma, Majorca, where the *Blake* secured alongside the west end of the Dique de

Quest Jetty at 9.15am. The four days spent in Palma coincided with the arrival of large numbers of British holidaymakers who were beginning to take advantage of package tours to this lovely island, which made for some lively evenings in the bars and local clubs. However, after leaving harbour on the morning of Wednesday 13 June it was back to work and more gunnery exercises with the two destroyers, during which the cruiser carried out long-range surface firings. The rest of the month was spent carrying out manoeuvres off Malta and on Wednesday 27 June the ships of the Mediterranean Fleet carried out a ceremonial steam-past of HMS *Surprise,* with the Governor of Malta taking the salute, after which the fleet returned to Grand Harbour.

The remainder of the *Blake's* summer was to be spent on a nine-week detachment to the West Indies where, flying the flag of Rear-Admiral J. F. D. Bush, she would represent the United Kingdom at the Independence celebrations of Jamaica and Trinidad. The deployment began on Saturday 14 July when, at 12.30pm, she left Malta to steam west for Gibraltar. After only a short stay alongside the colony's South Mole, during which time Admiral Bush inspected Divisions, the *Blake* departed at 3pm on Wednesday 18 July and set course across the Atlantic for Bermuda. The nine-day passage was uneventful, with the ship's company being fully engaged on their final preparations for the Admiral's Harbour Inspection which, in the event, was carried out at sea on 25 and 26 July, when the ship was off Bermuda. At 6.40am on Friday 27 July the *Blake* arrived in the old naval dockyard at Ireland Island in Bermuda to refuel. For those who remembered the base from pre-war days, when it was in full working order, it presented a depressing sight with broken windows, shattered roofs, weeds, rusty capstans and heaps of scrap metal. Not far away the clean, modern US naval base stood out in sharp contrast and it was clear evidence of the decline in British naval influence in the area. This decline was to be reflected throughout the West Indies detachment where it was obvious that the countries of the region were now looking to the USA for both political and financial support.

At 3.15pm that day, having completed her refuelling, the *Blake* slipped her moorings and steamed through the Dundonald Channel to secure alongside No I berth at Hamilton, adjacent to the main shopping street, an hour later. As always in Bermuda a considerable programme of entertainment was arranged both for officers and ratings, and the generosity of the local population ensured that there was little need to spend time in the shops. When the Royal Marines Band Beat Retreat in the main street the Governor of Bermuda, Major-General Sir Julian Gascoigne, took the salute in front of a considerable crowd of Bermudans and tourists. Although the visit to Bermuda was short, lasting only for the weekend, the *Blake* received good coverage from the local press, which was to be in stark contrast to the remainder of the deployment.

After leaving Hamilton at 8am on Monday 30 July, the *Blake* set course for Kingston, Jamaica, and on arrival there at 7am on Thursday 2 August with HMS *Whirlwind* found the frigate *Ulster* already at anchor, wearing the broad pendant of the Senior Naval Officer, West Indies, Commodore J. E. L. Martin. The *Blake* went alongside the Texaco fuelling jetty, where she spent three hours embarking furnace fuel oil. At 10.30am she left the jetty and steamed to an anchorage off the town for, although Admiral Bush had been offered a berth alongside, he decided the *Blake* would be much more in evidence in the stream where the US Navy's aircraft carrier USS *Lake Champlain,* the destroyer USS *Bristol* and the Canadian frigate HMCS *Iroquois* were also anchored. As far as Admiral Bush was concerned the celebrations did not get off to a good start, for no sooner had the *Blake* anchored than he received a letter from the Governor-General designate regretting that pressure of work made it impossible for him to visit the ship, or even to receive a call from the Admiral. After 307 years of British rule this was obviously a disappointing slight, for as he said in his report: 'HMS *Blake* had steamed some 4,000 miles specially to be at Jamaica at this time,' and with the Royal Navy in mind, and in particular the *Blake,* he went on to say: 'Had he (the Governor-General) come on board and received his gun salute on leaving it might have brought our presence more into the public eye and to the notice of the press.' However, the Admiral was able to call on the Jamaican Prime Minister, Sir Alexander Bustamante, who received him very courteously and gave him nearly an hour of his time. That evening the Prime Minister attended an official reception on board and he obviously enjoyed the event, for according to Admiral Bush: 'The same evening he arrived first, with signs of lipstick on his left cheek, at the reception on board and left nearly two hours later positively smothered.' However, despite his friendliness it was apparent that Sir Alexander was in the process of cutting his country's ties with the United Kingdom, whilst wooing both the United States and Canada for all he was worth. The USA had in fact sent Vice-President Lyndon Johnson to Jamaica as a special representative of President John F. Kennedy, and he had arrived with an army of aides and publicity men. To back up Lyndon Johnson the US Navy's Central Band, together with a drill squad from the US Marines, had flown in and US Navy helicopters were constantly overhead. It was, therefore, hardly surprising that the press gave pride of place to the USA, and virtually ignored the Royal Navy's more modest presence. For her part Canada sent two warships, a government minister and a fat cheque for the new Jamaican Government. It was another depressing reminder of the decline of British influence.

However, despite the lack of publicity which the Royal Navy received, the ships' companies of the *Blake, Whirlwind*

HMS *Blake* and the aircraft carrier *Centaur* at Malta in early May 1962.   *(Imperial War Museum MH 31276)*

HMS *Blake* at Bermuda.   *(Author's collection)*

The Prime Minister
of newly independent
Jamaica, Sir Alexander
Bustamente, visits the
Blake.

(Author's collection)

and *Ulster* played their part to the full in a very dignified manner. At the Independence Ceremony itself an extremely smart Royal Navy Guard of 100 men from the *Blake* was one of the main features of the flag raising ceremony and on the occasions when the Royal Marines Band played ashore they were, as always, very well received. However, the general atmosphere of indifference among the population was summed up by Admiral Bush when he wrote: 'The lack of enthusiasm shown by the public was, however, most marked. There appeared to be a general air of uncertainty about the future which reached down to the humblest citizen. Although no important speech, except that of HRH Princess Margaret at the State Dinner, made any reference to the part which the United Kingdom had played in preparing Jamaica for independence, I felt that there were at least some who were doubtful of the wisdom of severing the link.'

At 10am on Wednesday 8 August the *Blake* weighed anchor and on leaving Jamaica she steamed to La Guira in Venezuela, which is the port for the capital city, Caracas, about ten miles away. Throughout the cruiser's five-day stay the Venezuelan authorities were most helpful and they made it clear that the visit was most welcome. On the last day, at the invitation of the Venezuelan Navy, Admiral Bush travelled to the naval base at Puerto Cabello, stopping en route to lay a wreath at the site of the Battle of Carabobo (the decisive battle in the Venezuelan struggle for

independence from Spain). On his arrival at the base he was taken on board the Barrow-built destroyer *Nuevo Esparta,* which was similar to a Daring-class destroyer, where the ship's company manned ship and he was warmly welcomed. The base itself he found to be very clean and smart and run on US Navy lines which, with the British and Italian built ships, provided a curious mix. After a formal lunch with the Venezuelan C-in-C, Admiral Bush flew back to La Guira.

The *Blake* left Venezuela at 8am on Tuesday 14 August and next morning she secured alongside the North Wharf at Port Castries, St Lucia, for a four-day stay on the beautiful island. The ship's company received a large number of private invitations for picnics, swimming trips and rum parties, while on the official side Admiral Bush entertained the island's Chief Minister to dinner, the ship laid on the usual official reception and a children's party was held. It was a tribute to the officers and ratings involved in the latter event that everything went smoothly for, although invitations for 150 had been sent out, 300 children arrived on board. Happily no one was turned away and all the youngsters enjoyed themselves immensely.

After leaving Castries during the afternoon of Sunday 19 August, the *Blake* set course for Barbados and she berthed alongside the western breakwater of the new deepwater harbour in Bridgetown at 8.30am the next morning. For the first time during the deployment the visit of a British cruiser received good press coverage and the Royal Marines Band gave a number of performances in the town as well as on the local radio station. Finally, at 11.15am on Sunday 26 August, the *Blake* sailed for her final visit of the detachment to Port of Spain, Trinidad, and to Scarborough Harbour, Tobago, for the Independence Celebrations of the two islands. She arrived off Port of Spain early on the morning of Monday 27 August and having fallen in with the *Whirlwind* and *Ulster*, the *Blake* moored alongside No 2 wharf at 9am. Also in harbour for the event was the Canadian frigate *Iroquois* and the Venezuelan destroyer *Nueva Esparta,* both of which berthed astern of the *Blake*. From the outset it became clear that the celebrations in Trinidad were to go ahead with virtually no organization at all and, according to Admiral Bush, 'Throughout our stay counterorder and disorder prevailed.' However, despite this, there was one significant and very positive factor, in contrast to the celebrations in Jamaica, when the Royal Navy and the *Blake* in particular, was given pride of place while the US Navy's representatives were rather sidelined. One reason for this was the Prime Minister's lack of warmth towards the USA and his very positive attitude towards Britain. Such was the lack of organization that Admiral Bush, although being aware that he was expected to be at the local airport on Tuesday 28 August, to welcome the Princess Royal, only found confirmation of this when he read in that morning's newspaper that, 'Commander J. D. C. Bush is to be presented when Her Royal Highness alights.' Armed with the newspaper and a home-made windscreen sticker he then drove to the airport where he found that he was indeed expected. The story continues as told by Admiral Bush: 'From then on, playing entirely off the cuff, I met Her Royal Highness, sat on the royal dais, had champagne in the VIP lounge, toured the new airport building, saw Her Royal Highness to her car and finally drove in the royal procession to Port of Spain. I felt that at least I had achieved some prominence for the Royal Navy.'

At the flag raising ceremony the Guard from HMS *Blake* again presented themselves very smartly, and as all orders to the naval half of the Guard were given separately from those of the local regiment, their presence was given a great deal of publicity in the local press. On conclusion of the ceremony, after the Union Flag had been lowered, it was presented to Admiral Bush for safe keeping. This ceremony too was in marked contrast to the rather formal affair that had been held in Jamaica, being held in Port of Spain's main square which, together with the surrounding area, was packed with excited people. There was no doubt that despite instructions to the contrary, the population were out to enjoy themselves in a carnival atmosphere. The visit ended at just after midnight on Saturday 1 September and eight hours later the *Blake* anchored in Scarborough Harbour, Tobago. As soon as the ship was safely at her berth Admiral Bush left for the airport to meet the Princess

Royal once again, and he subsequently accompanied her to a youth rally, a formal lunch at Government House and a garden party, which concluded Tobago's Independence celebrations. After a stay of just over 30 hours, at 3.15pm on Sunday 2 September the *Blake* sailed for Gibraltar. As far as the ship's company were concerned the detachment was summed up by Admiral Bush in his report to the C-in-C Mediterranean thus: 'Throughout the cruise the officers and ratings of HMS *Blake* were fully extended as hosts at receptions, children's parties and "At Homes" on board, and as guests to overwhelming hospitality ashore. This experience was on a far greater scale than any they had had previously during the commission and they responded to it nobly. They were also able to get a fair amount of sport of all kinds and to make considerable progress with the non-swimmers. The behaviour of the ship's company ashore was very good throughout, although put to the test by rum which was always cheap and often free.' As for official matters, when responding to the question of whether the cruiser's detachment to the West Indies had been worthwhile, he wrote: 'As far as Jamaica and Trinidad were concerned, preoccupied as they were with independence and all that goes with it, the answer is probably No. No that is, in the positive sense. In the negative sense it is certainly Yes. Although it appeared on the surface that her presence did not matter much, there is no doubt that if a cruiser had not been sent, it would certainly have been noticed and criticized. This would have been particularly so in Jamaica where the press were often anti-British in tone, and where such headlines as, "United States Sends Carrier - United Kingdom Small Frigate" might well have appeared. In contrast there is no doubt that the visit to Venezuela was a great success, and the fact that Venezuela was the only "foreign" country to be visited did not escape notice and was clearly appreciated.'

As the *Blake* made her north-easterly transatlantic crossing the guns' crews were given some practice when Y turret carried out bombardment firings, and at 11.40am on Monday 10 September the cruiser arrived in Gibraltar and once again joined the Mediterranean Fleet. From Gibraltar she steamed east to Malta and in the last week of September she paid an official call at Istanbul which, as it transpired, was to be her last foreign visit as a conventional cruiser. After leaving the Turkish city on Monday 1 October the *Blake* returned to Malta and following a ten-day period of maintenance she left on Saturday 13 October for Gibraltar and then Devonport. She arrived in Plymouth Sound at just after 11pm on Sunday 21 October and at noon the next day, after receiving Customs clearance, she weighed anchor and, after firing a salute to the C-in-C Plymouth, she steamed up harbour with her decks fully manned to secure alongside No 8 wharf at 1.10pm, where wives and families were waiting patiently on the jetty. Next day destoring and deammunitioning began and the ship

The *Blake* alongside in Castries, St Lucia.
(*Author's collection*)

was prepared for an extensive refit at the end of a successful commission.

For the *Blake* Christmas came and went as she lay in No 9 dry dock, and on 20 February 1963 she was shifted into No 4 basin of Devonport Dockyard. Next day came an announcement from the Admiralty, which was a bombshell to the ship's company, that *Blake* was to go into temporary reserve in June that year just as soon as her refit was completed. The official reason given was that naval manpower in certain categories was temporarily under strength, but once again rumours began to circulate that all three Tiger-class cruisers were to be laid up. In the following month questions were asked in Parliament and the Civil Lord of the Admiralty denied reports that the *Tiger,* as well as the *Blake,* was to be cocooned in reserve. There followed an exchange of letters in daily newspapers and specialist journals, including the following which was sent to the *Navy News:* 'As a taxpayer I think it disgusting that a £13,000,000 ship like HMS *Blake* should be allowed

to rot in reserve fleet after only two years' service. Will the *Devonshire* be next?' In his reply to the correspondent the journal's editor wrote: 'It is understood that *Blake* will be "out of commission" for only a short period due, entirely, to a temporary shortage of highly trained technical ratings.' How wrong that statement would turn out to be.

Meanwhile, back on board the *Blake* in No 4 basin at Devonport, at 10.15am on Friday 8 March, Captain Clutterbuck addressed his ship's company for the last time, and half an hour later he left the ship. Two weeks later the *Blake* went into dockyard hands, by which time most of her ship's company had dispersed, many of them to the aircraft carrier *Centaur,* which was to undergo a five-month refit before recommissioning for service east of Suez. Later that year it was announced that the *Blake* would not rejoin the operational fleet unless an emergency arose. This announcement was deemed to herald the end for the *Blake* and for the next 15 months she lay idle at Devonport, being used as an accommodation ship.

Chapter Eleven

HMS *Blake* - Second Commission 1969-1970

When the *Blake* was decommissioned at Devonport in March 1962, there were many who thought that her short operational career was well and truly over and that she would never again put to sea under her own power, with only a bleak trip to the breaker's yard ahead of her. Fortunately, in January 1964, when top secret plans for the conversion of the Tiger-class cruisers to command helicopter cruisers were first put to the Minister of Defence, it had already been decided that if the conversions did go ahead, then the *Blake* would be the first of the trio to undergo the transformation. However, like the original construction work, the conversion was bedevilled by delays and it would be 1969 before the *Blake* got to sea once again. In his letter of 4 February 1964 to the Minister of Defence, the First Lord of the Admiralty, Earl Jellicoe, wrote: 'I am writing to you about our latest

proposals for new construction and conversions. There is one new development – the plan to convert the Tiger-class cruisers which I have already mentioned to you in passing. There are two main factors here: the vital role of improving our anti-submarine defence by employing A/S helicopters sooner; and the unavoidable delay we foresee in our escort cruiser programme.* By a thorough study of the problem we have therefore a scheme, of which the main features will be these. (A) Operational Case. The three Tiger-class cruisers would be converted to enable them to operate four Wessex A/S helicopters each. They would be a significant access of A/S strength to the Fleet. They could also be deployed with an effective military force on board and, in this role, troop-carrying helicopters could be operated from them. (B) Conversion and Equipment. The conversions would be carried out in the dockyards over the years 1965-1968; each would take about 18 months and cost (including long refit) about £5 million. (The cost of the long refit without conversion, would be some £3.5 million). The first ship would be taken in hand in early 1965 (and we therefore wish to start as soon as possible on the design work). The A/S helicopter procurement programme would be adjusted so that two new flights could be formed – one in 1967/68 and a second in 1968/69. The third flight would be found from present and planned resources of helicopters. (C) Financial Saving. Their refit and conversion should enable the Tigers to give a further 8 - 9 years' operational life. It would thus be possible to accept the deferment of the ordering of the first of the escort cruisers from mid-1966 until about mid-1970. As a result of this, the Tiger-class conversion scheme as a whole (including the extra helicopter buy) would produce a total net saving of about £25 million on the 1963 long-term costings for the ten-year period 1973/74.' In his final paragraph on the subject Earl Jellicoe referred specifically to the *Blake*: 'We are submitting a memorandum to the Operational Requirements Committee, and we shall be ready to have

HMS *Blake* in Portsmouth Dockyard's No 14 dry dock towards the end of her conversion to a helicopter cruiser. *(T. Middleton)*

* The escort cruisers to which Earl Jellicoe was referring were first envisaged in the early 1960s as 13,500-ton, 650ft, vessels armed with a twin 4.5-inch gun and Sea Slug missiles, capable of carrying nine anti-submarine helicopters. It was intended that these ships would accompany the fleet carriers on operations, and it was hoped that the first such vessel would be included in the 1962-63 Naval Estimates. However, with funds being sought for the new fleet carrier, CVA 01 it was clear that these smaller, but very expensive, ships were out of the question at that time. In the event, with the demise of the fleet carriers, the basic design of the escort cruisers was adapted for the 'through deck' cruisers or, as they became, the Invincible-class light fleet carriers.

Wessex helicopter 410 BL of 820 Squadron makes the first deck landing on board the *Blake* on 22 April 1969. *(Fleet Air Arm Museum)*

A Wessex helicopter of 829 Squadron carrying out deck landing trials on board the *Blake* on 8 May 1969. *(Fleet Air Arm Museum)*

whatever detailed discussion may be necessary with your Department and with the Treasury; but I think that you will agree that there would be operational and financial benefit from this change of plan. There would also be very definite political advantage in putting the Tigers to such valuable use over the next decade and in providing an answer to the very awkward questions which will be asked about our continuing inability to recommission HMS *Blake*.'

The *Blake's* conversion, like that of her sister *Tiger*, would involve the removal of the after 6-inch armament and the provision of a flight deck of sufficient size to range two Wessex III helicopters with rotors spread, together with a hangar for four Wessex helicopters. Beneath the flight deck there would be workshops and stores and also the additional accommodation for the squadron personnel. In order to provide helicopters for the converted *Blake*, improvised arrangements were to be made from the Navy's existing aircraft. As regards their complement, the cruisers would carry 49 officers and 365 ratings of the ship's company, and 17 officers and 80 ratings of the embarked air squadron. In addition the troop-carrying capacity was put at 50 officers and 500 other ranks, with an increased capacity for periods of less than 24 hours. Once converted the displacement tonnage would be increased to 12,080, the maximum speed would be 28 knots, and the endurance at 20 knots would be about 3,500 miles.

The conversion of the *Blake* was to be carried out at Portsmouth Dockyard and by the end of 1964 she had been towed from Devonport in readiness. In the event it was April 1965 when the work actually started, with the optimistic prediction that it would be completed in two years. In the summer of 1966 came the first delay when, on Saturday 16 July, fire broke out on an amidships mess deck. Both the Dockyard and City Fire Brigades rushed to the scene and it took over two hours for them to bring the blaze under control. The spokesman for the firefighters on the scene said at the time: 'It was an extremely hot and smoky job with intense heat and dense smoke, and firemen had to wear breathing apparatus.' Although damage to the cruiser's after section, where the 6-inch turret was being removed, was described as 'fairly extensive', it was stressed to the press that the damage was not likely to delay the completion date. However, six months later it was admitted that there would be a delay of 12 months, and that instead of Wessex helicopters, the *Blake* would carry the newly developed Sea Kings. In July 1967 came the news that the *Blake* would not recommission until early 1969 and this time the estimate was correct, but the work had taken four years.

On Monday 21 October 1968 the *Blake's* new commanding officer, Captain R. F. Plugge DSC RN, was appointed and he joined the nucleus of key personnel who were standing by the ship while living in the redundant aircraft carrier *Centaur*, which was acting as an accommodation ship. Just over four weeks later, on Thursday 21 November, the lower deck was cleared and the ship's company mustered in the hangar for the first time to hear Captain Plugge read the Commissioning Order. Just 11 days later, on Monday 2 December, with the *Blake* lying alongside Portsmouth's Middle Slip Jetty, the pipe 'Special Sea Dutymen to your Stations' was heard for the first time in more than six years. An hour and 40 minutes later, at 11.40am, the mooring lines were slipped and, assisted by tugs, the *Blake* was turned in the harbour before getting under way. At noon she passed Fort Blockhouse and 25 minutes later the pilot was disembarked off the Nab Tower. All afternoon and well into the evening the *Blake* carried out compass trials off the Isle of Wight before, at 9pm, she anchored for the night at Spithead. Next morning there was an early start as the ship got under way at 7.30am for a day of engine trials, during which the after engines were found to be performing satisfactorily. Unfortunately, the same could not be said for the forward engines which, after strange noises had been heard coming from the gearbox, suffered a total vacuum failure and had to be shut down to avoid any further damage. The mechanical problems meant an early arrival at the Spithead anchorage and the ship remained there the following day whilst the dockyard engineers worked on the faults. Fortunately, by 8.30am on Thursday 5 December the *Blake* was under way again and soon all engines were working at 160rpm on all four shafts. That day trials were carried out on the cruiser's main 6-inch and secondary 3-inch armament and next day, after a night anchored at Spithead, came the full-power trials over the measured mile south-west of the Nab Tower. By the end of that forenoon the *Blake* had achieved 28 knots at full power, and at 2pm she returned to Middle Slip Jetty for a weekend break. On Monday 9 December the cruiser slipped her berth at 9am, to commence four days of engine, gunnery and pre-wetting trials, anchoring each afternoon at Spithead before finally returning to Middle Slip Jetty at 6pm on Thursday 12 December. Next day she was shifted into C lock for two days of tilt trials, and on Tuesday 17 December, with her preliminary trials over, the ship's company moved into shore accommodation in the naval barracks.

With the Christmas and New Year celebrations having come and gone, everything seemed set for the Commissioning Ceremony which was due to be held on the last day of February 1969. However, on Tuesday 21 January, with the ship high and dry in C lock, fire broke out in a storage area on board the cruiser. Once again both the Dockyard and the Portsmouth City Fire Brigades were rushed to the ship, and the *Blake's* own fire and emergency parties opened the dry dock's sluice gates to let water in so that the ship's firemain system could be made serviceable. In the event it took two hours to extinguish the blaze, which created a great deal of billowing smoke over the dockyard. Despite the fact that a subsequent investigation

A very smart and newly converted helicopter cruiser, HMS *Blake*, leaves Portsmouth Harbour for the NATO Fleet Review at Spithead in May 1969.

(Maritime Photo Library)

ruled out sabotage as a cause of the fire, plans to commission the ship were delayed by almost two months.

On 15 April 1969 the ship's company moved on board, and seven days later, on Tuesday 22 April, the first helicopter landing took place, when a Wessex of 820 Squadron, which was bringing senior officers to the Commissioning Ceremony, landed on the new flight deck. It was a sure sign that the cruiser's long sojourn in Portsmouth Dockyard was almost over. Next day, to everyone's relief, with the ship alongside South Railway Jetty, the Commissioning Service took place on the quayside. Right up to the last minute rain had threatened to disrupt the proceedings, but it was decided to go ahead and hold the ceremony in the open air. The guest of honour, Vice-Admiral Sir David Clutterbuck, who had been the cruiser's first, and only other commanding officer, addressed the ship's company and their 1,000 guests. He was followed at 11am by Captain Plugge, who read the Commissioning Warrant, after which the White Ensign was hoisted at the masthead. As soon as the formalities were over, Mrs Plugge, assisted by the Master-at-Arms, cut the cake and the guests were then allowed on board to look round the ship and to have lunch. The proceedings were enlivened by the Royal Marines Band and the Detachment who provided the music and the Guard of Honour, and although the weather was cool, the threatened rain did not spoil this auspicious event. Two days after the ceremony the *Blake* sailed from Portsmouth Harbour for a shakedown cruise and the first phase of the work-up at Portland which, as work-ups always do, stretched everyone to the limit.

In mid-May there was a timely break in proceedings when, with 62 other warships, the *Blake*, flying the flag of the Flag Officer Carriers and Amphibious Ships, Rear-

Admiral M. F. Fell CB DSO DSC, took part in the NATO Naval Review at Spithead. The Review marked the 20th anniversary of the formation of NATO, with its pledges of mutual assistance against aggression, and by the afternoon of Tuesday 13 May the *Blake* and most of the other ships from 12 NATO countries had taken up their positions at Spithead. The earliest arrivals from foreign navies were the Italian guided missile cruiser *Doria* and the destroyer *Alpino*, together with the USS *Wasp*, which was the only aircraft carrier present. In addition to the *Blake*, the Royal Navy's contribution included the destroyer *Glamorgan* (Admiral Sir John Bush, Allied C-in-C Channel), six frigates, three submarines, two minesweepers and a fleet auxiliary.

Friday 16 May dawned as a fine but breezy day, and with all the ships dressed overall the Spithead anchorages were a splendid sight. During the afternoon HMY *Britannia* left Portsmouth Harbour and steamed past the beaches of Southsea where large crowds had gathered to watch the event. As the royal yacht reached the eastern end of the review area, and just before she began her passage down the lines of ships, a 21-gun salute crashed out and as an added touch of drama, the liner *QE2* steamed out of Southampton Water on only her second line voyage to Le Havre and New York. As she passed through the assembled fleet, close to the royal yacht, her master, Captain William Warwick, saluted the Queen by dipping his Blue Ensign and sounding three short blasts on the ship's siren. As the *QE2* left the area the Review began, and for more than two hours the royal yacht steamed between the lines of cruisers, destroyers, frigates and minesweepers, before returning to the dockyard where the Queen signalled to Admiral Bush: 'It has been a privilege to review the NATO fleet assembled at Spithead today and I have been greatly impressed by all I

Friday 16 May 1969 at Spithead. The *Blake* is dressed overall for the NATO Fleet Review to mark the Alliance's 20th anniversary. *(A.Middleton)*

During the 1969 NATO Fleet Review the *Britannia* steams past the *Blake* as the Squadron Personnel prepare to cheer ship. *(A. Middleton)*

On 1 July 1969, 820 Squadron embarked in the *Blake* for the first time.
(Fleet Air Arm Museum)

have seen of officers, men and ships. I and my husband have much enjoyed this unique occasion and send congratulations to all who have taken part.' For the *Blake* the end of the Review meant a return to her work-up off Portland, but by the last week of the month she was back alongside in Portsmouth Dockyard where, on Monday 26 May, she made newspaper headlines when the Dockyard and City Fire Brigades spent 90 minutes extinguishing yet another fire on board. Fortunately it was in a storeroom which contained only paper and cardboard boxes, and damage was minimal.

The first day of July 1969 saw the *Blake* steaming off the coast of Cornwall while the four Wessex III helicopters of 820 Squadron were landed on, and next morning, whilst in the Bay of Biscay, a request for urgent medical assistance was received from the German merchant ship, MV *Ulla*, one of whose seamen had severed a main artery. The German ship was some 120 miles away and the cruiser increased speed to 27 knots in order to close the distance and when she was about 90 miles from the *Ulla*, two helicopters were launched. They were quickly able to locate the vessel and the Medical Officer was winched on board to treat the patient. The last week of July saw the *Blake* in Torbay for the second Review of the commission, the Royal Review of the Western Fleet. The 41 ships of the Western Fleet were led by the aircraft carrier HMS *Eagle*, flying the flag of the C-in-C Western Fleet, Admiral Sir John Bush. It

was the largest gathering of the Royal Navy's warships since the Coronation Review at Spithead in the summer of 1953, but unfortunately the weather, in the form of mists and heavy rain, did its best to mar this latest fleet assembly. The Review started on Monday 28 July when the Queen and Prince Philip, accompanied by Prince Charles and Princess Anne, arrived by train from London and embarked in the royal yacht at Torquay. That afternoon, despite the driving rain, the royal party visited a number of ships, with the Queen holding a tea party in the *Blake's* hangar for the Fleet's Chief Petty Officers. That evening gales, rain and poor visibility caused some anxious moments and the ship to shore boat service had to be cancelled, with many liberty men being stranded ashore in Torquay. Fortunately they were picked up early the following morning, shortly before the Queen presented the new Fleet Colours in a ceremony which was held in the *Eagle's* hangar. This was followed by a fly-past by 89 Fleet Air Arm aircraft, starting with Wessex helicopters flying at 400ft, and at a leisurely 80 knots, and ending with Phantoms that roared overhead at 800 feet at a speed of 360 knots.

That afternoon all the ships put to sea where, ten miles east of Torbay, they staged a very impressive steam-past. The *Eagle* led the Review and she was followed by the newly converted, and now rather ungainly looking, command helicopter cruiser, HMS *Blake*. Next came the guided missile destroyer *Hampshire* and 12 frigates, before

An aerial view of the *Blake* at sea with a Wessex helicopter on the flight deck.

(A. Middleton)

HMS *Blake* carrying out Harrier trials in the Channel on 2 August 1969. *(Fleet Air Arm Museum)*

After a successful landing the Harrier is manhandled into position for its take-off.

(Fleet Air Arm Museum)

The *Blake* in Malta's Grand Harbour on 6 November 1969. *(Maritime Photo Library)*

HMS *Blake* leaves Portsmouth in February 1970 for exercises off Portland and Scotland, before leaving for Australia and the Far East.

(Maritime Photo Library)

the *Britannia* steamed in the opposite direction to take all the salutes of the second column led by the *Glamorgan,* which was followed by the nuclear submarines *Valiant* and *Warspite,* six conventional submarines and an array of minesweepers and fleet auxiliaries. At the conclusion of the Review and after clearing the area, the *Blake* rendezvoused with the royal yacht and embarked Prince Philip, Prince Charles and Lord Mountbatten by light jackstay. They subsequently flew off the cruiser in a Wessex of the Queen's Flight. Despite the miserable weather it had been a successful two days.

Following summer leave, the much interrupted work-up at Portland continued and the weekend of 2 and 3 August saw the first landing on the *Blake's* mini-flight deck of a Hawker Siddeley Harrier close support jet fighter. With the impending demise of the Royal Navy's strike carriers it had been decided to study the feasibility of operating the Harrier 'jump jet' vertical take-off aircraft from the helicopter cruisers, with a view to becoming operational

from the mid-1970s. The *Blake* was operating just south-east of the Isle of Wight when the Harrier, flown from Dunsfold airfield in Surrey by Hawker Siddeley's Chief Test Pilot, Hugh Merewether, flew in and landed without a hitch and successfully took off again. The last week of that month saw the *Blake* alongside at Portsmouth and on Tuesday 26 August she moved a step nearer to full operational readiness when her detachment of 35 Royal Marines, commanded by Captain D. L. Hunt RM, marched through Portsmouth Dockyard to join the ship. Included in the party were two buglers who were to be the last full-time seaborne Marine Buglers to serve in the Royal Navy. Preceding the Marines as they marched along Fountain Lake Jetty to the cruiser was the band of the Flag Officer Naval Air Command, and on the jetty to greet and inspect them was Captain Plugge. The Marines arrived on board just in time for the Navy Days weekend at Portsmouth, and three days later, on Thursday 4 September, the *Blake* left for Portland and the final phase of her work-up.

The gruelling work-up was finally completed in mid-October, after which the *Blake,* flying the flag of the newly appointed Flag Officer Flotillas, Western Fleet, Rear-Admiral J. E. Pope, steamed south for some autumn sunshine in the Mediterranean. The first official call was at Marseilles, where the wine was good but where the prices were exorbitant, and this was followed by a weekend in Malta. There were exercises with the aircraft carrier *Eagle,* and the Dartmouth Training Squadron, and another stay in Malta, this time for ten days which gave plenty of time for sport, banyans and make and mends. In mid-November the *Blake* spent two weeks in Gibraltar and for much of that time acted as guardship during the period of political tension which had started on 8 June that year when the government of General Franco closed the frontier crossing between Spain and Gibraltar. Having both the *Eagle* and the *Hermes* alongside as well ensured that the colony's bars and restaurants were always crowded. The foray into the Mediterranean was not all play however, for during the second period the *Blake* took part in two major exercises, 'Autumn Colours' off Malta and 'Emery Cloth' in the area around Gibraltar, then in early December came the last visits of the deployment. The first, at Gibraltar, gave the *Blake* some unexpected publicity when 50 officers and men raised £270 to provide an incubator for the local hospital by walking backwards for four miles through the town and up to the top of the Rock. The final visit, a few days later, was to Casablanca where the ship's company gave a party for Moroccan orphans and some members went on a coach trip to Marrakech. However, with Christmas approaching most were happy to leave the port as the *Blake* set course for the Bay of Biscay and exercises with the French Navy, before she returned to Portsmouth for seasonal leave and, for the ship herself, dry docking in C lock, in preparation for her next deployment, to the Far East.

It was early February 1970 before the *Blake* sailed from Portsmouth once again, and after a few days in the Portland area she steamed north for Scottish waters to exercise her main armament. This period ended with a full-power trial over the measured mile off the Northumberland coast, before the cruiser continued southwards through the Strait of Dover and course was set for Gibraltar. After another short stop in the colony the *Blake* pressed on south, for with the Suez Canal closed she had to make the passage east via Cape Town. On Thursday 12 March the cruiser crossed the equator with all due ceremony, and on the following day she anchored off Ascension Island. After eight days at sea there was the opportunity for some welcome recreational leave, but only after a rather hazardous transfer from boat to jetty and back again for the return journey. The helicopters of 820 Squadron were able to assist the local community by sowing some casuarina grass seed by air onto an inaccessible area of the island. Two days later the *Blake* anchored off Jamestown, St Helena, which at first sight

appeared to be even more barren than Ascension Island. Fortunately that impression was deceptive and those who ventured ashore to attend the church service at the island's cathedral were treated to the unusual and alarming experience of being crammed into rather ancient 'bone-shaking' trucks, which the locals optimistically called buses, and being driven at breakneck speed through the town, round some sharp hairpin bends on the edge of a hill, and up to the cathedral, set in magnificent gardens. The congregation included the island's Scout and Guide groups and the Boys' Brigade band proudly led the parade back to the town. The shore party then visited Napoleon's home and tomb which in those days was still situated on St Helena, before they returned to the ship and the *Blake* set course for Cape Town.

The visit to South Africa came at a time when political pressure the world over was beginning to affect various sporting events, and at the time of the *Blake's* arrival a South African cricket tour of England was about to be cancelled. Fortunately this atmosphere did not adversely affect the cruiser's visit and the officers and men were treated to hospitality on a grand scale, with invitations for receptions, barbecues, bus tours and private parties pouring into the ship. On leaving Cape Town on Wednesday 25 March the *Blake* headed across the Indian Ocean for Mauritius, where she was due to arrive on 30 March to hoist the flag of the Flag Officer, Second in Command, Far East Station, Rear-Admiral T. T. Lewin, when he flew on board from RFA *Stromness.* Initially there was some mild interest on board in two tropical cyclones in the area, Louise and Michelle, but when on the night of Friday 27 March, with H1 and H2 boiler tubes badly damaged and leaking, Louise changed course towards the cruiser, the mild interest turned to concern. With the *Blake's* power greatly reduced FO2 cancelled his proposed visit and Captain Plugge decided to turn 180° in an attempt to skirt round the outside of the storm, the eye of which was only 150 miles away. Fortunately this manoeuvre was successful, but even so the *Blake* came within 130 miles of the eye of the cyclone and met with Force 6 winds and heavy seas. The *Stromness* was not so fortunate and she went right through the storm, with its winds of 110 knots and mountainous seas. It was an experience which the *Blake,* with her reduced power, was lucky to avoid.

Following the cancellation of her Mauritius visit, the *Blake* continued across the Indian Ocean, stopping briefly at Albany to embark a specialist boiler engineer to work on the least damaged of the two units, before steaming across the Great Australian Bight to arrive in Port Adelaide on Saturday 11 April. The visit coincided with South Australia's celebrations of the Cook Bicentenary Year. During her one week's stay in the city the people of Adelaide did everything possible to make the ship's company most welcome, including inviting them into their

HMS *Blake* at speed.   *(Fleet Air Arm Museum)*

always, throughout the visit the personal invitations flowed in for the ship's company.

On Monday 27 April, during the visit to Sydney, there was a change of command when Captain R. D. Butt RN, who joined the ship direct from the shore establishment HMS *Dryad,* relieved Captain Plugge who, after 18 months in command, flew home to a well-earned retirement.

After leaving Sydney, which was unanimously voted the highlight of the commission, the *Blake* steamed north up the Australian coast and inside the Great Barrier Reef, bound for Singapore. Unfortunately, soon after leaving harbour there was a very dramatic 'flame out' in one of the boiler rooms, which left the cruiser with no power, forcing her to anchor very quickly indeed. By the following morning the engineers had restored power and the *Blake* was able to continue her passage to Singapore where, upon her arrival, she was placed in dockyard hands for major repairs to her damaged boilers. The repairs actually took 13 weeks, but there were few complaints from the ship's company who moved into the comfortable shore accommodation at HMS *Terror,* while the squadron went to RNAS Simbang from where they could continue their flying operations. The cruiser also missed a major exercise in the South China Sea, involving more than 40 ships from four nations, which was designed to bring vessels and men of the Australian, British, Malaysian and New Zealand Navies to the peak of efficiency when working together. Once again there were few complaints from the ship's company at the prospect of missing the exercise, although the *Blake's* engineers hardly had the easy option as they had to work hard to repair the damaged boilers and to put right the many machinery defects which had accumulated in the ship.

The *Blake* eventually left Singapore on Monday 3 August, bound for Hong Kong and for a much modified and shorter visit to Japan than had originally been planned. However, the arrival in Hong Kong saw the *Blake* alongside with more machinery problems, this time in the form of 'condenseritis', and once again the engineers were kept busy removing and fitting tubes, this time in an engine room, as they toiled to overcome their latest problem. Unfortunately, because of this setback the proposed trip to Japan had to be cancelled and when the cruiser sailed from Hong Kong it was on a homeward course by way of the Beira Patrol, Cape Town and Gibraltar, leaving the Chief Writer to work out what to do with the 10,500,000 yen he had obtained for the trip to Japan. Happily the main boilers and engines behaved well on the return passage, and despite all the programme changes which had bedevilled the commission, the *Blake* arrived at the Outer Spit Buoy at Spithead on the morning of Tuesday 27 October, exactly on schedule. Soon afterwards she entered harbour and berthed alongside in Portsmouth Dockyard. Although she was nine years old, it was the end of only her second commission.

homes. Back on board, however, the engineers were hard at work trying to repair the boilers, but it soon became clear that it would be necessary to retube both of them and arrangements were made for the work to be carried out in Singapore Dockyard. After leaving Adelaide the *Blake* steamed the few miles down the coast to anchor off Glenelg, and in so doing she became the first British warship to visit the town since the 1920s. Her visit coincided with the incorporation of Glenelg as a city in its own right, and the cruiser also acted as the guardship for a sailing regatta which had been organized. After leaving Glenelg the *Blake* set course for Sydney where she met vessels from several other navies, and the royal yacht *Britannia* which, with the Queen and other members of the Royal Family, was there to celebrate the 200th anniversary of Captain Cook's arrival in Botany Bay. The *Blake* was given a 'plum' berth at Garden Island, with an uninterrupted view of the Harbour Bridge and the Opera House which was then under construction. On Wednesday 29 April, which was Bicentenary Day, there was a spectacular water carnival and fireworks display and, as

HMS *Blake* at Spithead for the Queen's Silver Jubilee Review in June 1977. *(D.Smith)*

Flying her paying-off pennant, the *Blake* enters Portsmouth Harbour for the last time on 6 December 1979. *(D. Smith)*

Chapter Twelve

HMS *Blake* - Showing The Flag 1971-1975

In the early 1970s, with the introduction into the Royal Navy of 'trickle' drafting, the traditional recommissioning ceremonies became something of a novelty, and following the *Blake's* refit which ended in the spring of 1971 there was no formal ceremony to mark the start of a new phase in the ship's career. Instead it was straight to Portland for the inevitable trials and work-up period.

For the *Blake* the highlight of 1971 took place in the autumn of that year when, after visiting Caribbean ports, she made her transit of the Panama Canal and set course for Acapulco in Mexico, where the ship's company were able to take advantage of the sun and the surf at this well-known resort. On leaving Mexico the *Blake* headed for San Francisco to take part in 'British Week', which was the biggest commercial and cultural event ever staged in the city by another nation. However, soon after leaving Acapulco the cruiser met hurricane Olivia, which meant a change of course in order to avoid steaming through the centre of the storm, and as a result she was a day late in arriving at San Francisco. Nevertheless, the *Blake* made an impressive sight as she steamed under the Golden Gate Bridge with her decks manned. As she passed the Treasure Island naval base she fired a 13-gun salute to the Senior Officer, and the ship's company stood smartly to attention. As they tied up alongside, few on board had any idea of the extent of the hospitality which their American hosts were to lavish on them and the ship. The press had afforded 'British Week' a great deal of publicity, in particular by giving the *Blake's* friendly invasion a tremendous build-up which, in turn, accorded the sailors ashore almost a 'star quality'.

The event was opened by Princess Alexandra at the San Francisco City Hall, where a 100-strong Royal Guard from the *Blake* paraded for the opening ceremony. It was a rare and historical occasion, for it was one of the few times that a British Royal Guard had paraded on the streets of an American city since the Declaration of Independence in 1776. On conclusion of the ceremony the bands of the Royal Scots and the Royal Artillery headed the Royal Guard as they paraded the Queen's Colour on a two-mile march from the City Hall to Union Square, where most of the 'British Week' activities were to take place. That evening there was an official reception on board the *Blake* for 300 people who were closely involved with the promotion. The cruiser's ship's company took part in nearly every event of the week, from supplying guides in stores at the main exhibitions, to attending events such as the Highland Games and other specially organized British displays. On the day after the opening ceremony Princess

Alexandra and her husband, Sir Angus Ogilvy, toured the *Blake* and had lunch on board. Ashore the regimental bands, London 'bobbies' and buses, a Blackpool tram, a mock-Tudor pub, the Flying Scotsman steam locomotive, British goods in the big department stores and British drama and music in the city's theatres, ensured that San Francisco certainly had more than a flavour of Britain about it. The exhibitions included a large scale-model of HMS *Victory*, complete with various artefacts from the museum in Portsmouth Dockyard. The *Blake's* chaplain, the Revd D. Baxter, preached at a Battle of Britain memorial service at the city's Grace Cathedral, and the US Navy's aircraft carrier, USS *Ranger*, organized coach tours and social functions for the *Blake's* officers and men. One of the biggest events organized for the ship's company was a dance given by the British-American Club on Wednesday 6 October. It was attended by about 450 members of the ship's company and the success of the occasion was enhanced by the fact that the men were greatly outnumbered by the ladies, who were there in their hundreds. The *Blake* herself was opened to the public over three days, and she attracted some 12,000 visitors. The VIP guests on board included the film star Rex Harrison, the Lord Mayor of London and even 'Miss London Stores', a young lady who had won the beauty competition and the trip-of-a-lifetime. Another official visitor was the Minister of Trade who flew over especially for the event, but he was not nearly as popular as the group of fashion models who presented a televised 'In Fashion' spectacular on board the ship. The cruiser's rugby and soccer teams were in action, and even the cricket team got an outing in a country not noted for its love of the game. On Sunday 10 October, flying Nelson's famous Trafalgar signal, the *Blake* acted as guardship for the Corinthian Yacht Club Regatta in San Francisco Bay, before slipping out of a fogbound harbour next day on conclusion of the festivities, bound for San Diego.

Following this popular US sojourn the *Blake* made her return transatlantic passage by way of Tenerife where she docked alongside the harbour at Santa Cruz, not far from the local yacht club's old cannon 'El Tigre' which, according to a plaque on its side, fired the grapeshot which shattered Nelson's right arm when he attempted to capture Santa Cruz in 1797. After calling at Gibraltar, where the ship's company raised a further £300 for the local hospital by walking backwards from the ship to the top of the Rock, the *Blake* steamed east for Malta where she was to spend Christmas.

The island of Malta had been granted its independence

HMS *Blake* in the Channel in the early 1970s. Note the Sea King helicopter of 820 Squadron on the flight deck.

(FotoFlite)

Heavy weather in the Atlantic Ocean as the *Blake* steams into Force 10 winds and enormous seas.

(G. Malcolmson)

in September 1964, and the *Blake's* sister ship *Lion* had been present at the ceremony, but ever since the end of the Second World War the island's relations with the Royal Navy had been changing as successive British Governments made cuts to their defence budgets which, in turn, reduced the number of ships in commission. By the end of the 1960s the Royal Navy's small force based in Malta had become a shadow of its former self, and the buoys of Grand Harbour were dominated by cruise ships carrying vast numbers of holidaymakers, rather than the mighty battleships of pre-war days with their thousands of sailors. In 1964 a Defence Agreement had been negotiated which gave the British Government the right to remain in its Maltese bases for a further ten years, but even so the rundowns continued and there is no doubt that they hit the Maltese economy hard. When Mr Dom Mintoff was elected Prime Minister in 1971, he requested that the NATO Headquarters leave the island, and he also indicated his wish to renegotiate the defence agreement with Britain. Diplomatic relations between the two governments reached an all-time low and on 30 November 1971 the Maltese issued a demand for a financial supplement to an agreement which had been reached with Edward Heath at

Chequers. When this was refused Britain was ordered to withdraw its forces from Malta by 31 December 1971. The British Government agreed to this demand, but insisted that it would take at least three months. However, despite the diplomatic disagreements the withdrawal commenced, heralding a period of uncertainty and tension for the British service families and civilians concerned. Fortunately, the presence of the *Blake* moored in Grand Harbour was a reassuring sight as 'Operation Exit', the withdrawal from Malta, got under way. Besides their welcome 'presence' the *Blake* and the frigate *Euryalus* provided manpower and helicopters to move large loads of luggage and equipment to central collecting points. From the *Blake* as many as 150 ratings a day were ashore carrying out a variety of tasks, from helping families to pack their belongings and transporting them to the airport, to acting as couriers to ensure that families were on time for boarding coaches and aircraft at the Families Reception Centre at RAF Luqa. The RAF's fleet of VC10s carried out the airlift of service families, with six planes carrying up to 750 women and children. Meanwhile, for large items such as furniture and cars, the Manchester Container Lines made three of its cargo ships available to cope with the demand. The three

HMS *Blake* steams through the Panama Canal while a Sea King keeps a close eye on proceedings.

(Fleet Air Arm Museum)

main service schools on the island which catered for children of Navy, Army and RAF personnel did not reopen after the Christmas holidays and ratings from the *Blake* helped to remove and pack all the equipment and furniture which had to be returned to the UK. Much of the work consisted of manhandling heavy crates on and off lorries, while other members of the cruiser's ship's company operated fork lift trucks on the wharf and dealt with the inevitable paperwork. The *Blake's* shipwrights, meanwhile, were busy working round the clock to construct thousands of wooden crates, while the helicopters of 820 Squadron were particularly useful when they were temporarily converted to a cargo-carrying role. However, despite their demanding role in the hurried evacuation, one of the *Blake's* helicopters was still able to go on a mercy mission to lift a sick seaman from a Greek oil tanker some 90 miles from Malta.

The New Year was a hectic time but in a very different way from the usual Royal Navy celebrations in Malta, and the *Blakes* ship's company were greatly relieved to see the

arrival on Tuesday 18 January 1972 of HMS *Bulwark,* which had been sent to take over her duties. The arrival of the *Bulwark* was soon followed by the departure of the *Blake,* and the cruiser arrived in Portsmouth Dockyard on Friday 28 January to a very warm welcome from friends and relatives. There was even a musical greeting from the Band of the Royal Marines.

On 17 April 1972, whilst the *Blake* was in Portsmouth Dockyard, Captain B. M. Tovey RN took over command of the cruiser, and soon after this, with her maintenance and leave completed, the ship was back at sea once again and heading for the Mediterranean. On Tuesday 2 May she joined 90 ships from NATO countries for 'Exercise Dawn Patrol 72'. The aim of the exercise was to provide advanced training for naval air and amphibious operations, and the *Blake* was the command ship with Rear-Admiral A. J. Miller, the Amphibious Task Force Commander, flying his flag on board. It was in fact the first time that the Royal Navy had commanded the amphibious operations of such a large NATO exercise in the Mediterranean. The manoeuvres which began in the southern Aegean aroused considerable interest from Soviet naval units, which maintained a constant vigil on the ships, among them the USS *Guadalcanal, Albion, Blake, Fearless,* and the frigates *Aurora* and *Juno.* Bad weather marred the start of operations when a landing was carried out at Kevalla in Macedonia. Later the force sailed through the Aegean to Soudha Bay in Crete, with the passage being made against submarine and fast patrol boat attacks. The helicopters from both the *Blake* and the *Albion* effectively countered both forms of opposition, and at the same time their crews were able to see quite a lot of the Greek island scenery. In the final phase of the exercise the Commando Groups from the *Albion* and the *Guadalcanal* made a full assault landing into an area of southern Greece in Kyparissia Bay, where landing sites for helicopters were difficult to find, but where wild goats and ponies abounded. Following the conclusion of the exercise the whole fleet anchored in Phaleron Bay, Athens, for the official wash-up, and for a run ashore in the Greek capital.

In early July the *Blake* was back in home waters, and over three days between 13 and 16 July she took part in 'Exercise West Hoe' off the west coast of Ireland with other units of the fleet. They made up a strong force of ships, including the aircraft carrier *Ark Royal,* the commando carrier *Bulwark,* the destroyers *Caprice* and *Fife,* and the frigates *Achilles, Jaguar* and *Lynx.* Unfortunately, fog and poor visibility hampered much of the exercise and on its conclusion the fleet assembled at Devonport which was a welcome homecoming for the *Bulwark* following her Mediterranean deployment and the withdrawal from Malta. The first ship past the breakwater was the guided missile destroyer *Fife,* followed by the *Bulwark, Blake* and the destroyers and frigates. Next day the *Ark Royal* joined the 'armada', together with RFA *Tidereach,* and to complete the picture in Plymouth Sound were three units from NATO's Standing Naval Force Atlantic.

After the summer leave period the *Blake* headed north to take part in the NATO exercise code-named 'Strong Express'. It was the largest NATO amphibious exercise which had ever been staged in northern waters and once again the cruiser's helicopters were able to cross-operate with the commando carrier *Albion.* The manoeuvres involving 300 ships and 64,000 men started on Thursday 14 September in the North Sea and off the North Cape. The Royal Navy's contingent was headed by the *Ark Royal* and during the operations the men tested methods of anti-submarine warfare, minelaying and the control of merchant shipping, as well as carrying out a landing of 3,000 British, US and Dutch marines in Norway. On completion of the exercise a six-day wash-up was held at Rosyth, where the *Blake's* most popular visitor was not some foreign Admiral, but the glamorous 'Miss Fife', who made the draw in the ship's raffle. Unfortunately, her choice of ticket was not quite so popular, for the winner of the first prize, a brand new car, had left the ship on draft some two months earlier. After leaving Rosyth the *Blake* headed for Portsmouth, where she was to undergo a long refit.

It was in the early summer of 1973 that the *Blake* returned to sea once again, and for some weeks she operated from Spithead and Portland. During her Sea Days in the Spithead area she took two groups of nursing sisters from the Naval Hospital at Haslar to sea for a day to give them some idea of life aboard one of HM Ships, for prior to this most of the sailors whom the girls had met were usually in-patients at the hospital. Each group spent the day getting acquainted with the cruiser, steering the ship, viewing the machinery spaces and, as a highlight, taking a flight in one of the cruiser's Sea King helicopters.

In mid-February 1974 the *Blake* was one of 14 Royal Naval units which steamed west for the Caribbean and a series of exercises in the area code-named 'Caribtrain'. Although it entailed a good deal of hard work for the ships' companies it was an opportunity to enjoy some winter sunshine as well. During the deployment the cruiser berthed alongside in San Juan, and one intrepid Petty Officer decided to invite the pop star Engelbert Humperdinck and the film star Liza Minelli, who were appearing in cabaret in the city, on board the *Blake.* Much to his surprise and delight both of them accepted the invitation, and there is no doubt that Miss Minelli, with her irrepressible personality and charm, was one of the cruiser's most popular visitors. She was shown round the ship and, as a guest of 2G2 POs' mess, signed hundreds of autographs. As a reciprocal gesture she invited members of the ship's company to her show that evening. In the event the invitation spread to other ships in San Juan and in all 750 sailors turned up to see Miss Minelli give one of her very lively cabaret performances.

By the end of March the *Blake* was back at Portsmouth and on 22 April there was another change of command when Captain P. G. M. Herbert OBE RN took over from Captain Tobey. Essentially Captain Herbert was a submariner, but he had commanded the frigate *Venus* in the early 1960s in addition to the submarines *Scythian, Porpoise* and *Excalibur* and the nuclear-powered submarine *Valiant.* His first deployment after taking command was to northern waters for a visit to Gothenburg in company with the frigate *Llandaff.* They arrived to a musical reception on the jetty and the residents of the city went out of their way to make the ships' companies most welcome. When the cruiser was opened to visitors during the weekend over 2,000 people toured the ship. One evening the *Blake's* wardroom hosted an unusual reception on the cruiser's quarterdeck for members of the Royal Gota Artillery Regiment and their ladies. The regiment itself had been disbanded, but its 19th-century uniforms had been revived and the cruiser's quarterdeck made an ideal setting in

A view of HM Ships *Warspite* and *Falmouth* and the RFA *Green Rover* taken from the *Blake* during Task Group 317.2's deployment to the Far East and South America. *(G. Malcolmson)*

Refuelling at sea from RFA *Tideflow* during the Far Eastern deployment. *(P. Turner)*

which to entertain the guests who were all decked out in their colourful finery. Following this visit the *Blake* called at Wilhelmshaven in Germany which was another very popular run ashore. This time the cruiser was accompanied by the frigate *Lowestoft*, and Captain Herbert and Commander P. Dingemans RN, the *Lowestoft's* CO, laid a wreath to commemorate the Battle of Jutland. When the *Blake* was opened to the public here over 10,000 visitors flocked on board.

The summer of 1974 and Cowes Week saw the *Blake* in Portsmouth where she played host to the Italian square-rigged sailing ship *Amerigo Vespucci,* which had completed the tall ships race. The Italian vessel was berthed at South Railway Jetty, close to the *Blake,* and her crews were able to visit the cruiser to compare 'sail' with 'steam'. However, this was a diversion for the *Blake's* ship's company who were preparing the cruiser for her next duty of heading Task Group 317.2's nine-month deployment to the Far East and South America. The *Blake* was flying the flag of the Flag Officer First Flotilla, Vice-Admiral H. C. Leach, and as well as the cruiser the group comprised the nuclear-powered submarine *Warspite,* the frigates *Achilles, Diomede, Falmouth, Leander* and *Lowestoft,* with the RFAs *Green Rover, Olna* and *Stromness.* The *Blake* left Portsmouth on Tuesday 17 September, accompanied by the *Falmouth* and the *Lowestoft* and two of the RFAs. Although it was a fine autumn day when they left Spithead they soon ran into thick patches of coastal fog, but that evening they rendezvoused with the other frigates and course was set for Gibraltar. During the passage the group carried out 'Exercise Bashex', which was essentially a work-up for the ships' companies to get used to working together.

With the Suez Canal closed to shipping the group steamed south to Cape Town, and as they crossed the equator King Neptune visited the ships and subjected his victims to the traditional duckings. From Gibraltar a non-stop passage was made to Cape Town where, as always, the hospitality shown to the men was second to none. On leaving South Africa the group headed for Mombasa for maintenance, and during the seven days there the ships' companies were able to enjoy the nightlife and the beaches to the full. As the ships steamed into Kilindini Harbour crowds of British nationals lined the shore at Nyali to wave them in, for Kenya was now well and truly on the package-holiday itinerary. During the stay in Mombasa the *Warspite* berthed alongside the *Blake,* for prior to the deployment it had been planned that the cruiser would act as a depot and support ship for the nuclear-powered submarine, or 'the tube' as she became known. The *Blake* carried spares for the submarine, and her ship's company were able to use the cruiser's bathroom and laundry facilities as well as the dining halls. It was after the group left Mombasa that work began in earnest as they steamed north-east to join the US Navy units, including the giant aircraft carrier USS

Constellation, whereupon the joint fleet set course for Karachi which was the assembly port for 'Exercise Midlink', involving units from the host country, Pakistan, the USA, Turkey, Iran and Britain, all countries of the Central Treaty Organization (CENTO). The aim of 'Midlink' was to exercise all the ships in current aspects of maritime warfare, with an emphasis on the protection of convoys and task forces against air, surface and submarine threats. As usual with this type of exercise there were always uninvited guests, in this case they took the form of a Soviet Sverdlov-class cruiser together with its accompanying intelligence-gathering ships. Vice-Admiral Leach was in tactical command of the exercise involving 48 ships and 150 aircraft and also on board the *Blake* were the C-in-C Fleet, Admiral Sir Terence Lewin, and VIPs from the five CENTO nations involved. The finale included gunnery firings and a steam past by the *Warspite* and the US submarine *Plunger,* while the CENTO air forces staged a fly-past.

From the exercise areas the task group set course for Singapore, and on the way the cruiser's Sea Kings assisted in an unsuccessful search for survivors of an air crash off Sri Lanka. At Singapore the group berthed in the old naval base for a five-day maintenance period which came as a welcome break after the long spell at sea. During the brief stay in Singapore the facilities of the familiar old naval base were used to the full, but unfortunately, being on the island's north coast, it was a long way from Singapore City and so no one was too sorry to leave and head for the ever-popular run ashore of Hong Kong.

However, the stopover in Hong Kong over the Christmas and New Year holidays was not all play as the ship had to prepare for FOF1's Inspection. Meanwhile, the Sea Kings of 820 Squadron flew ashore and, with the rest of the squadron personnel, continued to operate from RAF Kai Tak on the outskirts of Kowloon. It was whilst they were ashore that, on Christmas Eve, the crews of the aircraft were called upon to assist in the search for an overdue yacht. Fortunately, shortly before they took off the yacht was spotted cruising safely off one of Hong Kong's outlying islands, and the squadron was able to stand down. However, early in the New Year two Sea Kings from the squadron were scrambled after an urgent request for medical assistance was received from a merchantman, MV *Able Reefer.* It was not this vessel herself which was in trouble, but the Panamanian freighter, MV *Asia Lake,* whose crew had abandoned ship about 180 miles out of Hong Kong after a fire on board had killed one member of her crew and injured four others. The *Able Reefer* had picked up the survivors, but with no medical facilities on board she had had to radio for help. Ably assisted by a Cessna aircraft of the Hong Kong Auxiliary Air Force, the two Sea Kings, flown by Lieutenants Mike Watson and Loring Nichols USN, with an RAF doctor on board to give immediate medical attention, soon found the *Able Reefer.*

The *Blake* refuelling at sea from the *Ark Royal* during exercises off the coast of Brazil.

(*P. Turner*)

The injured men were then winched aboard one of the Sea Kings while the other stood by, but with the helicopters operating at the limit of their range there was little room for error or delay. So tight was the fuel situation that the helicopter carrying the casualties had to refuel at Kai Tak before landing them at the Queen Elizabeth Hospital in Kowloon. During the stay in Hong Kong, as well as frequenting the bars and nightclubs of Wanchai, the ship's company found time for some sporting activities and joined forces with men from the *Chichester, Falmouth* and *Tamar,* to take on local clubs at rugby and soccer. In the event the Navy team won their rugby matches, but did not fare so well at soccer. The *Blake* herself was given a complete facelift, courtesy of Jenny's Side Party, with the whole of the superstructure and hull and a lot of between-deck spaces being repainted. No doubt many of the officers and men would have liked to remain in Hong Kong much longer, even if it did mean preparing for FOF1's Harbour Inspection, but all too soon it was time to put to sea again.

After leaving Hong Kong the *Blake, Diomede, Lowestoft, Warspite,* HMAS *Swan* and RFA *Stromness* steamed back into the South China Sea where they operated with the Thai Navy which, although it was small and consisted of mainly ex-US Navy ships, was very efficient. During a lull in the exercises they made a call at Kota Kinabalu (formerly Jesselton), where full advantage was taken of the idyllic banyan beaches which have now been discovered by package holiday companies, but which in those days were unspoilt and virtually deserted. A few hardy souls even managed to climb Mount Kinabalu. Once the exercises were over the *Blake* and her group, apart from the *Warspite* which visited the US Naval Base at Sattahip, paid a seven-day courtesy visit to Bangkok where they were warmly received, with the event being given wide coverage in the local newspapers and on radio and television. The general opinion on board was that, although expensive, Bangkok was a 'good run ashore'. On leaving Thailand, with Cambodia's long and bitter war coming to an end, and with the communist forces of the Khmer Rouge laying siege to the country's capital, Phnom Penh, the *Blake* was ordered to stand by to evacuate all non-essential members of the British Embassy in the city, and any other British nationals. In preparation the Sea King helicopters had the Union Flag painted on their sides, and their crews were given small arms weapons training, which mainly consisted of 'shooting-up' plastic gash bags as they floated by, and also the Met Officer's balloon. In the event the *Blake's* services were not required, and she left the area for Hong Kong once again. There the final touches were made to the cruiser's paintwork, before Vice-Admiral Leach carried out his Harbour Inspection and Chinese New Year was celebrated. During the Ceremonial Divisions which formed part of the Harbour Inspection, Vice-Admiral Leach presented Flag Officer Naval Air Command's Commendation to Lt R. W.

The *Blake* follows the *Ark Royal* into Rio de Janeiro Harbour. (G. Malcolmson)

Lewis of 820 Squadron, for his part in an air-sea rescue mission in mid-January 1974 when he had flown his Sea King in 100mph gale force winds to rescue seven people from a Danish coaster, *Merc Enterprise,* which had sunk in severe storms. A Russian trawler rescued four more survivors, but seven other crew members, and the master's wife, had lost their lives in the disaster.

It was on Monday 17 February 1975 that the *Blake* and her group left Hong Kong to head south once again, this time to Manila where they were suitably entertained by both the Filipinos and the Americans. More exercises in the Subic Bay area followed, before the *Blake* returned to Singapore to carry out an assisted maintenance period at the old naval base and to prepare for the long haul back home. Whilst the ship underwent her maintenance the Sea Kings of 820 Squadron were flown off to the Singaporean Air Force Base at Tengah, where the resident RAF Squadron proved to be excellent hosts. Before leaving South-East Asia for the last time there were yet more exercises, this time in the Strait of Malacca with Malaysian and Singaporean naval units, before the *Blake* and her accompanying vessels set course across the Indian Ocean bound for the Seychelles and Cape Town. Upon departure

from South Africa, Task Group 317.2 set course north-west across the Atlantic Ocean to the coast of Brazil where they rendezvoused with the aircraft carrier *Ark Royal,* the destroyer *Hampshire,* the frigates *Achilles* and *Leander* and RFA *Resource* which had all been on a deployment with the US Navy on their Atlantic Fleet Weapons Range off Puerto Rico. They were also joined by the Brazilian Navy's destroyers *Esperito Santo, Mariz E. Barros* and *Maranhao,* all of which were ex-US Navy units. After exercising together the Royal Navy's force dispersed to various Brazilian ports, with the *Blake, Ark Royal* and *Falmouth* visiting Rio de Janeiro which, for the cruiser and the frigate, was the highlight of the deployment. The other units of the force visited Salvador and Santos. While the ships' companies explored Rio and the exotic Copacabana Beach, the residents had a chance to visit the British warships, and when the *Blake* and *Hampshire* were opened to the public more than 14,000 people flocked on board. All too soon the end of the visit meant back to work and more joint exercises with the Brazilian Navy, before the whole force steamed back home to the UK, via Gibraltar, with the *Blake* arriving in Portsmouth in mid-June for leave and maintenance.

Chapter Thirteen

HMS *Blake* - The Final Years 1975-1983

Following her return from the Far Eastern and South American deployment in the summer of 1975 the *Blake* underwent a refit in Portsmouth Dockyard, during which time the ship's company took their summer leave, but by early September that year she was back at sea again. One of her first duties was to join a NATO exercise in the South Western Approaches, which also included three nuclear-powered US Navy warships, the submarine *Seahorse,* the cruiser *South Carolina,* and the world's biggest warship at that time, the *Nimitz.* By mid-September the *Blake* was back at Portsmouth and on Friday 10 October 1975 there was a change of command when Captain D. M. Eckersley-Maslin RN relieved Captain Herbert. Captain Eckersley-Maslin had entered the Navy in the late 1940s and he had qualified as a Navigation Direction Officer in the early 1950s. For two years he served with the Australian

Navy and in the 1960s he commanded the frigates *Eastbourne* and *Euryalus,* and the destroyer *Fife,* before being appointed to the Royal Navy's Presentation Team. It was from this latter appointment that he joined the *Blake.*

In early November Vice-Admiral Leach was succeeded as the Flag Officer First Flotilla by Vice-Admiral A. S. Morton, who hoisted his flag in the *Blake,* and the cruiser joined 'Exercise Ocean Safari' in northern waters. This major NATO exercise involved 75 ships and 17,000 men from the UK, USA, Canada, Denmark, West Germany, Holland and Norway. The Royal Navy's contingent was led by the aircraft carrier *Ark Royal,* and as well as the *Blake* it included the *Hermes, Devonshire, Bacchante, Eskimo* and *Tartar,* the submarines *Finwhale, Osiris, Otter* and *Sovereign,* and seven RFAs. The exercise was designed to provide the NATO navies with realistic training in all

The *Blake* exercising with the US Navy's giant aircraft carrier *Nimitz* in September 1975. *(P. Turner)*

aspects of maritime warfare under the adverse conditions found in the Norwegian Sea during the winter. The *Blake* was Commander ASW Group II, and needless to say this impressive presence attracted great interest from Soviet forces, making it right from the start a case of, 'We're watching you watching us.' The *Ark Royal's* Phantoms were kept busy intercepting the Russian Tupolev TU-95 (Bear) reconnaissance aircraft over the fleet, and conditions on the *Blake's* small flight deck were cold, wet and dangerously slippery. In the subsurface 'war' several 'kills' were recorded by her helicopters and the ship herself actually reached the Arctic Circle whilst refuelling, which earned the ship's company their 'Bluenose' certificates. In the *Blake's* case the exercise was followed by visits to warmer waters, calling at Gibraltar and the picturesque Atlantic island of Madeira, where she secured alongside the breakwater at Funchal.

Following Christmas and New Year leave and a short maintenance period at Portsmouth, the *Blake* paid a visit to Cardiff to liaise with the Bridgwater Sea Cadets, whose President was the Deputy Lieutenant of Somerset, Admiral Sir Mark Pizey. Later came 'Exercise Springtrain' with the *Ark Royal* off Gibraltar, and a spell of duty in the North Sea carrying out patrols in the area and escorting Russian vessels. At one stage she was nearly caught up in the fishing disputes between Britain and Iceland, which had resulted in the frigate *Andromeda* being rammed by an Icelandic gunboat, and the breaking off of diplomatic relations by Iceland as the disagreements escalated into what became known as the 'Cod Wars'. In May 1976 the cruiser was given the honour of showing the White Ensign during 'British Week' in the Dutch City of Rotterdam. Senior ratings from the ship attended a reception held by the City's Burgomaster, at which the guest of honour was the British Government minister, Roy Jenkins, while some more unusual guests included a Pearly King and Queen. At night the ship was a blaze of light when the floodlights were switched on, and during the daylight hours there were ample opportunities for members of the ship's company to see the city, and to relax in the sunshine with a glass of beer. From Rotterdam the *Blake* steamed north to make a transit of the Kiel Canal, and to visit the German naval base for the renowned 'Kieler Woche', where she represented the Royal Navy in the world famous sailing regattas. Also at this time 820 Squadron were awarded two trophies; the Kelvin Hughes Vectac Trophy and Best Aircrewman of 1975, which went to Leading Aircrewman A. J. Cooper. Both awards were presented by Flag Officer Carriers and Amphibious Ships, Rear-Admiral J. H. F. Eberle, when he visited the ship.

In early June, back at Portsmouth, the *Blake* played host to the powerful Russian Kashin-class guided missile destroyer, *Obraztsovy*, which was making the first official Soviet Navy visit to Portsmouth since the controversy surrounding the cruiser *Ordzhonikidze* in May 1956 when the naval diver Commander Lionel (Buster) Crabbe disappeared in mysterious circumstances resulting in strained diplomatic relations between Britain and the Soviet Union. Fortunately nothing marred this latest occasion and on conclusion of the Soviets' stay the Flag Officer Portsmouth sent the following signal to the *Blake*: 'I was well pleased with the efforts of all who contributed towards the success of the *Obraztsovy* visit. Clearly a great deal of hard work had been involved in planning and preparing the visit and equally in ensuring that the programme was efficiently and professionally executed. The Soviets were full of praise for the manner in which the Royal Navy hosted their visit and were particularly impressed by the friendly response that they received at all times.' As well as playing their part in ensuring that the Soviet Navy did not achieve its aim of world domination, the officers and men of the *Blake* had also played their part in fostering warmth and friendship which, in its own way, would one day help to bring about the end of the Cold War. During the remainder of June 1976 the *Blake*, wearing the flag of FOF2, Rear-Admiral F. D. E. Fieldhouse, carried out a programme of Staff College Sea Days from Spithead, before returning to Devonport to pay off and to undergo a long refit.

On Monday 6 December 1976 there was another change of command when Captain H. B. Parker RN relieved Captain Eckersley-Maslin, and in the spring of 1977 the *Blake* was at sea once again. During that summer she operated from Portland with the destroyer *Sheffield* and the frigate *Active*. On Tuesday 28 June 1977 the *Blake* joined her sister ship *Tiger* at Spithead for The Queen's Silver Jubilee Review of the Fleet. The event involved some 180 ships and was the largest fleet review since that held for the Coronation in 1953. It was also the first review held at Spithead in which battleships did not take part and the C-in-C Fleet, Admiral Sir Henry Leach, was flying his flag in the soon to be withdrawn aircraft carrier, *Ark Royal*. The *Blake* formed part of the First Flotilla which was led by the guided missile destroyer HMS *London*, flying the flag of Rear-Admiral R. R. Squires. For two hours on a cold and blustery day, the *Britannia*, led by the Trinity House vessel *Patricia*, cruised at eight knots down the 15-mile circuit of the assembled fleet, after which 90 helicopters took part in a Fleet Air Arm fly-past.

Following Christmas and New Year leave, in the early weeks of 1978, the *Blake* visited UK ports, including Liverpool, before steaming south to Gibraltar and the warmer waters of the Mediterranean Sea where she took part in a NATO exercise. This was followed by exercises off the east coast of Scotland and a visit to Hull. In May 1978 the *Blake* led ten ships of 'Group Seven Deployment', including the frigates *Ambuscade*, *Hermione*, *Leander* and *Juno*, the nuclear-powered fleet submarine *Conqueror* and three RFAs, under the command of FOF1, Rear-Admiral

HMS *Blake* closes to store from RFA *Regent* during exercises in the North Sea, in June 1975.

(George Mortimore/Action Photos)

R. R. Squires, on a seven-month deployment to the Pacific off the West Coast of the USA and Canada. En route the group exercised with the French Navy, and made a short visit to Brest before steaming on to Bermuda where a painting of the *Blake's* crest was added to the many others which were already displayed on the dockyard walls. During the passage to Bermuda 820 Squadron celebrated its 1,000th landing of the commission on the cruiser's flight deck. The destroyer *Birmingham* joined the group in the Caribbean and then the ships put in to the old Spanish town of Cartagena in Colombia. The small Colombian Navy proved to be excellent hosts, while the town itself afforded a warm welcome with good beaches and hot sunshine. The *Blake* reciprocated the hospitality with a party for local orphan children. Admiral Squires, Captain Parker and the British Ambassador to Colombia laid a wreath in honour of Simon Bolivar, the country's national hero, during an impressive ceremony in which the *Blake's* Guard exercised the Royal Navy's privilege of marching through the streets of Cartagena with bayonets fixed. On board the *Blake* Anglo-Colombian bonds were further strengthened when Admiral Squires presented engravings of

HMS *Victory* to two young Colombian naval officers who had passed out of the country's Naval Academy. The British Defence Attaché, Lieutenant-Colonel M. Liley, travelled to Cartagena from Bogota to assist with the visit and then took passage in the *Blake* for her transit of the Panama Canal.

Next on the programme for the group was a four-week assisted maintenance period at the US Naval Base at San Diego which, needless to say, proved extremely popular with everyone on board. This was followed by exercises with the US and Canadian Navies in the Pacific, and a visit to Esquimalt, the Canadian base on Vancouver Island. However, the highlight of the deployment was undoubtedly a visit to San Francisco where, despite a 'welcome' in the form of protests by small groups of IRA sympathisers, the sailors of the Group Seven Deployment went on to win the admiration of the local community. In the event the visit proved a particularly valuable contribution to Anglo-American relations. The local newspapers paid tribute to the good humour and restraint of the sailors in turning aside what they described as the 'contrived wrath' of the demonstrators, and winning the hearts of ordinary citizens. The *Blake's* cycling relay team even completed a marathon

1,057-mile ride from Vancouver to San Francisco. Camping out each night, they completed the journey in eight days and collected a substantial amount of sponsorship money for an old people's home back in Hull. Altogether the Group Seven ships called at 42 ports and took part in four major exercises with units of the Dutch, French, German, Canadian, Mexican, Dominican and US Navies. They had steamed 32,000 miles but, to everyone's relief, they arrived home in time for Christmas, with the *Blake* returning to Portsmouth.

On 3 January 1979 there was a final change of command when Captain D. J. Mackenzie RN took over from Captain Parker. Captain Mackenzie had entered the Royal Navy in 1943 and during the following 29 years he served in the East Indies, the Far East, Home and Mediterranean Fleets. He had commanded HMML *6011,* and HM Ships *Brinkley, Barrington, Hardy, Lincoln, Hermione,* and as Captain F8, the frigate *Ajax.* Four months later, in May 1979, the *Blake* was the star attraction for a very cold and wet Spring Bank Holiday Navy Days at Chatham when some 37,000 visitors crowded on board. Despite the wind and rain the cruiser's helicopters put on a search and rescue operation in the dockyard's No 3 basin, when two Wrens were 'saved' several times over the course of the three-day event.

Within a few weeks, however, it was becoming clear that the *Blake's* career was nearing its end, for on Thursday 29 June the government announced that the Armed Forces were suffering from a chronic shortage of 15,500 men. It seemed that many highly skilled soldiers, sailors and airmen had applied for early retirement because pay had lagged behind that for comparable work in civilian life. The Royal Navy was some 2,000 to 2,500 under strength and it was announced that, during the course of the next 14 months, six warships would be prematurely paid off into reserve to help relieve the acute shortage of both officers and men. The *Blake* was the largest of the ships to be withdrawn, the other five being Tribal-class frigates, all of which had been designed in the 1950s for service in the Persian Gulf. It was announced that the *Blake,* which was by that time the last of the Royal Navy's cruisers, would join the Standby Squadron at Chatham in December 1979. But before then, in August that year, she took the families of her officers and men out to sea for a day to observe manoeuvres with the fast patrol boat HMS *Scimitar* off the Isle of Wight. Also that summer, flying the flag of the C-in-C Fleet, she undertook a sunny and warm Baltic cruise, which included visits to Stockholm and Kiel.

The *Blake's* final deployment, in the autumn of 1979, was to the Mediterranean, where 'Old Snakey' as she was affectionately known, proved that she was still full of life by maintaining 30 knots during a full-power trial west of Corsica. Prior to entering the Mediterranean, she took part in 'Exercise Ocean Safari' in the Atlantic Ocean, and

during a six-day stay in Gibraltar a full-scale divisional sports competition was held, the outcome of which was decided on the sixth, and final, event – the Rock race. This was won by the Wardroom team, who took the overall prize for the whole event, in spite of a fine effort by 820 Squadron. In addition visits were arranged to Livorno and Genoa in Italy, during which one member of the ship's company managed an audience with Pope John Paul II, at St Peter's Square in Vatican City.

The end for HMS *Blake* came on Thursday 6 December 1979 when she fired her 6-inch guns for the last time. It concluded a century of tradition for the Royal Navy as the last of the big-gun warships fired her final salvo. On her approach to Portsmouth Harbour for the last time her Sea King helicopters flew overhead as she prepared to pay off, thus ending a decade's association between the *Blake* and 820 Squadron, which left to join the *Hermes.* The Royal Navy's last cruiser spent the early weeks of January 1980 at Rosyth Dockyard where she had arrived under her own steam, the biggest ship to enter the dry dock there since the depot ship HMS *Adamant* in 1962. During her stay in Rosyth the cruiser underwent essential maintenance and was dehumidified to protect her against the elements whilst in low category reserve. Her guns, radar and other equipment were sealed in plastic cocoons and all her deck openings were sealed up. In May 1980 she was towed to Chatham Dockyard to join the Standby Squadron, and for almost three years she lay alone and neglected, receiving only minimum maintenance.

In the autumn of 1982 came the final episode in the *Blake's* career when she was placed on the disposal list, and in early November she was sold to Shipbreaking (Queenborough) Ltd for demolition at the Scottish port of Cairnryan. She left Chatham on her final journey on Friday 30 October 1982, under the tow of two of the RMAS tugs, *Roysterer* and *Typhoon,* and six days later at the mouth of Loch Ryan two commercial tugs took over. She was finally secured alongside Cairnryan's deep water wharf to await her fate at the hands of the demolition team that had already dismantled a number of the Navy's capital ships, including the aircraft carriers *Centaur, Eagle* and *Ark Royal,* as well as a number of frigates.

One of the last people to see the *Blake,* still more or less intact, was Ian Johnstone from Glasgow who recalls his visit to Cairnryan on Saturday 15 January 1983: 'This was not the first time I had seen HMS *Blake.* As a boy, nearly 23 years before, I remember peering over the wall at Fairfield's shipyard to see her under completion in the fitting-out basin. This time, although her appearance had altered considerably, the view was essentially the same – the road to Cairnryan suddenly opened out to reveal the pale grey upperworks of the cruiser, stripped of her masthead radar, but unmistakable nevertheless with her squat tower bridge and slender funnels.

The *Blake's* 6-inch guns in action, and...

...the Sea Cat missile. *(P. Turner)*

A Sea King helicopter stages an SAR incident during FOCAS Inspection in February 1976. *(Fleet Air Arm Museum)*

tangled heap on the pier. A sudden shower of sparks indicated that work was in full progress on the hangar, the starboard side of which had already been shorn away. A large - tracked jib crane was busy manoeuvring a section of the hangar off the ship onto the pier for reduction to smaller bits.

Climbing up the gangway amidships, I made my way through the ship to the base of the forward superstructure. On board there was no lighting or power of any description, making a good torch an absolute necessity. If her external appearance was almost as normal, then devastation reigned inside. The decks were strewn with debris of all kinds, fittings had been ripped off their fixings, pipes and ventilation trunks were ruptured, and smashed telephone handsets dangled from their shock-proof mountings. All hatches and doors were open and, although I was not familiar with the ship's layout, I made quick progress to the bridge. Much of the equipment I had expected to find there, tele- graphs etc, had already been removed, and on the port side the breakers had removed one of the bridge windows to recover the metal frame which held it in place. The wind blowing across Loch Ryan was ripping through that space at what seemed to be something approaching supersonic speed. Many of the deck panels had been lifted to reveal a massive network of cables running to the Operations Room behind, and no doubt to every other part of the ship as well. In the Operations Room there were banks of cabinets full of dials, gauges, fuses, switchgear, vertical and horizontal displays, airborne warning plots, target indicators and fire control gear. The room was lined with vent trunks and louvres, pipes, cables and loudspeakers and so on, Much of this equipment had been smashed, presumably to ensure that it would never be used again.

Going down through the bridge, and after taking a series of wrong turns, I eventually arrived at the boat deck where the motor house was all that remained of the ship's crane. Descending another ladderway on the port side and keeping well clear of the breaking squad, I entered the after main super-structure. I now appeared to be in the ship's main galley and dining halls, but since I was more interested in seeing one of the engine rooms I moved further aft and arrived at a promising access which I promptly descended. After climbing down about three decks I arrived on the starting platform of the port outer engine room. By the light of my torch I could make out a complexity of pipes of all diameters, temperature gauges, valves and revolution

Cairnryan Pier runs parallel to the shore for almost half a mile. *Blake* was at the end of the pier to the seaward side, moored stem to stem with the Tribal-class frigate *Mohawk,* also awaiting demolition. I trudged through the mud, which seems to be the natural state of the ground in breakers' yards, and onto the pier, heading for the *Blake* in a wind which threatened to blow me into the sea. Apart from the absence of radar, from a distance the *Blake* appeared to be intact. Closer examination, however, revealed that the Sea Cat launchers and the ship's boats had gone, probably at the dockyard along with other reusable items prior to the voyage north. The breakers had not been idle either, as the jib of the cruiser's crane was lying in a

A Sea King carries out in-flight refuelling from the *Blake*. *(Fleet Air Arm Museum)*

HMS *Blake* at sea off the Isle of Wight during Staff College Sea Days, June 1976. *(George Mortimore/Action Photos)*

The *Blake* anchored at Spithead for the Queen's Silver Jubilee Review in June 1977.

(Robert Shopland/Ship's Monthly)

A floodlit HMS *Blake* presenting a spectacular sight.   *(P. Turner)*

A final view of the *Blake* at sea.

(*P. Turner*)

The *Blake's* last entry into Portsmouth Harbour on Thursday 6 December 1969 coincided with the acceptance into service of the mine countermeasures vessel, HMS *Brecon*. Here the two ships are seen together at Spithead.*(Fleet Air Arm Museum)*

counters and, of course, the turbine casing itself. It was difficult to restrain myself from visualizing the engine room in full operation, the noise, vibration and the smell of lubricating oil. Although the smell of the oil had lingered there was, of course, no sound or vibration at all, just an eerie silence. Before I left the compartment I stuffed my torch down the front of my jacket, and as I climbed the vertical ladder out of the blackened compartment it described a wild arc of light ahead of me.

Once out of the engine room I continued aft and I came to the wardroom area with the officers' cabins, which were small and fitted with wooden bunks and lockers. Lying on the deck in one of them was a letter to a senior officer which was scuffed and torn. It appeared to be from his wife who was bemoaning the fact that the *Blake* was steaming to the Pacific and sunny California, while she was stuck in England. I walked further aft and, suddenly, the clean smell of fresh air marked the end of a labyrinth of passageways and cabins. The fine lines of the once immaculate quarterdeck were criss-crossed by a tangle of heavy ropes

which secured the after end of the ship to the pier, and above on the flight deck a flurry of sparks down the starboard side was a reminder of the breakers' presence. Making my way back through the ship I emerged on the forecastle and looked through the twin 6-inch turret. Both guns had been immobilized and the thick glass of the sighting hood was smashed. After a brief look at the 3-inch turret I left the *Blake* to negotiate my way through mud and strong winds back to my car.

Two weeks later I revisited the *Blake*, only to find that the breakers had been about their business with great speed. They were cutting out the Airborne Early Warning Room to the starboard side of the bridge. Everything else from that area aft, down to the level of the boat deck, funnels, masts and hangar, had gone.'

The final weeks of the *Blake's* life meant extra jobs for people in the nearby town of Stranraer, and she provided British industry with some 850 tons of non-ferrous metal, about 100 tons of armour plate and 10,500 tons of ferrous metal, but it was a sad end for a once proud ship.

The *Blake* lying alongside the breaker's yard at Cairnryan on Saturday 15 January 1983. *(I. Johnstone)*

The 6-inch gun turret deserted and neglected as it awaits the breaker's cutting torches. *(I. Johnstone)*

By 29 January 1983 the shipbreakers were making rapid progress in cutting up the last of the Royal Navy's cruisers. *(I. Johnstone)*

The cruiser *Blake* as a destroyer depot ship in 1912. *(Maritime Photo Library)*

The first HMS *Blake* served in the Royal Navy between 1808 and 1816, and the only time she fired her guns in anger was at the unfortunate Walcheren debacle in 1809, where she earned the *Blake's* only battle honour. She ended her career as a prison ship at Portsmouth and she was finally broken up in 1858. The second *Blake* was completed in 1819 and she spent her entire service in use as a stores ship at Portsmouth Dockyard. She was broken up in 1855. The third ship of the name was a 9,000-ton cruiser which was launched in November 1889, but in 1906 she and her sister ships were converted to destroyer depot ships. During the Great War of 1914-18 she served with the Grand Fleet, providing facilities for the 2nd and the 11th Destroyer Flotillas. She was sold for breaking up in June 1922.

Battle Honour
HMS *Blake*

More Majorem
(After The Manner of your Ancestors)

Walcheren   1809

HMS *Blake*
Commanding Officers

Name:	Date Appointed:
Captain D. G. Clutterbuck RN	17 January 1961
Captain R. F. Plugge DSC RN	21 October 1968
Captain R. D. Butt RN	27 April 1970
Captain R. M. Tobey RN	17 April 1972
Captain P. G. M. Herbert OBE RN	22 April 1974
Captain D. M. Eckersley-Maslin RN	10 October 1975
Captain H. B. Parker RN	6 December 1976
Captain D. J. Mackenzie RN	3 January 1979

Acknowledgements:

My thanks to: Rear-Admiral Michael Stacey CB, commanding officer HMS *Tiger* 1973 to 1976 for reading through and advising on the manuscript and for kindly writing the foreword to this book: Mr Brian Conroy for his watercolour painting used on the dust jacket: Mr John S. Morris for his pen and ink sketches.

I must also thank the following for their help and, in many cases, for the loan of valuable photographs: -
Jim Allaway, Editor, *Navy News:* David Axford, Haslemere, Surrey: Roger Beacham and the staff of Cheltenham Reference Library: Glen Beck, Aylesbury, Buckinghamshire: Rt Hon Tony Benn MP, House of Commons, London: Derek Brook, Weston-Super-Mare, Somerset: J. R. Burt, Hawkhurst, Kent: Michael Cassar, Valletta, Malta: Vice-Admiral Sir Simon Cassells KBE, Hampshire: R. A. Cooper, Wadesmill, Hertfordshire: Charles Davis, Yealmpton, Devon: Neil Duffy, Buckhaven, Fife: Rear-Admiral D. M. Eckersley-Maslin CB, Hampshire: Frederick Green, Plumstead, Cape Town, South Africa: Derek Fox, Southsea, Hampshire: George Henderson, Plymouth, Devon: Richard Holme, Tunbridge Wells, Kent: Rob Jerrard, Budleigh Salterton, Devon: Ian Johnstone, Glasgow: Peter Kent, Dept of Photographs, Imperial War Museum, London: David Lippman, Portsmouth, Hampshire: George Malcolmson, Gosport, Hampshire: Kevin Marshall, Whitley Bay, Tyne & Wear: Tony Middleton, Hardwick, Cambridgeshire: Norrie Millen, Canada: Eric Mills, Ramsgate, Kent: George Mortimore, Action Photos, Ryde, Isle of Wight: Norman Muir, Bickleigh, Devon: Gerry Nunn, Chatham, Kent: G. A. Penn, Warwick: Tony Perrett, Royal Marines Historical Society: Vic Richards, Redditch, Worcestershire: Martin Rhys-Jackson, Chandler, USA: Walter Sartori, Southsea, Hampshire: A. D. Saunders, Southend-on-Sea, Essex: Robert Shopland, Editor, *Ships Monthly*: Jerry Shore, Research Officer, Fleet Air Arm Museum, RNAS Yeovilton: E. I. Shrimpton, Malvern, Worcestershire: Rodger Sloper, Middlesbrough: Don Smith, Selby, North Yorkshire: Ian Spashett, FotoFlite, Ashford, Kent: Derek Taylor, Colchester, Essex: D. A. Thorburn, Banff: Paul Turner, Bognor Regis, Sussex: J. S. Tunnicliffe, Salford, Greater Manchester: Adrian Vicary, Maritime Photo Library, Cromer, Norfolk: Bill Whalley, London: Finally to my wife Freda and my two daughters Caroline and Louise for their invaluable help.

Other Titles From FAN PUBLICATIONS

HMS *Eagle* 1942-1978 £18.95

HMS *Centaur* 1943-1972 £16.95

HMS *Victorious* 1937-1969 £21

Three *Ark Royals* 1938-1999 £23

SS *Canberra* 1957-1997 £21

Please add £2.50 p+p for the UK/EU
or £4.00 for worldwide surface mail

For current list write to:
FAN PUBLICATIONS
17 Wymans Lane
Cheltenham, Glos GL51 9QA
England
Tel/Fax: 01242 580290